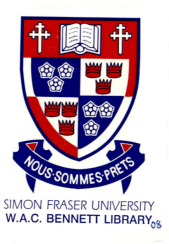

Doing Practitioner Research Differently

Why do some practitioner researchers break with convention and find their own creative and unique paths through their research? Why are they prepared, sometimes, to take methodological risks when they are studying for a higher academic degree? What do they gain from doing practitioner research differently, and what are some of the challenges and dilemmas they face in doing so?

These are the key questions explored in this book. They are examined through an original investigation in which the authors worked with six practitioner researchers who found individual and innovative routes through their award-bearing research.

The book presents edited versions of the practitioners' research reports and also explores the motivations which caused the practitioners to break away from conventional approaches. The investigation revealed that a variety of forces were at work. There were personal factors related to preferred thinking and artistic styles; professional factors related to purposes for doing research; and institutional factors related to the encouragement received and the models of research presented.

This book makes an original contribution to our undestanding of motivation and quality in practitioner research. It suggests that we may need to resist any form of dogma if practitioner research is to be effective. Instead, we may need to liberate individuals to make methodical choices that harmonise with their own purposes and predispositions – to free them to 'do it their way'.

Marion Dadds is Professor of Education at St Martins College, Lancaster. Her previous publications include *Passionate Enquiry and School Development* published by Falmer Press. **Susan Hart** is a Lecturer in Education at the School of Education, University of Cambridge. Her most recent publication is *Thinking Through Teaching*, published by David Fulton.

Doing Practitioner
Research Differently

Marion Dadds and Susan Hart
with Tish Crotty, Linda Ferguson, Ros Frost, Joe Geraci,
Jacqui Potter and Liz Waterland

London and New York

First published 2001 by
RoutledgeFalmer
11 New Fetter Lane, London EC4P 4EE

Simultaneously published in the USA and Canada
by RoutledgeFalmer
29 West 35th Street, New York, NY 10001

RoutledgeFalmer is an imprint of the Taylor & Francis Group

Editorial and selection © 2001 Marion Dadds and Susan Hart; individual
contributions © 2001 the contributors

Typeset in Sabon by Curran Publishing Services Ltd, Norwich
Printed and bound in Great Britain by St Edmundsbury Press, Bury St
Edmunds

British Library Cataloguing in Publication Data
A catalogue record for this book is available from the British Library

Library of Congress Cataloging in Publication Data
Doing practitioner research differently / Marion Dadds and Susan Hart;
with Tish Crotty ... [et al.].
     p. cm.
Includes bibliographical references and index.
1. Action research in education. 2. Education–Research–Methodology.
I. Dadds, Marion. II. Hart, Susan, 1947– III. Crotty, Tish.

LB1028.24 .D65 2001
370'.7'2–dc21
                                        00–050996

ISBN 0–415–23757–2 (hbk)
ISBN 0–415–23758–0 (pbk)

Contents

Figures

Tables

Acknowledgements

This book has been made possible by the willingness of the 'Darers' group: Tish Crotty, Linda Ferguson, Ros Frost, Joe Geraci, Jacqui Potter and Liz Waterland, to share the research carried out for their Masters' degrees with a wider audience. We appreciate the time and commitment they gave to this project, editing their own studies, reading one another's studies, and meeting to discuss them. Initially, before we received funding, the group met in the late afternoons and early evenings after a full day's work. Latterly, we have even met on Saturdays in order not to take time out from professional responsibilities,

We also thank the School of Education, Cambridge University for providing support for the project from the Research and Development Fund. This enabled supply cover to be provided to enable Darers to meet and also edit their own writing.

Further thanks are due to Ken Thomas and Kevin O'Connell for their willingness to share their innovative work in this book, allowing us to illustrate how other practitioner researchers can use, and have used, the examples and insights to support their own enquiries.

We are grateful, too, to the many other practitioner researchers – too numerous to mention by name – who have contributed to the ideas explored in this book; to Marion Blake for her help and feedback on the manuscript at draft stage; to Richard Winter also for feedback on the manuscript; to Christine Goad for her meticulous organisation and invaluable secretarial support; and to Thimble Press for permission to reproduce, in shortened form, Liz Waterland's *Not a Perfect Offering*.

Marion Dadds
Susan Hart

Chapter 1

Background and introduction

What motivates some practitioner researchers to take an unconventional, innovative direction in their research; to employ their powers of creativity in surprising ways; to think and do differently from the mainstream research they have met? This many-sided question engaged us – Marion Dadds and Susan Hart – for more than three years in the project which forms the basis of this book. It caused us to re-examine many of the assumptions underlying the learning conditions that are offered to practitioners who want to know about, and apply, research to their daily professional work. And it caused us to understand more clearly some of the drives and problems which shape the research of practitioners who choose to frame their work in a radically different way from mainstream approaches.

We had been working as higher education tutors and researchers at the Cambridge University School of Education (formerly the Cambridge Institute) for many years. Marion started her career there in 1981, Susan in 1989. Our work focused on supporting the continuing professional development of teachers and other practitioners through award-bearing courses and research projects. We shared a common interest, through our teaching and research, in methodologies that help practitioners to study and develop their work. The research project we share in this book emerged from that common interest.

The project began one afternoon when we met on the stairs in our workplace. We stopped to talk about the practitioner research studies we were currently validating for the Masters' degree on which we both taught. There were, we both felt, some challenging, innovative research studies being submitted for validation, which were worthy of sharing with a wider audience. We were not, at this stage, explicit about the particular qualities of these studies that led us to perceive them as 'innovative': we were simply responding at an intuitive level to features that set them apart from the kinds of work that we were used to supervising and assessing. Despite their engaging qualities, some of these studies had taxed the academy, as they transgressed more conventional notions of research, though most were awarded high grades on the Masters' assessment criteria. As we talked on, we were able to recall other such innovative studies we had encountered in the past.

As light turned to dusk and our legs grew weary from this stairway exchange, the idea grew for a publication that would make some of this research more widely available to other practitioner researchers. Our first idea was simply to edit a collection of studies that might provide example and inspiration for others to experiment with alternative modes of doing and reporting practitioner research. We had been concerned for some time that research methods teaching, and the Masters' degree criteria, could be constraining for some practitioners, deterring them from pursuing more adventurous approaches to inquiry and reporting. A collection of studies providing examples of different innovative approaches which had been judged successful according to conventional research criteria would, perhaps, give others encouragement to be inventive, to search for their own more empowering ways of fostering the development of professional thinking and practice.

After approaching practitioner researchers past and present in the following weeks, as well as being unable to trace others, we drew a group of six together, all of whom were interested and willing to see their work shared more widely in a publication. Liz Waterland, Ros Frost and Tish Crotty were working in mainstream primary schools. Liz was a headteacher of a city infant school, Ros a teacher of five and six year olds in a large primary school, and Tish was working for Cambridgeshire Multicultural Education Service as a Language and Curriculum Support Teacher.[1] Linda Ferguson was a class teacher in a school for children with severe and profound learning difficulties; Jacqui Potter was a physiotherapist educator, working on a course development team writing a new BSc Hons physiotherapy programme, and Joe Geraci was working as a substitute teacher at RAF Lakenheath, an American high school for Department of Defense dependants whose parents are attached to the US Air Force.

These practitioners' Masters' degree work started at different times, covering different courses, though each pursued, successfully, a Masters' programme at Cambridge. Liz and Jacqui followed a two-year, part-time course in applied research in education, accredited by the University of East Anglia. Joe, Linda and Tish followed the new Modular Masters' programme established when the Cambridge Institute became part of Cambridge University. Ros also followed the Modular Masters' course, but one year later than the other three, by which time considerable changes to the original course structure and to the graded assessment criteria had been introduced.[2]

---

1   Liz Waterland is also author of *Read With Me: An Apprenticeship Approach to Reading* (Thimble Press 1985).
2   Information about the assessment criteria and examining procedures used on different courses is provided in Chapter 9 (page 144).

What all the members of the group had in common was that, at some point in their research degree, they had made a decision to break with conventional ways of doing and reporting research, as they understood them. They reached out for their own unique ways of doing or writing up their research, in response to the perceived needs of their particular project and their own preferred thinking and representational styles. In this sense, they all found the courage to take a risk with their research. Thus we called the project, temporarily, 'Daring to be different', and the project members the 'Darers'. The naming seemed to 'stick' to the point where it is difficult now to think of it in any other way.

When we met to discuss the proposed edited collection, it seemed a good idea to explore with the group if they themselves saw their work as 'innovative', and if so, in what respects. As we began to engage in this discussion, however, a broader conversation emerged. As well as discussing the innovative qualities of the research itself, we began to focus on what the processes and experiences of being an innovative researcher had been like for those in the group. As our conversations developed, it became increasingly evident that we should be seeking to understand more about the Darers' experiences of being innovative researchers and that this should be expressed through their perspectives, voices and language rather than through our own.

A more complex project than that of dissemination was emerging. It was clear that we had something more profound and important to learn from the group about the experience of being an innovative researcher, something we had not previously understood in any significant way. Without our initially designing it to be so, a research-based project started evolving, in which we came face to face with issues and questions about the conditions in higher education that encourage, support, foster or inhibit quality innovative practitioner research. The project started to take a new, deeper direction. We became, spontaneously, enquirers into our own teaching and institutional practices, seeking, through collaborative research with the group, to understand better the minds, hearts and motivations of those who had developed the courage to 'do differently' within the academic context.

We discovered that, in their own ways, group members had each encountered tensions at some point in their learning between the models of research which seemed to dominate the resources offered to them by higher education, and the shape and direction they felt was right for their own research. Though most had found knowledge of established traditions helpful in certain ways, they felt a need to break from 'official academic genres' (Ely *et al.* 1997: 11) in order to follow their own intellectual as well as emotional desires and styles in their research. They wanted, and needed, to break new ground on their own terms, while working towards the criteria by which higher education would judge their work as worthy of a Masters' degree. They succeeded in doing so and, in the process, they implicitly created their own criteria for what constitutes worthwhileness and quality in practitioner research. This book maps something of the territory they covered as they accepted the challenges of shaping their own desires and purposes into research that was, ultimately, considered valid by academia, even though, in some cases, it diverged radically from mainstream research.

What we mean by 'innovation' in this book thus relates to the particular experience, understandings and perceptions of the participants in this research, who were studying on a variety of courses within a particular institutional setting. We realise that what we and they perceived at the time as 'innovative' may not be so perceived by others, even though the studies stood out as innovative in our own context. Yet we believe that two of our questions that emerged from the project, 'What motivates practitioners to take unconventional directions in their research?' and 'What conditions in higher education support creativity and methodological inventiveness?' are worthy of consideration whatever the context of study and however 'innovation' is defined.

Developing a methodology

A collaborative methodology soon crystallised for exploring the processes and outcomes of this innovative work. Funding from our internal Research and Development fund enabled us to meet regularly, as a group, over a two-year period (1997–9). At each meeting, one study was the focus of discussion. In advance of the meeting, the researcher whose work was being discussed prepared his or her reflections on the experience of doing the research, outlining motivations, challenges, difficulties. A second colleague prepared a critical reader response to the work which included questions that had arisen in the reading. At the meeting, the researcher's insights and experiences were shared and discussed. The reader response was then shared. Open discussion involving the full group followed. All these discussions were tape-recorded for later analysis. By the time the project was established, Joe Geraci had returned to the USA. We communicated with him via e-mail. As he could not be with us, he sent us a written account of his perspectives on, and experiences of, doing his research. During these stages, our own views as research tutors also became part of the database. Our methodology thus captured a range of perspectives on each individual's study and on the personal and institutional issues that arose from it. The epistemological basis for the project was therefore predominantly collaborative.

After this stage of the project the two of us met to analyse this mass of data. Before every meeting we each carried out an issues analysis of the transcribed discussions being considered. In the meetings, we compared and contrasted our individual analyses in order to develop a richer, more collective picture. During our analytical conversations, key issues and themes started to emerge.

We followed these backwards into previous transcripts and forwards into those still to be analysed. Thus, our issues and themes were emergent but were ultimately tracked across all the studies. This work provided the basis for the analytical narrative summaries which accompany each of the edited studies in Chapters 2 to 8. In these summaries we bring out the key features of innovation in the studies and the key issues emerging for the researchers from their experience of researching differently. All these summaries were shared with the group who offered critical feedback for the final drafts. All the practitioner researchers had the final say in how their own work was represented in both the narrative summaries and the editions of their research.

Concurrently, group members undertook an editing task on their own studies in order to preserve the key features while reducing the text to fit the requirements of the size of this book. Tish had done two distinctly different innovative research studies and it was ultimately decided to include both. Thus, we had seven edited studies and these are represented in Chapters 2 to 8.

When we had completed our analysis together and identified key themes, we took some time independently to think more theoretically about what had emerged. At this stage, we had no agreed strategy for doing this other than to go away and have a good think on our own.

Our 'good thinks' generated a remarkable similarity in the themes and hypotheses that emerged. When we next met we saw that we had, independently, clustered the themes into three major categories which we both saw as theoretically related. The outcome of this work is represented in Chapter 9, and gave us the theoretical basis for thinking about the practical implications of the project which we outline in Chapter 10.

The outcomes of this analytical stage were shared orally and diagrammatically with the group members for discussion and collaborative validation. Although the intention was methodologically sound, the outcome was, we both felt, strange. The group offered little in the way of response in contrast to the very lively and engaged previous meetings in which we had discussed the individual studies. We puzzled over this for some time and concluded that, perhaps, they had found it difficult to engage with the analysis and theory that had excited us simply because it *was* ours and not theirs. They had disengaged from the research process after the meetings in which we had analysed and discussed the individual studies. The rest of the research process had been ours. This explanation, if valid, offers a sound lesson in the nature of collaborative methodologies and epistemologies: what one does not participate in creating, one may have difficulty 'owning'. (Our meeting was also held on a late, hot July working day towards the end of an academic year. Herein might lie a second valid explanation. Indeed, when the same ideas were presented to the group later in written form, as an early draft of Chapter 9, they received enthusiastic endorsement.)

As a result of exploring the reasons why individuals had chosen to do what they did, different dimensions of innovation began to be identified. Some studies were innovative in their conceptualisation, some in the methods used to investigate them, some in the ways in which they have been written. Some were innovative in more than one way; some in all of these ways. For the purposes of this book, we have chosen to group them on the basis of a distinctive type of innovation shared by more than one study. Ros's and Jacqui's work, for example, was distinctive for its use of *visualisation* in the research process. Joe, Tish and Linda all adopted a *conversational* approach in their research in which the to-ing, fro-ing and changing of voice contributed to the development of ideas. Tish and Liz both adopted *fictional* forms to achieve their research purposes.[3]

We then moved on to the final stages of the project in which we explored the implications of the research for practice. We met with the group on two occasions to discuss what they felt the implications were from practitioners' points of view. The discussions were transcribed and analysed and used as the basis for the first part of Chapter 10.

We also had a two-way conversation in which we questioned one another about how the project had changed our own thinking as tutors. We then discussed the implications of these shifts in thinking for our own practice in supporting practitioner research generally and in the context of Masters' degrees particularly. Again, the conversation was transcribed, analysed and used as the basis for the second part of Chapter 10.

This, then, is the way we invented our methodological way through the project, designing the route to suit what we wanted to do and the ways in which we wanted to foreground the perspectives of the practitioner researchers in our analysis and theorising.

Drawing on prior thinking

This project, though small-scale, is nevertheless related to a wider field of practitioner research. In this work, therefore, we see ourselves as part of a growing research tradition which has crossed cultural and professional boundaries over the years. The associated research methodologies in this field have spread world-wide and into a variety of professional and community contexts: schools (e.g. Hollingsworth 1997), healthcare (e.g. Nichols 1997, Titchen and Binnie 1993), social work (e.g. Childs, Franklin and Kemp 1997), family support (e.g. Winter 1996), the police force (e.g Adlam 1998). Sometimes this research tradition is referred to as

---

3 This is not to suggest that these categorisations capture all that was innovative about these practitioners' work. A fuller analysis of the thinking that led to, and lay behind, individual studies is provided in Chapter 9.

practitioner research, sometimes as action research, and in the field of education it is referred to specifically as teacher research, especially in America (Hollingsworth 1994). While there may be characteristic differences in these several research methodologies, they share in common a central commitment to the study of one's own professional practice by the researcher himself or herself, with a view to improving that practice for the benefit of others (Dadds 1996).

Over the years of working together in this field, we have shared a common interest in alternative, creative approaches to practitioner research and research reporting. Marion Dadds supported an eclectic approach to research in her research teaching and was, herself, predominantly an action researcher with feminist leanings. She had, however, always been interested in practitioners' enquiries that diverged from traditional action research, not least because she realised that the tidy action research cycle was never that tidy in the practices of research. To this end, she supported inventiveness when it emerged, though she did not consciously and deliberately promote it. In 1984, she was successful in persuading the academic board of the institution to validate the use of non-traditional, alternative research outcomes that diverged from the standard research report or essay format, in order to enable teachers to match their research texts more intelligently to the cultures of teaching and schools. She conducted a small-scale study on some of the issues related to this work (Dadds 1995), but did not then delve as deeply into the perspectives of the innovative researchers as the Darers' project has subsequently allowed.

We had both observed that the more mainstream, traditional research approaches do not always suit the needs and available resources of practitioner researchers. Indeed, as a result of supporting practitioners in doing research on Masters' courses over a number of years, Susan Hart had begun to wonder if, for the purposes of practitioners' own enquiries, formal knowledge of research methodology could, in some cases, be deskilling rather than enabling. The message that some practitioners seemed to receive was that the expertise required for research is qualitatively different from the expertise acquired through practical experience of teaching. When carrying out their own enquiries, some would set aside their own sophisticated analytical and interpretive expertise, only to find themselves less able to think so effectively through the unfamiliar medium of 'research methods'. Susan had begun to feel uncomfortable about her own contribution to research methods' courses; to wonder if it would be more helpful to strengthen practitioners' own creative and critical thinking powers and to affirm these as legitimate and for some purposes sufficient resources for research (Hart 1995a).

Much action research and practitioner research continues to draw upon the methods and methodologies of traditional social science research. While this 'methodological borrowing' (Winter 1989) can be appropriate to some degree, we both felt that it is often not situationally appropriate for the professional contexts in which many practitioner researchers work, or for the kinds of research questions they choose to pursue. Examples of methodological inventiveness have emerged over the years (e.g. Convery 1993, Winter 1988, Hart 1995a, Hollingsworth 1994, Dadds 1994, Lomax 1994, Mellor 1999), but these have as yet led to few significant changes in practitioner research practices in higher education, although questions have continued to be raised about the nature of authentic methodologies for practitioner research (e.g. Day 1990, Elliott 1990).

At times, we have shared our despondency at the way in which we felt practitioner research was becoming increasingly controlled and narrowed by the constraints of higher education teaching and criteria. At other times, we have shared our unease, paradoxically, when practitioner researchers chose to go 'out on a limb', wondering if they would depart too radically from the academic criteria on their Masters' course and fail to achieve the quality standards set by the institution. More importantly, we have also shared a common sense of inspiration when practitioner researchers have reached out for exciting, unorthodox ways of doing and reporting their research and, as a result, taxed the mind of the academy, demanding new thinking about what constitutes legitimate practitioner research at Masters' level. This inspiration has given us a strong source of motivation for this project.

Power and responsibility

As the project developed, its importance for our work as higher education teachers became more and more apparent. Higher education colleagues, along with those in other legitimating bodies such as the Teacher Training Agency in the UK and funding bodies in general, are in a powerful position to influence the views of research which practitioner researchers develop; to portray notions of validity and appropriateness in relation to research which is designed to advance understanding and action in professional work; to influence how the research gets done, written, disseminated; to determine what practitioners learn about research, how and why. In this sense, it is a responsible position, one in which legitimating and funding bodies can shape the methods and methodologies of practitioner research for better or worse.

Given that such methodologies are designed primarily to improve the circumstances of those for whom the practitioner holds responsibility – children, patients, parents, communities – it matters how this work is supported and conceptualised, so that the most appropriate conditions are provided to enable practitioner researchers to give of their best in pursuit of improvement. Opening one's professional practice to critical scrutiny demands courage, curiosity, fortitude and a willingness to accept that there are always opportunities for further development. It often means that the practitioner researcher renders himself or herself vulnerable to critique, from both self and others. Yet such open attitudes, we believe, signal one of the highest forms of professionalism. Such professionalism deserves fostering and respecting in climates of optimum growth.

The practitioner researchers who formed the project group are but a few. Yet they are part of a growing number working in a variety of contexts – funded, unfunded, award-bearing, non-award bearing – who are engaging in research in order to improve their professional practice. They are also part of a growing number who experience a need to break with the traditional conventions where these do not fit, in order to research with validity in a different way. What they have to say and share deserves our attention. What they have to offer to other practitioners who are seeking courage to research differently, seeking to find new ways into and through their research, is significant. What we have to learn from them about the personal and professional experience of researching innovatively is of practical and theoretical relevance to those who shape and legitimate practitioner research, as well as to those who conduct it. We hope that this book will enable others to understand some of that learning – along with the implications for practice – which the project has generated for us.

Structure of the book

We have structured the book to reflect the sequences of learning which we have experienced, while at the same time enabling different readers to relate to it flexibly in response to their own needs. Those wanting to have immediate access to the practitioner research studies can move through Chapters 2 to 8, omitting the narrative summaries at the end of each chapter of the researchers' accounts of their experiences of doing their research differently. These narrative summaries could also be read together, independently of the studies to which they relate, by those interested in gaining an overview of issues of innovation arising from the project.

One practitioner research study is represented in each chapter. A full reading of each of Chapters 2 to 8 will give insight into each individual author's experiences of conducting his or her research project, as well as the edited version of the research itself. Chapter 9 then goes on, as we have said, to highlight and discuss the themes and issues which emerged from our cross-case analysis. This takes us into our theoretical discussion about the complementary and interrelated roles played by the practitioner researchers' individual needs, interests and styles, the climate and values of the supporting institution or agency, and the demands of the research project itself. In Chapter 10, we share our thinking and that of the practitioner researchers about the implications which the study has raised for those choosing to engage in this kind of research, and for those who support it. Then, in a brief final chapter, we describe some specific developments in our work arising from the project. Here, we provide some examples of how other practitioner researchers have already used the Darers' ideas and experiences as springboards for developing their own innovative approaches, and how we ourselves have already been drawing on those ideas and experiences in our teaching.

When the idea of this book was first put to the group, most responded with considerable enthusiasm because they felt it would have been a great help if such a book had been available to them at the time they were making decisions about taking an innovative route in their own research. The examples in Chapter 11 go some way towards evidencing the validity of that view, and consequently the value of the book as a useful resource for practitioner researchers. From our own perspective as tutors, the research has provided not only new insight but also a renewed sense of optimism about the importance of supporting innovative work. Innovation, we argue, can be a vital force for quality in practitioner research.

Part 1

Visualisation as a method of enquiry and reporting

Chapter 2

Children with special needs, teachers with special needs

Ros Frost

> I feel overwhelmed, detached, dizzy, they're coming at me, I wish they would go away, I'm past my point, I can not stay in here any longer, I want to get out . . . (*I stay*). . . . I need to get out. . . . I must stay. . . . (*I stay*) . . . I must get out . . . nothing is as important as getting out of here . . . RIGHT NOW. I get to the staff room as a colleague takes my class over. I cry . . . I sit . . . I think. . . .
> *How am I ever going to get back in that classroom again?*
> (My own classroom. Thursday 30 November 1995, 2.30 p.m.)

This study is a reflection on my attempts to answer this question and is of an exploratory, problem-solving nature. I am taking you on the same journey that I made between September 1995 and February 1996. I want you to travel with me and see what I saw as I met the issues that faced me. It has not been my intention to look in depth at all the issues I have encountered along the way. When new signposts have appeared I have had to consider the merit of continuing further on a particular track or, using the

---

1 On the Cambridge Modular Masters' course, at this time, there were three pieces of assessed work: two 6–8,000 word assignments, and a 15,000 word dissertation. Individuals selected their own topics for research.

compass of my reasoning, keep travelling over unknown land with my sights set on returning to work. It would have made me very unhappy had I not been able to do so.

I will outline the layout and furnishings of the train we will be riding, introduce your fellow passengers and myself, your guide. Before doing this, however, I will take some time to explain the rationale behind the research methods I have used to aid my exploration.

It became clear to me from the outset that this study would be of an exploratory nature, that I would be like Spradley's explorer 'trying to map an uncharted wilderness'. Spradley (in Hitchcock and Hughes 1989) likens the positivistic researcher to a petroleum engineer who already knows what he is looking for, how to look for it and what to expect. I knew that it would be unlikely to be this way for me. Faced with an inability to cope, in a situation that I would normally have been able to cope in, sent urgent messengers out from my brain, scouting for the reasons why this had happened. In order to sort through each layer of my experience in the classroom, and out of it, I considered that I would need a more interpretative approach, one that allowed me to set my general direction, begin gathering information, but change direction and tools as and when appropriate; to be rigorous yet flexible. I found Cochran-Smith and Lytle's (1993) description of purposeful teacher research helpful in this matter, finding rigour in their theoretical underpinning yet flexibility in their methods, particularly as they drew on sources I as a teacher was familiar with and knew to be helpful in my everyday teaching 'research', for example, the use of personal reflective journals. They define teacher research as 'systematic, intentional inquiry by teachers about their own school and classroom work' reflecting their desire to make sense of their experiences. Berthoff (in Cochran-Smith and Lytle 1993) states that teacher research need not involve new information but rather interpret the information one already has. She calls this 'REsearching'.

In keeping with Berthoff's thinking, then, this is in part a 'REsearch' study about revisiting the old to inform the new. Yet it is also a systematic and intentional inquiry into fresh questions generated from the combination of old information in a new context.

I will be 'revisiting' two areas in particular: the conclusions that I formed from my first three years of teaching; and the effects of teacher/school communication on myself as a pupil at secondary school. I have used the personal documentation of a termly evaluation from my second year of teaching and an annual school report to aid my thinking.

I have also used classroom observation as a method for gaining further insights into my own practice and children's behaviour. By direct observation of one pupil in his familiar environment I wanted to find out more about what the pupil was doing and how this related to everyday classroom factors. Before setting off, then:

Your itinerary for the journey

After an introductory talk by your guide about your travel arrangements, fellow passengers and destination, you will be calling at all stops along the way including:

1   Harried Hill   (Not for the faint-hearted)
    A new academic year and new challenges. An introduction to the pressures faced and stress experienced.
2   Mount Development   (A scenic viewpoint)
    The vantage point received from gaining insights into the current Special Educational Needs debate. The light it shed on my own experience of school and the management of the children in my class.
3   Finder's Sharers   (A voyage of discovery)
    Further exploration into behaviour management. Surprising findings from a classroom observation of one pupil.
4   Crisis Point   (A lemming's paradise!)
    The smouldering fire of stress becomes consuming.
    The lethal cocktail of pupils' disruptive behaviour and too many hours worked for too long.
5   The Path of Approach   (The final destination)
    From Initial Teacher Training through recent educational change. A proposal for return.

So, welcome aboard!

You are asked to observe the health and safety regulations of the train and to be aware of any *FLASHBACKS* encountered. Please consult the guard when you see one as these electrical occurrences have the potential to delay or advance the train's journey.

Refreshments will be served prior to arrival at some stops. They will be served by the guard from a personal selection of thoughts.

The train you are on is educational. The School Express has over 500 passengers, 10 per cent of whom are staff. The pupils range in age from four to eleven.

The guide has been a passenger on this School Express for the past three and a half years. Before this she was a passenger on the Initial Teacher Training Intercity for four years, specialising in the teaching of seven to eleven year old passengers and of art, and before that she spent the previous thirteen years as a keen 'guard and passenger observer' on the same Local Education Authority's Network service from the ages of five to eighteen. Your guide joined the School Express just after the train's National Curriculum time-tables had changed for the second time, and a year and a half prior to a further National Curriculum re-timetabling. The carriage this study is based in has adequate space, water and toilet facilities. Resources are satisfactory to deliver the school's aims effectively.

Within the carriage there are thirteen children working towards National Curriculum level one and fourteen towards level two in English and maths. Thirteen children receive extra language learning support; of these, nine are also on the Local Education Authority's Stages of Assessment with specific programmes for supporting a variety of needs in speech, hearing, learning and behaviour. The majority of family housing is privately owned, and four pupils receive free school dinners. There are also other health considerations such as asthma, eczema and toileting needs to be taken into account. The guide receives four and a half hours' classroom/welfare support and two hours' learning support a week, with two hours' support from parent helpers with reading each week. One-third of the class are girls, and all of the pupils have English as their first language. This does not fully explain the diversity within this carriage, but it may help to set a context for understanding the purpose of this study.

The journey begins.

Harried Hill

I had started the new academic year with a change of age group, from teaching Year 2 and 3 to Year 1, to which I was looking forward. In the nine months prior to this new term I had also experienced some personally taxing situations outside work, which had left me feeling emotionally drained but not exhausted. These involved an intimate bereavement, the break-up of a relationship, concern over a serious family illness, and domestic problems. I had also been in the process of buying a house. However it was the beginning of a year, and I looked forward to embarking on new challenges and leaving time to heal the upsets of the last few months. I was not far into the new term before my initial enthusiasm became strained, as I realised that I had more of a challenge on my hands than I had anticipated.

Although it was early in the new academic year, the behaviour of two boys, Eddy and Todd, in the class was already starting to cause me concern. The following summary is taken from notes I kept about their behaviour between September and November. The following were displayed by one or both most days:

- attention-seeking noises at inappropriate times
- not sitting still
- talking when others were talking
- bad language
- hurting other children
- taking others' property
- damaging others' work and school property
- refusal to work

- refusal to co-operate/enter classroom
- sometimes rude and dangerous behaviour to classroom helpers
- out of classroom problems, such as bullying before and after school, at break and lunchtimes.

It became increasingly difficult to maintain a calm working atmosphere within the carriage and direct my energies to teaching. How should I deal with this old but new situation?

FLASHBACK I had experienced similar behaviour with one of the children's relatives in my first year on the Express. I knew that I would still have to meet the same standards of teaching and learning, even with continual disruption to my practice. Could I cope with this for another year, with the knowledge at that time that there would be no extra classroom support, and of all that it had meant last time in terms of personal strain and disrupted teaching? How could I use my concerns to prevent what I feared from happening, rather than allowing them to act as a self-fulfilling prophecy so early on in the year?

I could feel the pressures begin to mount around and within me. At first I perceived these as challenges, but as the weeks went on I became increasingly worn out from dealing with the unpredictable behaviour of the two children, as well as that of a small handful of others in competition with them. I knew from previous reading on stress that a fair amount of pressure, seen in a positive way, helps improve performance (Dunham 1992: 95). But I recognised in myself the symptoms of excessive pressure. Appley (cited in Dunham 1992: 94) proposes that individuals pass through stress thresholds when attempting to cope with pressures, starting with early warning signs such as anxiety and irritability, and moving on to loss of concentration, psychosomatic symptoms such as skin irritations, exhaustion and eventually burnout.

Dunham in his book *Stress in Teaching* says of the fine line between pressure and stress:

> The extent to which work demands made upon a teacher result in stress depends on a number of factors including pressures from sources external to teaching, personality and previous experience of similar demands.
>
> (Dunham 1992: 2)

I had certainly experienced similar demands before, which had left less than favourable expectations for the current year. There had been, and was still continuing, a considerable amount of pressure on me outside work. Dunham defines stress as:

> A process of behavioural, emotional, mental and physical reactions

caused by prolonged, increasing or new pressures which are significantly greater than coping resources.

(Dunham 1992: 3)

Normally I would have coped with these pressures by putting more time and energy into my work. However the physical, emotional and mental demands of managing difficult behaviour now, while needing to maintain thorough planning, assessment and record keeping, had totally depleted these resources. I listed all the areas from which I felt under pressure, and identified from these three elements which concerned me most: difficult behaviour in the carriage, workload, and the meeting of contractual obligations. These were important departure points for me on my journey which needed to be addressed. The next three sections are devoted to their consideration. In retrospect it is easy to see how pressures in these areas built up to such a pitch, yet at the time I was so busy reacting that I was unable to step back and gain a clear perspective on them.

After discussion with the Special Educational Needs Co-ordinator, Todd and Eddy were placed on Stages 2 and 3 respectively of the Local Education Authority's Stages of Assessment, with individual programmes drawn up to support behaviour development. Through the advice of a visiting behaviour specialist I was able to recognise patterns in Eddy's behaviour. What struck me was that in drawing up programmes to manage Eddy's behaviour, there were considerable implications for my own practice. For example, when he became aggressive upon entering class, was his frustration in part owing to inappropriate classroom organisation on my part?

Although the Special Educational Needs Co-ordinator and I were planning for desired changes to Eddy's behaviour, I questioned where the safeguard was for the child against unhelpful teacher behaviour, within the Staged Assessment procedure. I could see that, if I wanted them to be, all the behaviour problems in the class could be attributed to problems in the children, and they could have programmes to sort them out. Yet I had seen that the teacher and school had very real responsibilities in this. Such sharing of responsibility for change, to meet the special needs of children, became even more apparent over the following months.

REFRESHMENT It appears that not only the pupil but the teacher and the school need to be prepared to change to meet the special needs of pupils.

Mount Development

Prior to beginning the Masters' course in October 1995, I had read the selected pieces forwarded to us over the summer (Barton and Oliver 1992, Martin 1988). Reading these was like coming home, bearing in mind the concerns that I already had regarding joint responsibility for change. The following quote is from one piece at the beginning of the course which particularly echoed my thinking:

> Special educational needs are needs that arise within the educational system rather than the individual, and indicate a need for the system to change further in order to accommodate the individual differences.
>
> (Dyson 1990: 59)

Dyson draws this conclusion making reference to the 'individual change' model of change in Special Needs education, influenced by the Warnock Report (DfE 1978) and the 1981 Education Act, where it is the pupils who are expected to change their behaviour regardless of their environment. Warnock's proposal talks of an alternative 'system-level change', where an environment which is not favourable to the child should consider changing itself instead to accommodate the pupil more effectively.

FLASHBACK I remembered a similar conflict myself from secondary school. Achievements that I had made appeared to be given less formal recognition when they were in areas that I perceived were valued less highly by the school at the time.

During our first week on the Masters' course we were invited by a tutor to think back, and reflect on, a learning difficulty that we had experienced at school.

I did not think that I had had a particular learning difficulty at school, except that my time at secondary school had left me with a very negative view of my abilities, further confirmed by my exam results. Although these events had taken place years before, their effects remained with me. I could not believe that I was this same person now beginning a higher degree. This might have been hilarious if there had not been a down side to it as well, the handicapping of myself through insecurity about my own ability. Purkey describes the results of continual affronts to our self esteem:

> Even the most insensitive parent or teacher can usually recognise and take into account a crippling physical handicap. Negative self-esteem however is often overlooked because we fail to take the time and effort it requires to be sensitive to how children see themselves and their abilities.
>
> (Purkey 1970: 37)

I knew I had caused some disruption at school, but equally knew, from my position now as a primary teacher, that there was more to it than purely blaming the teacher or the child. I did not want to pass on the same handicap that I still experienced but now was in a position to prevent. I was concerned to help Eddy, not hinder him.

FLASHBACK Could my teaching and communication leave Eddy with the same negative impressions of himself as a learner that I had felt at school?

Dyson again contributes that:

> Every event in a pupil's life may have some bearing on his or her capacity to learn. When 'normal' individuals show an inability to learn in school, yet are perfectly capable of learning in other situations, *one should be driven to consider what aspects of the society are creating negative attitudes to schools and whether changes are necessary in the schools themselves.*
>
> (Dyson 1990: 55, italics added)

It is with such an exploration, through observation in the carriage, that the following section is concerned.

REFRESHMENT A full and thorough consideration of the child and his or her life experience as a whole should be taken into account when planning learning programmes.

Finders Sharers

As already noted, it was Eddy's behaviour that caused me the most concern. I wanted to see exactly what he was doing in the carriage and not make ill-informed judgements based on inadequate evidence. I decided that I would observe him at work.

I asked the pupils to think about a special person that they would like to come to their house, and then to draw and colour a picture showing this guest and the kind of preparations they would make in order for this special visit. I did not tell the class that I would be observing Eddy, yet I was glad that he gave me an indication he knew I was watching him. As I looked for patterns within my written record I became aware of looking at Eddy's actions and considering different ways of interpreting them; first with the insight of seeing the full picture from my position in the class observing, and second to ask myself, 'How else might I have interpreted his behaviour when under greater stress myself, and what actions might I have taken?'

FLASHBACK I was much more relaxed as I observed Eddy. In fact the absence of a 'stressed' teacher trying to 'control' him all the time probably did his behaviour the world of good! I was prepared to see the lighter side of things rather than feeling, 'I must be on top of Eddy's behaviour always', and that, 'If he misbehaves it is my lack of classroom control and I am therefore a failing teacher', regardless of the other twenty-six children behaving 'well', who could also be said to be the 'product' of my classroom management.

I have summarised in Table 2.1 the main points I drew out from the observation of Eddy, my initial interpretations of them and an alternative interpretation.

Table 2.1 Alternative interpretations of Eddy's behaviour

Time	Action	Relaxed interpretation	Stressed interpretation
9.32	Talks when working	Helpful automatic self-expression	Disturbing concentration of others
	Joking	Values friends and humour	Lack of concentration
9.35	Visits friend's table	Needs to relate to others	Disturbing concentration of others
	Asks politely for something	I may have missed this good behaviour from across the room	
	Sharpening pencil	I forgot to organise the helpers	Work avoidance tactic
	'Wooden Willy' action	E's humour; he's happy	Inappropriate behaviour
	Tells friend colour of eyes	Helping his friend	Lack of concentration
9.41	Propels rubber using ruler with description of mechanical catapult	Understanding of technology	Throwing rubber – disruption
	'B' for balloon	Initial sound practice	Disturbing concentration of others
	Birds have stripes	Knowledge of natural world	Disturbing concentration of others
9.45	Discusses friend's eyes and choice of pencil	Accuracy and attention to detail	Disturbing concentration of others
9.46	Stands up and colours at table	Comfortable working position	Disturbing concentration of others
9.50	Describes picture	Expression about relationships	Disturbing concentration of others

To me this observation illustrates how one action can have so many interpretations held in the hand of the teacher. I consider this serves to reinforce the importance of open-ended exploration before making conclusions about reasons for behaviour and setting the wheels in motion for dealing with 'deviance' or 'disruption'. Martin (1988: 501) suggests the use of a broad evaluative framework for assessing children, as an alternative to the 'expert'-led, jargon-riddled and straightjacketed formats that she found unhelpful. We should consider seriously:

The child's stance in the world, the child's emotional tenor and disposition, the child's mode of relationship to other children and to adults, the child's activities and interests, the child's involvement in formal learning, the child's greatest strengths and areas of greatest vulnerabilities.

(Carini, in Martin 1988: 496)

REFRESHMENT Should we build a similar sensitivity to the one Martin suggests towards our staff as well as pupils? Teachers who feel they are 'failing' need as much support as the children who feel they are failing. It would make an interesting study to explore the similarities and differences with which pupils and staff facing difficulties are managed, especially regarding the use of the concept of 'failure'. Hence the title for my study: Children with special needs – teachers with special needs.

In the following section I will be considering the nature of the 'special needs' in my own experience as a teacher on this journey.

Crisis Point

At this point there may appear little to suggest that there was about to occur the 'crisis point' which prompted this study. The observation of Eddy shows the everyday antics encountered in the classroom. It is when we look at the personal events outlined briefly in the introduction, and the concerns regarding the children's behaviour listed in 'Harried Hill', that it is possible to see how the tinder of frayed nerves from a demanding summer could so easily be ignited by the sparks of daily conflicts within the carriage. I could have dealt with each of these demands separately, yet coming one after the other, and drawing on depleted reserves, they became increasingly difficult. I have highlighted in italics, in the opening statement, the conflict I felt between my own need and my professional duties. I had faced this hurdle of overwhelming pressure before, but this time I was not able to round up my strength and carry on. I was exhausted. I could see my targets but had no way of meeting them. When I pulled back the throttle, nothing came out. I was just too tired. My health was suffering. I had lost my appetite, was unable to sleep or relax and was prone to tears, anxiety and panic attacks. I suffered skin complaints and could not remember things, make decisions easily or keep things in perspective.

In returning to the question, 'How am I ever going to get back in that classroom again?', I began to consider what was preventing me from doing so. Obviously something was stopping me. I asked myself, could I go back tomorrow? My answer was 'no', because nothing would have changed. The pressures would still be the same. I began to look at which of those pressures could be changed, and what I could do about changing them. I have already considered the difficult behaviour of some pupils within the class. The Special Educational Needs Co-ordinator and I appeared to have exhausted our strategies within the carriage, and it was to be a while before further external help, such as the educational psychologist or counsellors, would be available. So, what of the other pressures?

This was not the first time I had experienced such stress. As a first strategy I decided to revisit my earlier experiences to see what help they could offer me in this new situation. The following extract is from a personal evaluation written at the end of my second year of teaching.

> By half-term I had had enough. Too many hours, no clear attainable objectives, too many requirements it appeared, but still wanting to do a good job and be a person. I found an excellent book, *Stress in Teaching* by Jack Dunham – a great encouragement and help . . . An inspector came in and praised another member of staff and myself for 'outstanding teaching' in the lessons he had observed . . . Becoming a Teacher Governor helped me to gain a better understanding of where the school is going – an overview.
>
> (July 1994 reflection on Summer Term 1994)

For the first time Dunham (1992) set my then present experience into a context of national change, that of the effects of the 1988 Education Reform Act into which I had walked as I began my teaching career. It was reassuring to know that there was a national cause for the local and personal pressure of work that we were feeling. If the national scene was turbulent and the management team within the train was doing its best to negotiate new tracks, it was not surprising that the passengers or guards could find no firm frame of reference from which to approach their journey.

Becoming a teacher governor at this time was invaluable in helping me to see light at the end of the tunnel. It was demoralising that the pressure was on to deliver higher standards of achievement, yet the most effective and efficient way of doing this was not clear yet. Thus I spent many hours in my first three years of teaching struggling to plan not only individual lessons, but also a framework of continuity and progression for each term and year, which I knew was essential for the children's achievement. Now in 1995, a year and a half later, I was back at this point of feeling overwhelmed. Although I had with me the knowledge that we had moved on, both nationally and locally, I observed that I was still working the ten to twelve hour weekdays and six to eight hour Saturdays needed in order to deliver in class the quality provision I took pride in. This was in November. The following and final section considers what happened in my thinking during the time that I was absent from work.

Path of Approach

I did not realise at the time that my concerns about planning at the time could be found in the voices of many others. Whether reports such as

Curriculum Organisation and Classroom Practice in Primary Schools echoed my thoughts or gave rise to them is hard to say.

> With the introduction of the National Curriculum and the School Development Plan initiative, there has been a recognition that teachers must plan together to ensure consistency and progression across classes and year groups and that formally structured short and long term plans are essential to effective classroom teaching.
> (Alexander, Rose and Woodhead 1992: 20)

I had also been trying to find my own philosophy for effective teaching practice while ducking the pendulum of change that was swinging again in educational ideology. I was very much aware, from my Initial Teacher Training period, of the polarisation between 'progressive' and 'formal' methods. At times I found myself lacking in confidence when faced with situations that required more formal teaching skills than I was used to. Alexander *et al.* also noted, giving regard to recent research into children's learning, that 'recent studies . . . place proper emphasis, on the teacher as teacher rather than "facilitator"' (Alexander *et al.* 1992: 18). Again this was largely contrary to the messages that I had received during my training. It has taken me a long time to shake off the shackles of prejudice regarding certain teaching methods, such as whole class teaching, and develop my confidence in a wider range of skills. It became clear to me that effective links between Initial Teacher Training, Newly Qualified Teacher induction and continuing in-service provision, for the continuing development of teaching skills, are of great importance for confident and effective teaching. The management on the School Express also demonstrated their commitment to this by funding my higher degree.

I realised that through these first three years I had not only been experiencing the stress of meeting requirements with inadequate skills in some areas, for example when more 'formal' methods would have delivered a teaching point more effectively, but had also been depriving myself of the chance to develop these skills through fear of doing 'the wrong thing'. One of the blessings of 'falling apart' as I did was that many unnecessary burdens were shown to be just that: unnecessary. I could not expect to do everything, and I became more able to put things in perspective.

December had passed, January was coming to an end and I was about to return to work. I was no longer exhausted. Something else had happened in me on my journey. I had shed the weighty luggage of the many unrealistic expectations that I had of myself and the children, and gained a new confidence in my teaching ability through my research. I was pleased to become acquainted with new insights into children's learning, especially in the work of Vygotsky and his theory of 'a zone of proximal development'; which 'refers to the gap that exists for children between what they can do alone and what they can do with help from someone more knowledgeable or skilled than themselves' (Vygotsky in Bourne *et al.* 1994: 24). This helped dramatically to increase my confidence as a teacher and confirm my reason for being in the carriage. I was not just a facilitator who drew out what children already knew, but someone who had skills and knowledge to help them develop. If this was the case, though, how could I hope to provide adequate quality interaction to aid development in twenty-seven pupils by myself? I could see that I would have to plan well but lower my expectations of myself. I found this hard, knowing that the greater the input I could give in the early years, the greater the benefits would be as the pupils matured. Fortunately, though, during my absence a teaching assistant for Eddy and Todd had been allocated for five mornings per week, thus providing the opportunity for much more of this desired interaction and support.

So the train has pulled up at its next destination. I have left much baggage behind but I have also gained some. Through reflecting on the educational experience of the children I teach, and myself as learner and teacher, this study has enabled me to deepen my understanding and develop my classroom practice. It has also helped me to locate my personal experience within the insights of others and to draw strength from this, to use this time as a period of growth. Regardless of the varied educational terrain travelled, it is this element of reflection on personal circumstance and practice, informed by the wisdom of others and supported by rest, that has enabled me to put events into perspective and return to the classroom.

* * *

NARRATIVE SUMMARY I

Issues arising from Ros's innovative research

The approach that Ros devised was not modelled on any existing description of practitioner research; it was tailor-made to draw creatively on a combination of childhood experience, current and prior reading, and classroom research. Her use of observations of a child in her class as a resource for reflecting on her *own* experience and needs is an unusual and distinctive feature of the study.

Ros had an urgent personal need to come to terms with the difficulties that she found herself experiencing, so she searched for a methodology for addressing those difficulties that would allow her both to give expression to her feelings and to find a positive way forward. With the emotional need providing the inner drive for her inquiry, she used these various resources to create a dialogue with herself that would ensure that her thinking was also sufficiently challenged to lead to new insight and understanding. She felt that the academic demands of the course were helpful to her purposes because they made her be rigorous and therefore 'honest' with herself; they required that she engage with the ideas and perspectives of others as a route to understanding, rather than pursue a purely introspective path. If she was not rigorous in her thinking, nothing would change. She said, 'If there hadn't been the criteria then I would have given myself my own criteria.'

She developed the metaphor of the train as a way of bringing structure and cohesion to the disparate parts of her study. Feeling uncertain about how to set about structuring her essay, she drew on her strengths as an artist to help her find a form of expression for her ideas. She said, 'I just sat there and thought, how is this going to hold together? And I had images in my mind that needed to progress, so there is obviously a start and an end.' The image of a train gradually took shape because it seemed to correspond to the range of ideas that she wanted to incorporate. 'There were sections within a whole, like the carriages within a train, and there were flashpoints, as I called them, which were danger awareness points . . . written in red (in the original) . . . the other thing that I wanted to have was a running summary going through each time I reached a certain point, like a refreshment person coming round train carriages.'

Although many of the ideas that she was dealing with were painful ones, she had fun playing with the metaphor of the train and exploring how it could support and stimulate thinking. She found the image engaging and motivating, and felt that it would be a successful way of engaging the reader's interest and communicating her ideas with clarity. She was not drawn to an academic style of language; she wanted to express academically rigorous thinking in a way that would be accessible and enjoyable for the reader. She felt that she was given encouragement to be experimental and follow whatever approach appealed to her personal style by the group of students that she was currently working with, and by her supervisor. She admitted that if she had not had this encouragement, the study would probably have ended up more like a traditional essay. She said, 'If my tutor had been a dragon, it would have been academic.'

Ros' study was so important to her that gaining a pass for her essay was actually less important than answering the questions that she had set herself. The drive to achieve the best possible quality work arose from this personal investment in the work. Nevertheless, she recognised that the academic demands of the course also made a significant contribution to the development of her thinking. Indeed, she became more convinced of the relevance and legitimacy of those demands as a result of the part that they had demonstrably played in helping her to find a way forward in her teaching.

Chapter 3

Visualisation in research and data analysis

Jacqui Potter

Editorial note

When Jacqui carried out this research she was employed on a course development team writing a new BSc Hons Physiotherapy programme. The participants in her research were studying on a physiotherapy course in a hospital-based physiotherapy school where she had previously worked. She was following a two-year part-time course in Applied Research in Education, accredited by the University of East Anglia and based at the Cambridge Institute of Education. The chapter describes an innovative, visual approach to analysis used in her final thesis. It is not an extract from the thesis itself.

Introduction

When I look back on my experience of the Masters' course I can see that the visual image was an important element in my thought and learning processes from the very first piece of work set for the course, which was to observe two students in a learning situation.

I was a little apprehensive of this task: I did not know what was expected of me. I was a foreigner, a therapist sitting in the midst of a group of teachers who spoke a foreign language. I was a teacher, and had been for thirteen years, but I taught physiotherapy, and that was different. I was a physiotherapist first and a teacher second. The subject was more important than the method used to transmit it.

I was not too worried though. Physiotherapists are good at observation. We watch people all the time: patients walking into the department, patients doing exercises, the public walking in the street or pushing trolleys around supermarkets. It is amazing how quickly you can diagnose all kind of ailments in quite short bursts of observing human activity. I observe students as well. I observe their hands and their stance, when they practise massage on a fellow student. I observe their technique, when they set up an electrical machine. I even observe how they relate to the patients in their care. What is so different about watching two students learning?

I found this activity to be something of a revelation simply because I had not really taken time out to do it before. In spite of having been involved in education for many years I felt that I was now for the first time seeing many things that I had totally missed before. More importantly, the things that I had been missing could have had a great effect on my teaching practice. One possible reason for this is that my experience of education was confined to physiotherapy courses. Physiotherapy, like many of the health professions, is more concerned with the content of the curriculum than the process of education.

Having worked for so long in what can only be described as something of an educational backwater, I knew not of 'structured observation' or 'time charts'. So, on the day before the work was due in, I strolled into somebody else's class – with their agreement – and set about observing two students learning. I had no expectations, no predetermined criteria. I had an open mind. I was just going in to see and write down what happened. Perhaps that was why I found it such a revelation. I saw two students, who I thought of as friends, working together on a task and yet not really communicating with each other or helping each other. Had this sort of thing been going on under my nose for all these years, without my noticing it at all? I walked into that room with a head empty of thoughts. I walked out with a thousand questions buzzing through my brain: questions not about the physiotherapy techniques they were working on, not about the subject matter, but about the learning process. When two students are working together, does it matter who practises a technique first? Does doing something first make that person more knowledgeable than the one who goes second? Why do they behave as if it does? The experience was a revelation to me: it shook my belief in what I had been doing all those years.

This really is a story about an individual who was accustomed to observing with one pair of eyes, those of the practitioner, but who learned to use another pair, those of the researcher. In particular, the story describes how I came to develop a model of physiotherapy education using a process of visualisation.

Background to the study

Physiotherapy is a paramedical profession which conforms to Schön's (1983, 1990) concept of professional practice in which professionals cope daily with unexpected, unforeseen, previously unknown, uncertain and unique human situations. Although reflective practice has not been widely understood by many physiotherapists in the past, research by Higgs (1990, 1992a, 1992b, 1993), has made physiotherapists more aware of the concept. Her work explored the clinical reasoning skills of physiotherapists and identified them as a hallmark of expert physiotherapy professional practice. She defines essential clinical reasoning competencies as including 'the ability to utilise cognitive skills, to use skills of reflection, review, evaluation and metacognition, and the ability to access one's knowledge base' (Higgs 1992a: 576). The research therefore presents expert professional practice as a highly complex process in which the interrelationships between formal theory, practical skills, personal knowledge and reasoning processes form vital elements. The research of Barrows and Tamblyn (1980) and more recently Boshuizen and Schmidt (1992) suggest that the knowledge structures that allow integration of these elements only occur after exposure to patient care in authentic situations. As I have come to understand the research, my belief in the importance of clinical education has been reinforced.

For many years the process of learning through practice has been largely neglected by educational institutions offering physiotherapy courses, and practising clinicians are still responsible for educating students in the clinical environment. Although given the title of clinical educator, these individuals, who are clinical specialists in a variety of fields, often have little educational expertise and receive little support to carry out the role.

My role as organiser of clinical education placements made me very aware of the problems that this caused. Students were consistently telling me how the quality of their experience (and consequently their learning) varied from placement to placement. It seemed to me that if students could be encouraged to view their clinical educator as one of many resources and to take more responsibility for their own learning, they might be able to cope better. However, before plunging into strategies intended to develop independent learning skills, I felt it was necessary to explore whether it was happening already or not.

I therefore set out to discover whether the physiotherapy students in one educational establishment were displaying effective self-directed learning behaviour during their clinical education placements.

Method and design

The driving force behind the overall research design was to develop an approach that would most appropriately demonstrate the learning behaviour of a variety of individuals in the complex setting of clinical practice. During the Masters' course a number of pieces of research-based work had been set that provided me with an opportunity to experiment with various methods of gathering data. I had tried out interviews, questionnaires and observations, but I had become dissatisfied with the results of using such methods in isolation. Abercrombie's (1989) writing on perception and Kelly's (cited in Ewen 1984) work on learning had helped me to understand that an individual will have a limited understanding of any situation. I felt that by gathering only one type of data you gain what is a superficial view of one small part of a very flat picture. I was interested in adopting a more holistic approach. I wanted to look at the three-dimensional structure, and was concerned to place the students' learning behaviour within context. I therefore chose to include staff and students from a range of levels within the participant group, and used interviews, meetings and observations held in the natural environment. Taken as a whole, the method was consistent with the principles of ethnography, and I found that I was able to justify my methodology by reference to this one set of principles which have been summarised by Hammersley (1990).

The interviews were informal, although a degree of structure was incorporated by adopting the 'critical incident review' approach (Flanagan 1954). The technique had been effectively adapted by Benner (1984) in her study of professional nursing behaviour. Benner used the approach to provide a focus for discussing abstract or hidden elements of professional behaviour and the factors influencing that. Physiotherapists working in the clinical field adopt a very practical and patient-centred approach, and having little knowledge of educational theory, they are not accustomed to discussing or even thinking about their own learning processes. Critical incident review guidelines were provided to the participants, which encouraged them to consider their approach to learning by reflecting on specific experiences. The focus for discussions was very loosely identified as 'good and bad learning experiences', and no questions were pre-set. The guidelines, therefore, provided a personal background for the interviews but did not dictate their direction.

I consciously made an effort to see the whole picture and ensure internal validity (Robson 1993) by using a process of respondent validation. The interview transcripts were given to the students and clinicians, who were invited to make any additions, deletions or changes that they wished. Following the interviews a group meeting was held, in which the participants discussed the issues they had individually identified. This discussion generated an observation schedule which was used in the observation of student and clinicians working together.

The emergence of the model

My approach to data analysis was also influenced by my experience on the Masters' course. I had found that simple category analysis involving cutting, pasting, colour coding and so on seemed to reduce the data to relatively unconnected, often uninteresting and unhelpful chunks which were at times difficult to put together into a coherent whole. I felt that depth of information and the 'thick descriptions' (Hammersley 1990) characteristic of ethnographic research were best developed by exploring the interrelationships between data and sources. I therefore decided to 'keep the data whole' rather than breaking each transcript into constituent parts. The transcripts were not merely words on a piece of paper, they represented complex individuals.

However, I began my analysis in traditional mode by identifying a large number of first-level categories (Miles and Huberman 1994). The labels I chose to give them were generated from the scripts themselves, but were also influenced by my reading of the literature. There was an endless list of categories, and I felt myself falling into a mire of reductionist scraps. I felt I was getting bogged down, and I made a decision to stop, step back and think.

For me, thinking is a very active process often conducted on paper. There are lots of words, mind maps with lots of arrows, and lots of torn-up sheets in the rubbish bin. I ended up with four key words arranged on a piece of paper. These comprised more meaningful second-level categories or themes (Miles and Huberman 1994), into which all of the earlier categories could be aggregated. They represented four learning resources which consistently appeared within the data. I referred to them as pillars, and pictured them as white marble columns (perhaps in my mind linking the themes of learning to the civilisation of ancient Greece).

This stage became a crucial point in developing my process of analysis. By representing the themes as three-dimensional structures placed in an architectural relationship to one another, I had created an imaginary location populated by the participants in my research. The whole transcripts represented the views of the populace, and I was able to explore the topography by asking questions of the transcripts. Each stage of the analysis added more details and generated more questions to ask of the data. I was able to use the information provided by them to guide me through a journey of discovery. In this respect I felt that I was observing that well-quoted maxim of qualitative research, 'let the data speak'.

Although I often refer to this as 'building the model', I feel that it was more a process of 'discovering an image'. I never felt the model was my invention. I was merely a tool. I found myself in a process that was self-perpetuating. The questions and answers were not mine, they came from the data. I suppose in my own mind I had achieved what I had set out to do. I did not look for things, I found out what was there.

The final model that emerged, and the learning that it represented, are explained later. In the sections that follow, I show how the model progressively evolved as I thought about, and interacted with, my data.

The basic map

In my doodling I had placed the four resources which I called formal theory, experts, patients and peers at the four points of the compass. This represented a simple topography which I called the basic map (see Figure

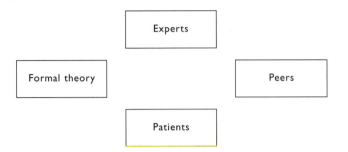

Figure 3.1 The basic map

3.1). By using the themes as questions to ask of each set of data, I began to develop substantial and consistent explanations of them.

Formal theory

Formal theory comprises the body of knowledge underpinning clinical practice which is available from textbooks, journal articles and formal teaching situations:

CLINICIAN D: If I know there is something coming up I don't feel very confident about, I always try and read up about it before I have to do it. Because I think some theory is extremely helpful.

It consists primarily of the medically related sciences together with the results of experimental research studies:

STUDENT 2: I think it stems back to being in school and doing basic anatomy and physiology and pathologies and being told that with a certain syndrome you will have these problems.

The rapidly progressive development of medical science dictates that formal theory does not remain static but is constantly changing and evolving.

Formal theory from other caring disciplines, which the learner perceives to have relevance to physiotherapy, may be included:

CLINICIAN C: They did a whole section on the visually impaired. It really brought it home to me, the problems associated with that client group. . . . I apply that now, especially things like wheeling people around in wheelchairs with a sensory handicap.

Formal theory is an example of propositional or objective knowledge, 'knowing that', in which 'since the formal affirmations of a theory are unaffected by the state of the person accepting it, theories may be constructed without regard to one's normal approach to experience (Polanyi 1958: 4).

Experts

Experts are primarily physiotherapists with a recognised level of knowledge within a specialist field:

CLINICIAN E: Because they have done more courses than I have, they have been qualified a lot longer so they have got more patient management skills.

Other health professions such as medicine, occupational therapy, speech therapy, social work and nursing also provide experts:

CLINICIAN E: I think you do learn a lot from the medical and nursing staff. You can't be a physio and just come on and do what you want and go off the ward again, you have got to pay attention to what everybody else is saying. But I also think that you teach them too.

Where the learner is exposed to a wider group of professions such as teaching or clinical psychology, they too are incorporated into the learning resource:

CLINICIAN C: I have learnt a lot about how other people operate including clinical psychologists, psychiatrists, special needs specialists. It is a multi-disciplinary approach . . . I have been learning quite a lot through that.

The experts appear to offer their personal, practical experience of the field, and help the learner to develop a better understanding of the relevant formal theory:

CLINICIAN D: It is just your basic skills that you are passing on, because I think that is actually what we, it is those little tricks that you have popped up your sleeve that you use every single day, your tone of voice to motivate a patient . . . but I think sometimes the clinical educator should be reminded that that is their forte.

Patients

Patients provide the data and opportunities through which the learner's personal and practical knowledge (Polanyi 1958) develop. Personal knowledge is an individual's personal understanding of a situation, and influences their ability to respond to the circumstances. Interaction with patients contributes to the process of developing personal knowledge in a variety of ways:

- Evidence supporting the formal theory: the patients are living examples of the conditions contained within the formal theory. Subtle differences in presentation between patients expose the learner to the range of possibilities they may encounter:

   CLINICAL EDUCATOR 1: I think what they are doing is actually trying to put what they can read about into practice. Start actually observing patients as people. You can't pretend to be a certain condition, you can't be a student pretending to be a stroke.

- An opportunity to acquire sensory knowledge: interactions with, and handling of, the patients allows the learner to develop tactile, audible and visual knowledge of clinical features such as alterations in muscle tone, breath sounds or abnormal movement patterns:

   CLINICIAN B: It is more a question of becoming very much more alert to how something feels and how to loosen it off when it is tight or how to stimulate it when it is floppy. . . . It takes a long time to get the feel of spasticity, and that comes from just having your hands on.

- Feedback: the ways in which the patients respond to the learner's interventions provide the learner with information on the effectiveness of their techniques:

   CLINICIAN E: It is what they are doing, I suppose, if they are not getting any better then that teaches you that either your treatment is wrong or ineffective. If they are really tired all the time after you have treated them, then you treated them too long. It teaches you to be more efficient and effective.

- Generalisable knowledge: exposure to several patients with similar problems allows the learner to test the generalisability of their personal knowledge. Approaches used successfully with one patient may be used with subsequent patients and adapted according to their response:

   CLINICAL EDUCATOR 3: It is easier for us because we have come across perhaps a similar situation before. You see a post op patient and they have got A, B, C and D, and you think, well, I will do this.

Peers

Peers include colleagues working within physiotherapy as well as those from other professions:

CLINICIAN A: Group discussions as well . . . essentially the ones that I work amongst, the occupational therapist if they are there, the speech therapist if you come across them. The doctors are very helpful and supportive, the social workers as well, and carers in the community.

The different experience of peers generates development of a different personal knowledge base, which allows an alternative viewpoint to be brought to a problem:

CLINICIAN D: I am the only person on Care for the Elderly here, I use the resources of the senior on neuro a lot . . . if they can just give me time to give an assessment of a problem I am having with a patient.

The learner: differences in the use of learning resources

Having filled out the substance of the pillars, I focused my attention on exploring how each participant related to each resource. The main differences between the individuals occurred in their use of the four learning resources, and I was able to use this to plot their position on to the basic map. Although there were several individual differences, three patterns of use became apparent: those used by students, undifferentiated practitioners, and specialists (see Figure 3.2).

Students

The students demonstrated a high level of dependence on the expert with whom they were working, and extensive reference to formal theory:

STUDENT 3: Well, first of all a good learning experience involved a lot of

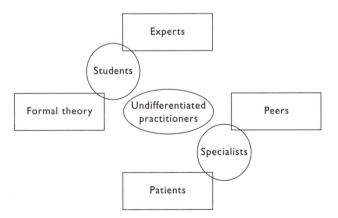

Figure 3.2 Differences in the use of learning resources

information being given to me, and a lot of feedback on what I was doing, so I knew whether I was doing the right thing and what bits I had to change to make it right.

The bad experience was a definite lack of feedback and a lack of information being given to me. Also, in the bad one, I didn't know where I could go to get the information, who was my senior, who was the person responsible for me, (who) was there for me to talk to or to ask questions. So you end up trying to work it all out for yourself and it is not as effective as when you have got somebody else to ask.

STUDENT 6: I used an Orthopaedic assessment textbook, a relatively new one that is very good, excellent. In fact it was so good I am going to try and buy it, which is saying something. It was the most excellent book, absolutely brilliant. I tried to wade through a bit of Maitland and Grieve, but I find those sort of technique text books very difficult, very difficult to exactly visualise what they are trying to get at. . . . They are very much more reference books than reading books. Someone has a problem and you think 'How am I going to mobilise that?' and you go away and look it up. It is very difficult to actually sit down of an evening with no particular patient in mind and just try and wade through them. The orthopaedic assessment book, I read all the relevant chapters.

However, there was little intentional use of either patients or peers:

The students reported that they had not really thought of patients as contributing to their learning. Patients were there to be helped, not to help the learner. Some students reported that they perhaps saw the time with patients as being a time away from learning.

(Fieldwork notes)

STUDENT 6: I do discuss things with some people. S (a friend) and I often discuss things, although I am quite a loner as well. I tend to discuss things with people who I feel I can learn from. So I will quite happily take advice from, discuss things with a senior, and feel quite at ease doing that.

Undifferentiated practitioners

Clinicians who had recently qualified were working in rotational posts and were in the early stages of specialisation. They appeared to use the four learning resources equally, and were grouped within the centre of the field. Their distribution showed less variation than the student group and that which did exist appeared to be related to the period of time they had been qualified:

CLINICIAN E: We have two very good seniors here and it makes it really interesting. I really am interested in that field, going on the normal movement course with Mary Lynch was just an inspiration, because she is just so good, and I felt 'I want to be her, I want to get my skills up to that level.'

CLINICIAN E: I look at my journal every month, but I don't read every article, some months I don't read any articles. . . . Some articles you think, that is not relevant to what I am doing.

CLINICIAN E: You learn a lot from every patient. They teach you that you can't have recipes and you can't have standard treatments. You have to really alter your treatments to, really tailor it to the individual patient.

Specialists

The specialist group retained contact with both formal theory and experts:

CLINICIAN B: Before, I would have read an article and thought, 'That is good'. Now I say, 'That is rather unreliable, I don't like the way they have done that. That is not a very valid measure to have taken.' . . . I prefer reading articles and criticising them, but I also think it would be difficult to measure that. I suppose they have done the best they can, but they still haven't taken account of this.

CLINICIAN B: I still contact colleagues that I think can help me, either here, or we have good links with the National Hospital for Nervous Diseases, I liaise with them quite a bit. I know my Bobath tutor quite well and I discuss things with her.

However, the emphasis in their learning process was focused more on patients and peer support, these two resources in fact forming the mainstay of their continued development:

CLINICIAN B: Mostly it is from the feel. . . . If I am not doing the right thing, the feel doesn't change. Then I can make a subtle alteration to what I am doing and the feel will suddenly change quite dramatically.

CLINICIAN D: Those times that I am not progressing with a neuro patient, I might ask a colleague where to go on a particular problem I might be having . . . if I have lost direction of what I am trying to achieve with a patient.

The specialists, therefore, form a closer grouping placed near patients and peers. The three groups' relative use of the learning resources available within clinical practice allowed them to be positioned at different points within the basic map.

The learning pathway

This relatively linear relationship between the three groups could be interpreted as representing a learning pathway, mapping the progression from novice (in the top left-hand corner) to expert (in the bottom right-hand corner) (see Figure 3.3).

Creating a pathway through the pillars, and perceiving the learner as progressing along it, strengthened the three-dimensional structure. The Grecian theme persisted until it developed into almost an Aegean island. It became a place in my mind that I could visit through my thoughts. The inhabitants represented by the whole data acted as tour guides, so that all I had to do to find out more about the details was ask a question. The answers were all there in the data. The model and its inhabitants grew stronger with each visit, and I really felt that I had become 'immersed in the data', the second maxim of qualitative research that is so often quoted but not necessarily perceived at first exposure.

The emergence of a basic map with its learning pathway generated more questions with which to search the transcripts, and exposed new interpretations of the data gathered. By examining the relationships between resources that were adjacent on the map, and questioning what separated

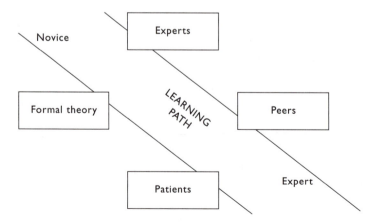

Figure 3.3 The learning pathway

those on either side of the pathway, I found that three zones appeared, each dominated by a major theme: the learning path itself; the area above and to the right, dominated by the theme of relationships; and the area below and to the left, dominated by the theme of knowledge.

The relationship zone

This area, which is placed above and to the right of the learning path, includes the learning resources of experts and peers. Within both these features, the inter-personal relationships between the learner and others have a significant role in the learner's ability to access the resource (see Figure 3.4). Moving diagonally from left to right, there is a shift from inequality to equality within the relationships. At one extreme, the learner often sees the expert as knowledgeable, inspirational and a figure to be emulated:

CLINICIAN B: That was what interested me in the first place, I had never seen anybody clinically improve a stroke patient or a head injury patient in a treatment session until I went on an assessment course. ... This hemiplegic sort of hobbled in to see [name] on the Saturday afternoon, and she turned him into a man who strode out. I thought 'I would like to do that' ... I just thought, 'My eyes are opened'.

If the expert does not fit this picture, the learner feels disappointed and let down:

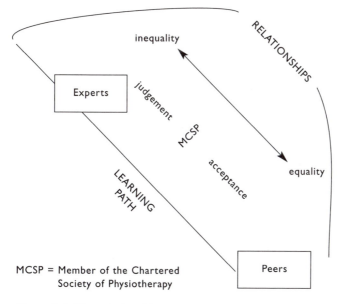

Figure 3.4 The relationship zone

STUDENT 6: She treated, I don't know, a couple of patients a day. She would spend an awful lot of time talking to other professionals, very little time with her hands on patients, and her treatments, what treatments she did give, were very textbook-like and not geared to the individual. . . . The few patients she did treat, that was what she did, regardless of whether they needed it or not.

At the other end of the spectrum, peers are, of necessity, equal, trusted and non-judgmental. Perceived inequality prevents interaction from occurring:

STUDENT 6: I do discuss things with some people. . . . The particular person I was with was having a lot of problems and I don't think it was appropriate for me to discuss my patients with her.

Within the zone there is a major barrier to be overcome: the attainment of qualified status. The existence of this barrier is demonstrated in the undifferentiated practitioners' experience of the change in relationship that occurs. Prior to this, the relationship between the learner and professionals is perceived as being judgmental. After the barrier is breached, the now intra-professional relationships are characterised by acceptance:

CLINICIAN F: Sometimes as a student you are expected to know things, whereas now it doesn't matter if you go and look at the book in the staff room, nobody is going to look at you and say, 'The student doesn't know something'. I sometimes think that you were expected to know things as a student, whereas now it doesn't matter. It is more relaxed in that way, you don't feel such an idiot asking, because everybody is asking each other questions.

This is an example of exclusivity within professions (Schein 1972), in which a potential member must demonstrate his or her 'fitness' to belong, but once accepted can enjoy the full support of the professional group.

The knowledge zone

This area, placed below and to the left of the learning path, incorporates the resources of formal theory and patients (see Figure 3.5). The learners' ability to utilise these resources is most strongly influenced by the nature of the knowledge itself. I expected that the development of professional interpersonal relationships with patients would exert a major influence. However, the students and clinicians alike reported no great problems in this area.

Formal theory is the first feature, and its application to patients in an experimental process leads to the development of personal knowledge. But as personal knowledge begins to grow, part of the formal theory relevant

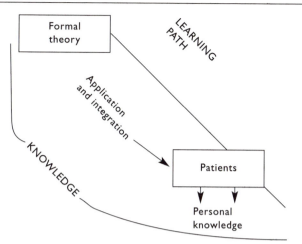

Figure 3.5 The knowledge zone

to the specialist interest is absorbed into it and becomes inseparable in the learner's mind:

STUDENT 6: To start with it is all very divided in your mind, into textbook knowledge and placement knowledge. Then it does all begin to gel. All of a sudden you turn around and you begin to think, 'Oh, where did that piece of knowledge come from?' and you are not quite sure, but it doesn't really matter, it is something you have learnt somewhere along the line. So I think it begins to gel more and more. You begin to start applying your lecture and textbook knowledge more in the clinical setting.

This is not always an easy process, and the students found moving from one point to the next a difficult and often confusing process:

STUDENT 3: I tried to go on what I had learned in school. But it is very different when you are in the clinical situation . . . because there are lots of different pressures on you. You have to think on your feet a lot more. It was an outpatients' department so it was all very busy and lots of people rushing around. I hadn't done that sort of assessment before, so I felt as if I didn't know anything.

When connections were made, learners were able to recognise their achievements and transfer their skills to other specialist areas:

STUDENT 1: What I did in my outpatient placement was, actually a couple of cases where I felt I had really seen the connection between the problem and the answer and the way of progressing it, I actually wrote them down. . . . Really I only made that link on the day before my assessment. The night before, she [the clinical educator] said go and read this, it was one of the books that had a lot of case histories in the back. . . . It suddenly clicked, it just made sense. . . . It carried over into everything else, even medical . . . the fact that I had done my outpatients first and that problem, what caused it, what can we do about it sort of approach.

Personal knowledge (Polanyi 1958) is developed through individuals' experiences and strongly influences their approach to problem-solving. The expert has often reached a stage where much of the relevant formal theory has been integrated and absorbed into his or her personal knowledge base, a factor also identified in Stengelhofen's study of speech therapy: 'Knowledge which is secure and well integrated appears to become embedded at a deep level and is used tacitly' (Stengelhofen 1993: 12).

The interconnections between the learning path and the adjacent two zones are the learning strategies which allow the learner access to the four learning resources. The specialists' group occupies the most advanced section of the learning path, and therefore may be regarded as demonstrating the most effective use of the four resources available within the clinical environment. However, effective learning was demonstrated by individuals within each of the groups. These resources, when amalgamated, may be regarded as providing guidelines of good practice. Individuality of learning style is an important factor to consider when determining effective learning strategies. This study set out to investigate learning within the clinical setting, and for the researcher to make judgements about the effectiveness of learning strategies is inappropriate. Effectiveness was therefore regarded as being present when the individuals themselves reported the benefits gained from specific strategies.

Further elaboration through literature and dialogue

At this point, the developing model appeared to suggest a linear, hierarchical structure, in which students were only able to interact effectively with formal theory, and only specialists benefited from their experience with patients. However, this was not accurately reflected within the data. Although the students were less adept at maximising their patient-contact experience, they still found it very beneficial. In fact, the model lacked depth. However, it was possible to extend the three-dimensional viewpoint to create a model which showed the learner accessing the resources with different levels of sophistication via a learning path which formed an ascending spiral.

One decision I had made in the early stages of planning was not to begin with a detailed analysis of the literature. I had begun to look at the literature on learning theory, but it was so vast and there was so little that directly related to learning in a clinical setting, that I simply did not recognise which aspects would be most relevant to my particular focus, and I did not want to impose an agenda that was not appropriate. I did not want to go in looking for something, I wanted to go in and see what was there.

During the process of analysis it became apparent that I needed to draw upon the literature relating to learning theory to find some explanations for my interpretations. This process of addressing the literature after collection of the data rather than before had been recommended to me on an earlier occasion. It is a practice which allows the data itself to determine the direction, rather than allowing the literature to influence the research. On this occasion I found it most appropriate, as the model of learning generated by the study provided the focus from which the literature could be addressed. Through the analysis I was able to discriminate between relevant and irrelevant theories by judging their application to the model. The literature allowed me to develop stronger theoretical explanations for the images I perceived.

Within the literature, two main areas contributed substantially to the conclusions drawn. They comprised the concepts of personal knowledge and effective learning. Polanyi's (1958) extensive discussion, in which he sought to clarify the nature of personal knowledge, was important in identifying the factors which contributed to the problems associated with clinical education, and Kelly's personal construct theory (Ewen 1984: 313–44) reflected the complexity of an individual's development through clinical practice.

For me, the relationship between theory and practice (or theory and experience) is an important professional issue. The fact that I had found literature that directly related to or explained a situation I had encountered was very significant. It reinforced my belief in what I was finding.

An important element in qualitative research is the consideration given to the role and influence of the researcher in the process. In particular, I felt that the relationship between the data, the literature and the analysis could be interpreted as rather incestuous and of my invention. In recognition of this, I chose openly to state my own situation and how it might influence the interpretations I was making, and to attempt to externally validate (Robson 1993) my interpretations through a process of peer consultation. My employment as part of a team developing a new undergraduate physiotherapy programme meant that during the course of this study I was also engaged in an exercise in which physiotherapy education was subject to much discussion and analysis. The two activities inevitably overlapped, and I found that there were occasions in those discussions when some comments influenced me either to revise, or to progress with, my analysis. The interpretations drawn were therefore founded within three elements: the data collected for the study, the literature that the data led me to explore, and my coexisting professional experiences. This may be viewed as an exercise in triangulation or as an idiosyncratic account. To refute the latter accusation, I have been concerned to ground my conclusions within the data (Strauss 1987), and have sought to validate my interpretations by subjecting them to the scrutiny of colleagues from both the Masters' course group and the institution in which I am employed.

The fully developed model of learning

The completed model is represented by a three-dimensional structure in which four learning resources appear as fixed pillars. These comprise experts, formal theory, patients and peers. A learner progresses along a learning pathway which forms an ascending spiral between the pillars. The position of the learner on the learning path reflects the learner's level of learning development, and is determined by his or her relative utilisation of each of the learning resources. Novices who are most reliant upon experts and formal theory, and have weaker links to patients and peers, are positioned at the beginning. Experts, who utilise patients and peers consistently, and select from experts and formal theory more discriminatingly, are placed towards the top (see Figure 3.6).

The learner's ability to access the resources is determined by the learning strategies he or she has developed, and by the characteristics of the resources themselves. Experts and formal theory represent a didactic and theory-based approach to learning on which novices rely, but which experts are able to question. Patients and peers demand the more experimental and reflective

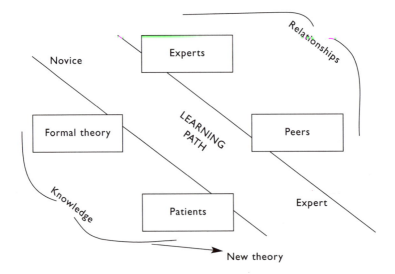

Figure 3.6 The fully-developed model of learning

approach characteristic of experiential learning and acceptance of diversity. Access to experts and peers is strongly influenced by the personal relationships between the learner and significant others. Formal theory and patients are influenced by the changing nature of knowledge, from an early reliance on propositional knowledge, through a process of application and integration, to an ability to utilise and develop personal theory (Polanyi 1958).

Reflections on what was learned

The written report of any piece of research tends to present the process as logical and orderly. In the beginning there is the question, which is investigated by a process, and the answer comes through analysis. The reality is not like that at all. My experience was one of a chaotic deluge of information, ideas and perceptions. Creating a visual image to facilitate data analysis helped me to organise the data and locate it in meaningful relationships which I still believe, portray a realistic model of learning through clinical practice.

* * *

NARRATIVE SUMMARY 2

Issues arising from Jacqui's innovative research

Jacqui had a desire to find a wholeness in the research. This wholeness emerged as a conceptual wholeness through the development of the theoretical model. The use of metaphor and conceptual imaging helped to create, develop and preserve this sense of wholeness for her.

Jacqui's experience was that the visual approach to analysis seemed to impose itself on her, rather than being something that she decided to do herself. It was as if the writing and thinking were beginning to control themselves, rather than being controlled by her. 'I was sitting there looking at the data and it started by accident really, the metaphor of the road and the pillars.'

The theoretical model became a secondary world which, at times, took over Jacqui's sense of reality. 'It was a place I could go and walk around and visit,' she said. Visiting it and exploring it became a form of theoretical discovery.

She moved aspects of her theoretical model around, visually and imaginatively. This created new thinking, new questions and new insights. The method of inventing questions from her model and then returning to the data to answer them was one of the innovative qualities of the work, although Jacqui did not see what she was doing as particularly innovative until the institution assessed it as such.

This visual mode was related to Jacqui's dominant thinking style, as she thinks in pictures. It was also related to the role of observation in her professional life. As a physiotherapist, much of her work is based on observation of patients. This has become generalised into her life such that she observes people spontaneously in a variety of situations, and especially in supermarkets. So the dominant thinking mode of her research emerged from this background. 'I had to match it to the mode of thought that helped.'

In no sense did Jacqui feel she was at odds with the academy nor fighting academic conventions. She said 'I didn't have any qualms. The message I picked up was that . . . as long as you can justify what you are doing that would be OK'. The norms, expectations and messages of the course validated what Jacqui was doing, and this made her comfortable with the path she was taking. She had a respect for the academic, because the course and aspects of her reading gave her authorisation for her own ideas and research processes. She used it for self-confirmation.

She did, however, depart from suggested academic convention in two ways. First, she did not read around the subject as her first step of enquiry, but rather moved straight to the gathering and exploration of data. Part of the reason for this was that when she started reading around learning theory, there was 'just so much literature [that] I could have spent the entire time on that'. She preferred to use literature later, during the analysis phase, to help her to make sense of, and reflect on, her data. Second, she did not start the research with a specific question. Although this had probably caused her supervisor some frustration, she 'felt more comfortable not having specific questions'. She wanted to begin her research in an exploratory way within her topic, letting her questions emerge from theorising her data.

Jacqui's way through her research was, therefore, individual and innovative, with distinct departures from some academic conventions. At the same time, however, those conventions provided support and validation for aspects of her research. There was a productive, symbiotic relationship between innovation and tradition.

Part 2

Conversation as a method of enquiry and reporting

Chapter 4

Towards an understanding of autism

An outsider's attempt to get inside

Joe Geraci

Editorial note

When Joe carried out this study, he was working as a substitute teacher at RAF Lakenheath, an American high school for Department of Defense dependents whose parents are attached to the US Air Force. He was in the second year of his Masters' course, and this was his final piece of work. The chapter has been edited by Joe from a 15,000 word dissertation.

I remember the world as I began to understand it when I was a young child, a world where I felt safe, a world where I was safe. In my world I could understand and imagine many things, but I could also wonder about and question many more. The first question I can recall asking my mother concerned automobile windscreen wipers. It was a rainy spring day and I was watching from our second-storey apartment window the traffic buzzing through the busy city streets. Fresh-smelling rain filtered in through the screened window, and I could feel the occasional drop of water passing its screen test to become mist upon my face. I asked my mother why was it that some cars' windscreen wipers went back and forth in the same direction together, while the wiper blades on other cars went opposite each other. I phrased the question differently, I've forgotten the exact wording, but I do remember using my hands to show the direction of the windscreen wipers so that my mother could better understand my question. Though I don't remember my mother's response to my question I do remember her sweet laughter, and that I felt safe, protected and secure.

Why do I relate this tale from my world, this little boy's story from when he could not have been much more than three years old? What can be the significance of a 'my world story' to this story of autism? By sharing my observations with my mother, I could gain another insight into my world, into our world. Children with autism would most likely never ask their mothers to help them make sense of their worlds, because the world of autism is a different world from the one that people without autism share. I convey my personal reminiscence as an example of a child learning by sharing his observations with another person. From a small group of people with autism who are called 'high functioning' we are beginning to understand the world of the person with autism from their sense of understanding. Writers such as Donna Williams and Temple Grandin are sharing insights of the world as perceived through the minds of people with autism.

It is the intention of this writing to journey into the world of people with autism so that a better understanding of that world may be reached. As an initiate into the world of autism, I hope to show how an 'outsider', a person who is familiar with the non-autistic world, can go about learning the world of autism.

I began my journey towards an understanding of the world of autism when my university tutors asked for volunteers to read books written by people with 'disabilities', about their disabilities, over the Christmas break, and report back to our seminar group the understandings we reached through these readings. Having never understood the disability called autism, I elected to read *Nobody Nowhere* by Donna Williams (1994). Fascinated by experiences Ms Williams endured as a child with autism, I felt that simply to report in a lecture format would not be adequate to express how moved I was by *Nobody Nowhere*. By developing a game in which my university peers could begin to enter the world of autism, I felt I could better share my understanding of the disability.

Before I committed myself to investigating the world of autism, I telephoned a local residential home for adults with autism and met with the manager. My personal impressions are related in the following section. (Throughout this essay I use a mode of personal reflection which is shown by a distinctive font as follows.)

Approaching the door of Middle Field Manor I notice a man walking around the perimeter of a large room. Each time he passes the door he momentarily stops and glances in my direction. It takes me a few of his passes to realise that this person might be a resident and probably will not open the door for me, so I ring the door bell. Observing Barry's travels, I realise that each time he passes the door and glances in my direction I can discern a slight smile cross his face. After waiting for a few minutes during which no one comes to the door, I let myself in and make my way to the unoccupied reception office.

Waiting by the office, I hear a sudden and shrill scream, followed by stomping feet. The noise is coming in my direction. Not knowing exactly what to do, I position myself about 45 degrees from the source of the noise. Emily bursts into the room, looks at me, throws herself on the floor and begins banging her head on the carpet. Following her is a woman who quite calmly removes a cushion from the nearby sofa and places it under Emily's head.

'Good morning! You must be Joe. I'm Elizabeth.[1] *Come right in the office.'*

I feel rescued. The only knowledge I have of people with autism I've gained from reading Nobody Nowhere *which, while an excellent autobiography, has not prepared me for the face-to-face realities of autism. How does one begin to learn to help people with autism? What kind of training is available to begin to work with this disability?*

First steps towards understanding autism

In my attempt to develop an understanding of the world of autism, I first read Uta Frith's *Autism: Explaining the Enigma* (Frith 1989). In her lucid text, and those of other professionals interested in autism (see Happe 1995 and Wing 1996), a chronicle of the disorder is traced to figures from history who are described as 'so-called feral children' (Frith 1989: 16). I learned that it was not until Hans Asperger and Leo Kanner first identified a set of criteria of behaviour that a working definition of autism began to be developed. While this definition has gone through various changes, the following criteria of behaviour have been established to describe people with autism:

> Qualitative impairment in reciprocal social interaction.
> Qualitative impairment in verbal and non-verbal communication, and in imaginative activity.
> Markedly restricted repertoire of activities and interests.
>
> (Frith 1989: 11)

Recently there has been much written about the 'triad of impairments' and the spectrum aspect of autism (see Frith 1989, Happe 1994, Jordan and Powell 1996, Wing 1996). These writings concur that people with autism have 'in common absence or impairments of social interaction, communication and development of imagination'.

The first day of observations at Middle Field Manor is quite intense. Although I've seen people with autism from a distance, I am not sure what to expect. The first stop is at Cambridge House. While I am sitting at a table discussing with the carers what I am trying to accomplish, Barry is again pacing the perimeter of the room. Charlie, who I met on the Studio Three Course, 'Meeting Challenging Behaviour', which Ian had invited me to attend, is explaining to me how at the end of every shift each resident's key worker has to complete a log of the activities the resident took part in during the day. Also on the log are annotated residents' behaviour, medication,

---

1 All names of residents and staff are pseudonyms. However, the manager of Middle Field Manor has requested that I use the actual name of the home and his name in this writing.

dietary observations and other information that might be pertinent. Sitting at the table I notice Barry is gradually decreasing the size of his route around the room; he is coming closer and closer to me, and finally reaches out to 'pat' me on the back of the head. Charlie smiles and tells me that he only does that to people he likes.

I meet other residents of Cambridge House. Paul asks me to spell words for him, the plural spellings. Richard, sitting in the television room staring not at the television and not acknowledging my presence, gives Charlie a cuddle and a kiss on the top of her head. Richard is approximately six feet, three inches tall. Mary is outside, working on a sun tan to such a degree of burn that the staff, to protect her, had to get her a bottle of sun screen, remove the label and tell her it was a lotion to increase the effects of the sun, otherwise she would not have used it. Chloe, a resident of Cambridge House who doesn't instantly avoid eye contact says hello; and there is Chris who I don't get to meet because she is in her room.

How am I supposed to address these people? What is the most beneficial way in which to interact with them? Beneficial for whom? Ian gave me a copy of the staff induction manual, Important Guidelines to Remember when Working with People with Autism, *which was useful, but how many of those statements can I remember?*

I find I am becoming very self-conscious about the way I am speaking to the residents. Realising I am using a tone of voice I normally reserve for my eighteen-month-old son and his group of peers, I feel I am belittling these people. When I later expressed my concern to Ian he said to 'be as natural as possible, be yourself – hell, at least you're talking to them. People come in and out of here as though the residents don't even exist.'

After Cambridge House I go to Norfolk House. Here residents are just finishing lunch, others are sitting in the garden enjoying the long awaited English spring. I sit at the picnic table with Sharon who avoids all communication, both verbal and nonverbal, but occasionally asks when the bus is going to leave. (After lunch the residents are to attend a drama session at a local hall.) Greg joins us and asks who I am and wants to shake my hand. Until then I hadn't offered my hand in friendship to any of the residents because I believed from my readings that most people with autism avoid physical contact. Eddie comes out into the garden listening to his radio which he holds up to his ear. Finishing his lunch, Wayne enters the garden and asks me how big the engine of my Harley-Davidson is. When I tell him it's 1200 cc he wants to know how many horsepower that could be. I tell him I don't know but will find out for him and let him know the next time I see him. Emily remains in the television room along with Cindy who is colouring in a book. One other resident of Norfolk House is away.

Watching the residents I become very aware of the fact that I am assessing them, and suddenly think how presumptuous it is of me to impose on these people in their home. How would I like it if people I didn't know barged into my home to observe me? Sometimes I think that does happen, but I can always throw these people out if I want to. Do these residents have the same power that I do? I begin having doubts about ethically conducting research in this setting; I'm beginning to question my own credibility too.

While the triad of impairments is a straightforward way of starting to understand the characteristics of autism, the idea of a spectrum disorder caused me some anxiety. As I began looking at autism as a spectrum disorder, I began to see the triad of impairment in everyone to some degree. My wife catches me counting how often she checks the alarm clock setting before she can go to bed. That is of course *after* she has completed her routine of making sure all the doors are locked, the cooker turned off, the refrigerator door closed tightly, and all the handles on our wardrobe are facing downwards. Sally Tomlinson, in *A Sociology of Special Education*, quips that in the early 1960s no one really knew much about autism and there were only a few people diagnosed with the disorder but by the late 1970s the number of people with autism was expanding astronomically and if we weren't careful we'd all be autistic by the turn of this century (Tomlinson 1982).

Sandra Harper, Middle Field Manor's assistant manager, directed me to review my reading on 'theory of mind'. Perhaps there I could find some help in working through this dilemma.

> The theory of mind . . . provides us with the ability to predict relationships between external states of affairs and internal states of mind.
>
> (Frith 1989: 156)

Theory of mind: the big difference

Developments in 'theory of mind' tests explored children's ability to understand other people's minds. In one experiment, children were given a scenario in which three people are involved. John, Mary and an ice-cream man are at the park. John wants to buy an ice-cream, but doesn't have the money. The man tells John that he will be in the park all afternoon, so John goes home to get the money for an ice-cream. However, while John is away the ice-cream man drives his van to a church, sees John and tells him he will be at the church. Mary meanwhile has gone home. Later she goes to John's house, where John's mother tells her that John has gone to buy an ice-cream.

Once this scenario is presented, the child was asked where he or she thought Mary thinks John has gone to buy the ice-cream. Nine out of ten 'normal' children gave the pass response, that is, 'Mary thinks John went back to the park.' Six out of ten children with Down's Syndrome also responded with the pass answer, but zero out of ten 'high functioning' children with autism could give a pass response.

Sometimes readings I uncover seem distanced from human sciences. Researchers speak of 'subjects' and 'autistic people' instead of 'people with autism'; the identity of the person is lost to statistical analysis and disability-specific jargon. For me, the people I have come to know and care about at Middle Field Manor are people first and people with autism last. While

I believe 'theory of mind' helps explain the enigma of autism and is a useful tool when working with this special group of individuals, it cannot overpower the fact that these people have ways of thinking which do not necessarily make sense to me, but may be the strategies they have had to develop to cope with the world.

Going on an outing with residents to a local park. The one day of English springtime has come and gone and it's chilly, so our walk doesn't last very long. On our way back to the van, Greg expresses his need to go to the toilet. Being the only male without autism in the group, I tell him I will show him where the toilet is. Approaching the newly-constructed building in which we presume the men's room to be, much to our dismay we find that the toilets aren't finished. Greg, already at a heightened level of stress because of his personal needs and the strangeness of the environment, becomes more anxious. Walking back to the van, I explain that we will find another toilet nearby to take him to. Returning to the van I tell the carer, Elaine, what has happened and she tries to soothe Greg:

> *'Get into the van and we'll go to the toilet,' explains Elaine.*
> *'No! No! Greg doesn't want to go to the toilet...'*
> *'It's okay, we'll find one just up the road. You can hold on that long, can't you?'*
> *'Does Greg have to go in the van?'*
> *'Yes Greg, we'll get in the van and Joe will take you to another toilet.'*
> *'Yes, Greg will get into the van and Greg will take Joe to the toilet.'*

In this moment of stress, there are evident many difficulties of coping with understanding the world in which the brain functioning of a person with autism is different. Greg's level of stress heightens to a near-hysterical pitch when Elaine inadvertently tells him to get in the van and go to the toilet. Literal understanding of language is often the case with people with autism. The look of fear that crosses Greg's face when told to go to the toilet in the van is obvious. He begins rocking and banging his head with his hand. I think that his heightened stress is a result of his inability to understand the mind of Elaine. Also evident in this episode are Greg's echolalic statements and confusion of personal pronouns, both characteristics of people with autism (AHTACA 1985, Frith 1989, Happe 1994, Jordan and Powell 1996, Wing 1996).

What sometimes seems to get lost in an individual with autism is the level of learning to cope in the outside world that has been accomplished. Greg knows that he isn't supposed to go to the toilet in the van, that it would be inappropriate behaviour. In many texts I came across there is a section on inappropriate behaviour in people with autism, but I question the value system we're placing on these people. Inappropriate behaviour for one may be acceptable for another. I understand what is meant by labelling certain types of behaviour as inappropriate, but I think we on the outside of autism need to try and look at the world of autism from the viewpoint of those with autism.

Towards a working definition of autism

Some outsiders, looking into the world of autism, begin with statements like: 'Autism is a disorder characterised by severe impairments in social and communicative development, and by abnormalities in flexible behaviour and imaginative thinking' (American Psychiatric Association 1987, in Holroyd and Baron-Cohen 1993: 379). It is only very recently that insiders' views, views from people with autism, are beginning to be explored. It is from these views that I can give my understanding of autism greater depth. Donna Williams, in a Channel 4 production called *Inside Out – Jam Jar,* ' renders the following provocative argument about academics coming to some kind of understanding of autism:

> We understand, we've read all these textbooks and we understand about autism and we're much more reasonable than other people and we're not ignorant and we treat people as equals. That's an outside-in approach. So everyone goes from their own perspective, from out here and they all see everything through their textbooks; and in him (the person with autism), he has his own system, and it's not an infantile version of their own system they haven't learned his system even if he, moving in their world has learned their system like a second language. So, who are they to say, 'Oh, we've read a textbook from somebody who's looked at lots of people like you from the outside,' and then they bring all their questions, what they think's relevant, what they think might speak this one's reality. So he says, 'hold on a minute, you've never lived my system, you don't know my reality from the inside; I'll have to show you what it is and then you just have to work out how to put it in the camera or in the sound. But you can't start with what you presume is happening in me.'
>
> (Williams 1995)

When confronted with this illuminating viewpoint I first felt a degree of indignation, a sense of being 'called out onto the carpet'. At first, I was not so sure, but as I worked my way through my thinking I realised that I was beginning to agree with Ms Williams' assertions, and again my confidence in working with people with autism started to shatter. And not subordinate to these feelings of my own capacity were ethical considerations of observing, commenting and judging people with autism from my outsider's view. After all, who am I and what qualifications do I have to affect the lives of these people?

Autism: can an outsider ever really understand?

Autism: An Inside-Out Approach is a remarkable book in which Donna Williams cuts through all the categorisation, statistical analysis and coding of aspects and tells her theory of autism. The symptoms of autism are due to the inability of a brain to make sense of a world which is constantly bombarding it with information. Sound, light, touch, smell, taste, all are sources of information those of us without autism take for granted (Williams 1996).

The traffic light turns from yellow to green and I am able to edge my car a few feet forward before the light turns red again. I'm stuck in a traffic jam in Cambridge city centre; the only new thing here is it's a warm summer day. The sun beats through my windscreen and the glare makes it difficult to see; buses pull away from the curb with impunity, spewing diesel fumes that must finally rest on Jesus Green which, by the way, is finally green and so is the traffic light as I'm reminded by the person in the car behind me. With the car radio playing something by Pachelbel, I drive on and avoid stopping in a 'keep clear' zone as, yet again, traffic comes to a standstill. Watching the people crossing and playing on Parker's Piece, where there is anything but peace, I realise how much information my brain is handling at once. Sights and sounds from the city, the sun tanning my arm resting on the car window, the feel of the car's clutch as I race towards the next red stop light almost 50 yards away – and yes, the smell and taste of the buses' fumes as I gag in the traffic.

When functioning at this level of stress, I don't think about my brain's processing capabilities. How do I sort out all this data into understandings and cope with literally hundreds of bits of information each minute? What if I become stressed to the point that, to protect itself, my brain shuts off just one of my sensory processing stations? Losing eyesight processing could be deadly; hearing for that matter could be too, the guy behind me will become upset if I pause at the next green light. However, it might be nice to be able to shut down my olfactory processing awhile!

According to Donna Williams, part of the difficulty people with autism face can be traced to the brain's mis-functioning. The brain shuts off certain aspects of information processing for some people with autism. For others, one or more sensory inputs becomes hyper-active and causes the brain to overload information. And yet still for others, there is a combination of hypersensitivity and/or shutdown of brain functioning. All of the possible combinations of these events can occur for various lengths of time ranging from continuously to sporadically instantaneous little bits. It would be like flipping a light switch on and off very rapidly, an activity often observed in people with autism. Other observed activities of people with autism may be similar reactions to sensory over- or underload. The flapping of hands to break up the light waves, or the shading of the eyes to prevent fluttering light waves from causing distraction is often observed. Clapping, tearing paper, breaking glass, rocking, jumping, these are just a few coping strategies people with autism develop to help them handle sensory information (for a more extensive list see Williams 1994, 1996).

Working with people with autism

During the first National Autistic Society seminar that I attended, I began to see the potential for pursuing my developing understanding of autism through direct experience. This seminar presented a structured teaching model, TEACCH (Treatment and Education of Autistic and related Communication-Handicapped Children). The TEACCH approach begins with the need to understand the culture of autism; the logical premise being, you need to know about the people you are trying to help.

Different ways in which people with autism think make it difficult for them to understand our outside world. Sometimes people with autism have difficulty making connections between one thing and another, between cause and effect. Often people with autism will focus on what we in the outside world would consider irrelevant details. For example children with autism when playing with a toy car may focus on the turning of the wheels and not understand how a 'normal' child would play with the whole car. This difficulty may be related to not being able to deal with two ideas simultaneously, which could also help explain why people with autism do not develop social communication skills very well. The inability to connect what you are saying to another person's thoughts and what they are saying may make conversation difficult. Also, people with autism will take things more literally: they may focus on the concrete, sometimes to such an extent that behaviours develop into rituals. Upon this general outside world knowledge of autism TEACCH is based; using these difficulties, rather than working against them, is how the TEACCH approach helps people with autism learn about our world.

It occurred to me that studying TEACCH at Middle Field Manor might prove interesting, to help me learn more about people with autism and about TEACCH itself, attempting grounded research, that is, research the focus of which is 'initially on unraveling the elements of experience' (Moustakas, 1994: 4). I wanted to find out what TEACCH tries to do and how this could help me understand autism. As a case study, TEACCH would be an experiential vehicle to explore the broader question of what you need to know to work with people with autism.

Methodology

My field research therefore took the form of participant observation in two contrasting settings: the National Autistic Society seminars and Middle Field Manor. The seminars were already proving to be an invaluable source of information from the 'experts'' standpoint, and my readings reinforced the understanding I gained. In addition, by observing and participating in TEACCH implementation, I hoped to gain experience in working with people with autism, and I would have access to others with greater experience in working with people with autism.

The best way, I decided, to gain access to the thoughts and feelings of the carers at the Manor was simply to work alongside them and observe as far as possible the daily events of their lives. This experience, together with the seminars, allowed me to find out how people on the outside of autism work with people on the inside: how programmes were begun, how training of staff was conducted, where funding came from, where parents fit in ... many important factors were discovered about working with people with autism. Yet something was still missing ...

Another day at the Zodiac Centre. The TEACCH transition board tells us that we are going to have music therapy today at eleven thirty, right after tea. Wandering around the centre, watching the people, talking to the residents and carers, I become aware that here at the centre the stress levels of the residents and carers are lower than at the Manor.

As we enter the common room area I have a brainstorm, I decide to tape-record the session. After asking Mike, Zodiac Centre's service coordinator, and Karen, the music therapist, if that would be okay, I place my recorder on a shelf and we all settle down to singing.

The session comes to a close and while we're putting away the instruments I see Emily pick up my tape recorder and study it carefully. Feeling a wave of embarrassment coming over me I am ashamed of myself. Sure, I had asked permission to tape-record this session, but who had I asked? Flooding into my mind all at once are the ethical considerations I had been trying to stifle since beginning research at the Manor. Words like disempowerment, human rights, barriers, imposition, access ... the whole bundle of 'whose life is it anyway' expressions bring me to stunned silence.

Emily places the recorder back on the shelf, its menacing red eye still indicating 'record'. I walk over to the machine, turn it off and make a note to destroy this tape when I get home. And I do.

Validity and ethical considerations

While I have trust in the data and the findings, the most important viewpoints to this project are missing: the viewpoints of the people upon whom the research is being conducted or imposed, the viewpoints and feelings of the residents of Middle Field Manor.

However, in this setting, that most important data cannot directly be conveyed by traditional means. It is important to keep in mind, when working with people with autism, that they most often cannot and/or will not share their feelings or their ideas with us, so we need to interpret their actions and reactions to be able to adjust to their needs as much as possible.

But we must be sure to keep in the forefront of our minds the ethical considerations of researching into areas of human science where the participants are not able to give their consent. Research into areas such as autism are important, so that we will always be aware of what we are attempting when working with people; but more importantly we need to remind ourselves that these peoples' rights come before our rights as researchers and carers. In our attempts to help ourselves and others to understand, we must not further our understanding at the expense of the individuals we are trying to help.

At Middle Field Manor no one was forced to partake in the TEACCH programme. During my observations there were instances when residents did not want to go to the transition area, or attempt the task that was assigned. These people were given the opportunity to opt out, exit the field. There were also instances when I felt my presence was causing undue stress and I would opt out, exit the field. Luckily the 'permission to record' instance occurred early in my field work. I could reflect back on it throughout the research and always remember that permission to conduct this research had never really been given, that I was a guest in a home and that was a privilege.

A matter of style

In the remainder of this study I draw on the issues raised by the various data sources to explain how my learning and thinking about people with autism has evolved. This is my attempt to tell the tale of my learning about autism; therefore, I have decided to write in the narrative mode. To begin understanding we need to start with an understanding of ourselves, how we think and feel, how we are affected by the real world. According to Middleton, 'Academic thinking, researching, and writing should move freely between the personal, the theoretical, and the political/institutional dimensions of experience' (Middleton 1995: 91). I feel the inclusion of the experiences I have written about should help the reader grasp the personal side of my experience while also provoke thinking. I am hoping that this style of presentation will 'encourage readers to experiment with unorthodox, multiple, and idiosyncratic readings' (Middleton 1995: 88).

Getting to know the residents as individuals

Observation of the residents at Middle Field Manor proved to be the data collection method which I found most fulfilling, and was personally the most rewarding. By combining what I had learned from the seminars with the data collected using survey methods, that is, staff interviews and questionnaires, I began to get a picture of the world that people with autism face every day, and how different that world is.

One point that comes up repeatedly is that the best way to help people with autism is to know people with autism. Each seminar presenter stressed that knowledge of the individual with autism is the key to understanding. Both interviewees commented on the importance of knowing the individuals, and through many instances of observation I could see the carers helping the residents before problems arose. However, there were occasions when I felt that perhaps I was intruding on the privacy of the residents.

My first trip to the Zodiac Centre is with the clients ... I am really beginning to dislike that term 'clients'. Lawyers and business people have clients, I much prefer 'friends'. Anyway, the first time I arrive with my friends from Norfolk House at the Zodiac Centre, we begin with a trip to the TEACCH board. Each person, with the help of Mike, the Centre Director, checks the board to find out which tasks they will be working on. The first task of the day is different for each person. Emily goes right into the 'Snoezelen' without checking the transition area, her routine is down pat. Eddie, Cindy and Sharon's tasks are at small motor skills work stations where they practise stringing beads or putting together jigsaw puzzles. Wayne goes to the art centre to do some drawing. Greg is anxious, and rather than attempt his TEACCH assignment, sits in the lounge. Mike can spend individual time with Greg because the others are quite happy to get on with their tasks.

> *'Greg, you don't have to worry, you've got the key to the bus so no one can leave without you.'*
> *'Greg's got the key, is it time to go now?'*
> *'No, Greg, we're going to have a cup of tea in a little while and then we're going to have some music and then ... Let's see, come and look at the board with me.'*
> *'Greg doesn't want to look at the board.'*
> *'But it shows us what we're going to do today, come and look at the board.'*
> *'Greg will look at the board ... is Greg going to have a cup of tea now?'*
> *'In a minute, first let's look at the board. See, here's when we're going to have a cup of tea, see the picture? And this picture shows us we're going to do music after we have our cup of tea, and this shows us that after we do some music, Greg is going to go into the 'Snoezelen' and then we 're all going to go back to the Manor. Okay Greg?'*
> *'Yes, Greg will have a cup of tea now, thank you.'*
> *'Okay, you can come and help me get the tea ready.'*
> *'Greg will help you get the tea now. Hello, Greg would like to shake your hand now.'*

This is the first time I have seen a TEACCH programme in action. Greg becomes very nervous when he first arrives at the Zodiac Centre. His fear is that he will be left behind, so he's given the key to the bus and knows that no one can leave without him. Talking him through the board, Mike can relieve some of Greg's anxiety, which is evidenced by a gradual decrease in Greg's rocking and hitting himself. At no time does Mike reach out to touch Greg, nor does he attempt to make eye contact with Greg. By the time Mike talks Greg through the TEACCH programme, Greg is relaxed enough to offer to shake hands with me – again.

It is interesting to observe the differences among the three divisions of Middle Field Manor. When I first started learning about autism, I thought that it would be less difficult to get to know and understand people with Asperger's Syndrome than others with 'more severe' autism. From this research exploration, I found to be true the points brought out in the seminars (Howlin 1996, Mortlock 1996a, 1996b) on how much more difficult it is to work with high-functioning and Asperger's people. Though I always spoke to each resident every time I saw them, the only resident of Crossways who would speak to me was John. Now I understand this behaviour, but at first the silence of Crossways was almost haunting.

My first visit to Crossways is a quick one to introduce myself and say hello to the residents and staff. Approaching the door I notice a young woman standing by the window looking out but making no signs of coming to the door. Having learned from my earlier experience at the Manor, I ring the doorbell.

The home is very neat and tidy; almost too tidy, almost sterile. I say hello to the young lady at the window and am answered with silence. A staff member introduces us and asks her if she can say my name.

'Yes', says the woman and she walks away.

I ask if the other residents of the home are out and am surprised to learn that everyone is home – surprised because how quiet a house for eight residents is. I am assured that it isn't always this quiet but usually the residents do choose to stay in their rooms and don't interact socially. As I'm to find out, 'that seems to be the way'.

During lunch at one seminar I am sitting next to a young mother who learned less than a month ago that her four year old daughter has autism. I am impressed with the manner in which she answers some very personal questions. As I listen to the conversation I wonder what I would do in that situation:

> *'Well, I don't want to be rude,' a woman sitting across the table asks, 'but didn't you notice anything strange or different about your daughter before?'*
>
> *'No, why should I have? This is my first child, I just thought she was being a brat.'*
>
> *'Why do you say that, what was she doing?'*
>
> *'Well as near as I could tell she wasn't doing anything really. Sometimes she wouldn't come with me when we went out but usually I just forced her to come.'*

Visions I'd conjured while reading Nobody Nowhere *came to mind, visions of a mother dragging her child kicking and screaming into ballet lessons, visions of a mother who'd never heard of autism and couldn't understand why her child didn't behave like other children, visions of a mother who developed a hatred for her daughter because of her behaviour.*

Finally gathering enough courage, I ask this young mother, 'How did you feel when you found out that your daughter had autism?'

'I wanted to kill myself,' she says, as she drew her finger across her neck, mocking the motions of slitting her throat.
'I'm sorry, I shouldn't have asked . . .'
'No, no! That's quite all right. I'm learning now, I know there's nothing I could have done and now we must get on with it and do the best we can.'

The mothers and fathers of children with autism I have had the privilege to talk to have been among the most informed and knowledgeable people within the field of autism. As all of the seminar presenters emphasized, parents are the key to developing an understanding of the individual (Mesibov 1996, Howlin 1996, Mortlock 1996a, 1996b; Peacock 1996), while researchers – those of us on the outside – may be the key to enabling the parents to understand the signpost that is autism.

Using TEACCH at Middle Field Manor

The focus of this section will be the experiences of the residents and staff of Middle Field Manor in their work to initiate and adapt a TEACCH programme. The service coordinator of the Zodiac Centre succinctly described TEACCH as nothing more than a 'structure using as many or as few visual, physical, tactile prompts', to help people with autism 'get through a period of the day . . . and [is] a means of communication' which should lead to understanding. Therefore, training in the use of that system is a logical place to start. And not just staff training: the residents of the Manor also require training in the use of the structure.

Early in the interview with Mike, Zodiac's service coordinator, we talk about the importance of staff training: 'If I had to change anything I think I would have changed the staff training. I think we should have started with everybody . . . all the staff knowing what is going on.' In conversations with Ian what continually arises is the 'need for the whole house staff to grasp TEACCH with the same vigour that those who have been on the course come back with.' It is important to be trained in the correct methods involved with TEACCH, as can be evidenced by Mike's ability to use the TEACCH board as a communication device (discussed earlier). However, John Mortlock shared with us an experience he had with a teacher who had some idea of what TEACCH was all about and was trying to implement a programme with a student of hers. While what she was doing was not TEACCH exactly, it was a structured programme that was successful. John believes that any structure is better than no structure when working with people with autism (Mortlock 1996b). Actual TEACCH theory goes beyond Mike's definition of 'a way to get through the day' but what is being done at the Manor is a start and is better than nothing.

On one of my last visits to Norfolk House the way the staff and, to a degree, the residents have grasped TEACCH is quite evident. Besides the TEACCH transition area board being accurate, concise and easy to read, the residents are all partaking in structured leisure activities. Eddie, the 'music star' as Mike has named him, is listening to his radio; Cindy and Greg are swinging on the swing set, an activity many people with autism enjoy (Williams 1994). I once thought swinging could become an obsession but with the TEACCH structure the next activity, drama therapy, is soon to follow. Emily is looking at pictures in a catalogue and Wayne is working with the ground's keeper in the garden. Not a lot has changed since my first visit to Norfolk House but the atmosphere is relaxed and calmer; perhaps one could say I've become accustomed to spending time with these friends and now understand better their behaviours – I don't know, I'm sure that is true to a certain extent. But what I do know is that as I leave Sharon is not incessantly asking to go to the bus and Emily looks up from her catalogue, says goodbye and gives me a 'Forrest Gump' wave.

Logistics: it's not logical always

Initiating a structured programme is not an easy process. Besides having to deal with materials not being delivered when promised, developing age- and ability-appropriate material for each resident, going beyond the educational setting and stretching into leisure time, finding funding (Ian's typical response was, 'If you need it just go and buy it'), there were subtle logistics that had to be coped with. How do we initiate a structured routine, a purpose of which is to relieve anxiety, without upsetting the current structure and raising anxiety levels of both the residents and staff? And what about parents: how do we allay some of their fears about regime implementation?

During an early May meeting I am invited to attend with Ian and the service coordinators, we discuss TEACCH readiness and the concerns of some parents are brought up. In a flash of inspiration (Ian is always getting these, I think actually they're not 'flashes' but preplanned ideas), Ian decides to introduce and explain TEACCH at the upcoming Parent/Carer Workshop to be held on 19 May. At this workshop Ian wants each service coordinator to cover an aspect of TEACCH and then discuss the progress made to date. Great idea!

> *'Right, we'll do it then, let's set the agenda. After the introduction and a quick talk by me about what's transpired over the last six months we'll have the accreditation award, then Sandra can talk about the International Convention in Barcelona, Judith will then cover personal*

Development and Sessional work, then we'll do TEACCH. Joe, when would you like to speak?'

'What?'

'Well, since you're like . . . the guest, I thought I'd give you the choice of when to speak to the parents about what your involvement in what we're doing here is. Would you like to go first?'

'Ah . . .'

Looking around the tiny office, meeting each person's gaze, I realise that I'm not going to get out of this one. Mike is especially enjoying watching me squirm – he looks as though he is about to burst! (Talk about theory of mind under-standing!)

'Ah . . . first, yeah okay, I'll go first. What day is it?'

'It's Thursday, Joe.'

'I know that, what day is the workshop?'

'I don't think he's been listening . . .'.

19th May

After a brief introduction by Ian, I find myself in front of about 500, well, maybe it was only 50, parents of the friends I've been working with. While explaining what my role is in the implementation of TEACCH at the Manor, I get stuck on the word 'society', as in National Autistic Society. After four or five attempts to get the word out I look over at Ian, who can just relax the grin off his face long enough to shout,

'Is it society you're trying to get out, Joe?'

'Yeah, thanks Ian.' After the chuckling subsides and looking to my wife for support, I can continue with explaining TEACCH.

Concerns of some parents are the same things that concern us. First, is this a programme that is appropriate for my son or daughter? Does it belittle them in any way? To that I would respond that actually the programme will lead to greater independence for the child. Second, is this a regime set up to control my son or daughter? There is the potential for the system to be misused or to develop into a behaviour modification plan, but that is not the purpose; and, with parents monitoring along with the National Autistic Society, it will not be abused. (Most of these questions were responded to by the three service coordinators, my role at this point was to keep saying 'society' in my mind.)

At the end of the meeting one or two parents approach me and thank me for attending. I was asked to attend the House Workshop back at the Manor but am required to be elsewhere during the afternoon. From what the carers told me most of the parents were quite receptive but there were still some who were sceptical – that's good, that's quality control.

Resident response: more than a few surprises

The fear of the unknown is perhaps the greatest fear of all. Staff members and I were concerned that the introduction of new ideas and physical structures into the environment would cause enough stress in the residents to make them want to destroy some materials. TEACCH boards, which have to be quite large to hold schedules for six to eight people, were placed in the least conspicuous areas that could be found; the pictures for the boards are encased in plastic.

Gradual introduction was considered, but it was decided that the full programme would be introduced all at once. I thought it best to wait until a week after the start before I went to the Manor to observe. My reasoning was that I wanted to give the staff time to help each other learn their system without my intrusion.

When I returned to the Manor, Ian and I spoke in his office before I went out into the home. His feelings were that at this early time it was difficult to see much change, but on the bright side, not one resident had attempted to pull down or dismantle any of the TEACCH material. Ian felt that with time the programme would take hold – he would not let it fail.

28 May   Day nine of TEACCH
Cambridge House field notes

Paul's response to anything with a bed on it is to go to sleep so we have to be careful with what we put up. Since he has this obsession to spell, we're going to try words for Paul. Richard has virtually no verbal communication so we're going to use the speech therapist to help us figure out which pictures he understands and try to find a way to get him to understand others. During rebound therapy ('trampolining') a resident went a little too high and scared herself. She became very upset and waited in the bus for the rest of us to finish. When we got back to the Manor she walked straight over to the board, removed the picture with the trampoline on it, held it in front of my face and tried to tear it up. It was being communicated to me that she didn't care much for 'trampolining'.

'Better communication with and understanding of the client' – TEACCH.

TEACCHing from here

By attending National Autistic Society seminars, undertaking further extensive reading, questioning carers and other experts, participating and observing and reflecting on my thinking, I believe that my knowledge base on autism has vastly increased. And because of this experience and knowledge gained, my confidence in my ability to help people with autism has increased. When Richard approaches me from behind and nestles his nose in my hair, I've learned that he's showing affection in his way; when Paul holds my hands down at my sides and invades my personal space, I know that it's spelling time and this is the way he interacts.

While the effects of this project on my practice are important, my practice will continue to evolve; what I've really gained from this experience is a set of new friends, friends who I'll remember for the rest of my life.

My last research day at the Manor; the house is in turmoil, a resident is missing. I join the search party; implications of theory of mind really hit home as I try to think about where I would go if I were Chris. During our search we decide to go to the village post office and ask if anyone has seen her. The man behind the counter is quite concerned and asks me what Chris looks like. Trying to give her description I'm embarrassed at how little information I can give him; realising I am describing her behaviour, I am ashamed of how little I've learned.

Chris is found back at the house safe and sound. After much worrying and walking through the fine English rain by eight staff members and two police officers everyone is relieved; some of us can even see the humorous side. But I am still ridiculing myself for not being able to describe one of my friends. I tell myself that Chris is a friend who spends a great deal of time in her room, has virtually no communication, and has never glanced in my direction. How can I know the colour of her eyes? But that doesn't work. Other questions about other residents come to mind: what sort of music does Eddie the 'music star' listen to, how often does Greg go home, what is Wayne's favourite gardening machine?

I haven't done my last day at the Manor yet. I'm not looking forward to it – I hate goodbyes. I'll be going back to the States at the end of July but I will keep in contact with my friends here. I want to know what colour eyes Chris has; I want to know if Mary is still following the TEACCH board and only going out in the sun for a safe amount of time.

There are all kinds of questions to ask as I sit watching the rain, still wondering why cars' windscreen wipers don't go the same way.

* * *

NARRATIVE SUMMARY 3

Issues arising from Joe's innovative research

Joe's study had such a unique impact on him that he felt he had to present his findings in a unique way. He came to care so much for the people with autism with whom he had worked that he sought a mode of representation that would be capable of engaging his audience, along with him, in understanding and identifying with people with autism.

Joe felt that an academic style of writing would be completely inappropriate for his research. He had begun to feel dissatisfied with traditional research reports that 'suck the life out of the research'. The conventional 'monologic' style eliminates the reader from responding to the work. It provides a single authoritative interpretation that does not leave space for the reader to question or challenge ideas. He questioned the validity of 'stand-alone' research, where 'a reader isn't even needed for the research to have validity'.

His background in literary studies served him well in deciding the kind of text that he wanted and needed to write. His knowledge of reader response theory led him to try to create a text that would engage the reader emotionally, that would have all the engaging characteristics of fiction, and make people care about people. These were criteria dictated by his own purposes and the nature of the ideas that he had to communicate. They were quite independent of the academic criteria that the work would need to satisfy for accreditation purposes.

Joe's use of the two-font technique was intended to 'free up' the reader to engage actively with the ideas presented. Normal font provides a narrative account of the research process as it unfolded; italics represent the more 'interpretive' parts of the research, as Joe reflected on the data generated from a variety of different sources. Neither of these voices has more validity than the other, in Joe's view, although he found the interpretive aspects more enjoyable to write and imagined that these would also be more enjoyable to read.

It is interesting that, although Joe's literary background was a resource available to him prior to starting the course, he did not make active use of it until his third study. He describes a process of evolution in his work, through which he gradually came to believe that his own thinking was valued, and of value, within the academy, that a more personal style of writing was acceptable. It seems that it was not until he developed sufficient confidence to define his own approach that he was able to draw fully on his personal fund of resources.

This process of evolution was influenced by other like-minded members of the course who were also experimenting with divergent approaches. It was also helped, he says, by 'the attitude of the institution' which actively encouraged and validated a range of styles of reporting. Most importantly, Joe says, 'I was allowed to feel that I was the establishment I was writing for. The challenge was a personal challenge. I was guided through that personal challenge and enabled to succeed.'

Success was certainly important, yet the work itself took on such significance for Joe that success became a secondary consideration. The people who were part of his research were more important to him than the acceptance of his findings, more important than the grade awarded, more important than personal success. This is reflected in his sense that 'my research topic has become part of my life'. After completing his study, he made a career change and took up a post working with children with special learning abilities, including autism.

Chapter 5

Perceptions of purpose for children's writing

Tish Crotty

Editorial note

When Tish carried out this study, she was working for the Cambridgeshire Multicultural Education Service as a Language and Curriculum Support teacher, and was based in a large multi-ethnic school in Peterborough. This was the first piece of research undertaken for her Masters' course, and the chapter has been edited from a slightly longer, 7,500 word essay.

Through open curtains
On words dance shafts of sunlight
Windows in my mind.

In common with countless other students I have an assigned piece of writing to complete, some research to undertake. For weeks I have procrastinated (at times even the ironing seemed an attractive proposition), but the deadline for completion draws sickeningly close. It is not that I suffer a dearth of ideas for potential areas to investigate; if anything quite the reverse. It is not that I dislike writing. In fact writing is an activity I engage in constantly for all sorts of reasons, usually with great pleasure.

No: my head in the sand approach, my protracted delaying tactics, are far more complex. They result, I am sure, from a combination of factors, not the least of which is an acute awareness that this particular piece of writing acts like both a mirror and a window. It will be read almost certainly by some of my colleagues and tutors, by people whose views I value and whose opinions I respect. How will they react to it, either openly or in private? This work inevitably reflects my attitudes and ideas. It becomes possible to view almost at first hand my thoughts and feelings. I find this idea uncomfortable. I am conscious of my own vulnerabilities and I am only too aware that once written down, words lose their evanescent qualities and *become permanent portraits, able to be studied and reflected upon. This after all is part of their beauty.*

This piece of work is an exploration into writing. The area of study is children, their attitudes to and perceptions of writing. In recent years few studies have investigated the perceptions of writing held by children, especially related to their own written work. This seems rather surprising considering that writing tasks consume much of the school day for children.

This study begins with questions rather than a hypothesis. It searches for answers using what could be called an 'emergent' model of research, sharing some of the characteristics of what have variously been termed interpretive, reflective and creative approaches to research. Pollard and Tann (1987) suggest that at the core of interpretive research lies a concern with opinions and perceptions, seeking to describe these things. According to Bassey (1992), reflective research involves critical and systematic thinking about previous and present research findings; while 'creative' research is concerned with the devising of new systems, novel solutions, using critical enquiry. 'Emergent' is used here in the sense that new understandings and new questions might come 'into view' as a result of description, enquiry and questioning.

So, to work. Immediately the feeling of panic is almost overwhelming. Why? Is this normal for writers? I am reminded of something Ted Hughes wrote; it describes so perfectly my emotions.

> *It is when we set out to find words for some seemingly quite simple experience that we begin to realise the huge gap that exists between our understanding of what happens around and inside us, and the words we have at our command to say something about it.*
>
> *(Hughes 1967: 119)*

Do children feel like this when they write? A blank computer screen stares at me malevolently. I have chosen to use the computer but I'm not sure why. At this particular moment in time I fervently regret the choice, made perhaps because I am aware of the huge advantages computers have for editing work, for changing font and text style at will. On the other hand maybe it is just a perverse determination to overcome my phobia with all things technical, especially computers; an attempt to move forward if only in a technological sense. Will its use influence my writing or change the finished product in some way? Inevitably it must, I can only hope for the better!

Armed with my notes, my tapes (interview and music!), my ever-present half empty/full lukewarm mug of coffee, door firmly closed against potential intruders, I commence battle. I spend a moment to muse on my analogy to war, deciding that past experience has taught me that inherently within the act of writing lies potential conflict: conflict between writer and reader, writer and language, writer and skill, understanding and meaning-making. Experience has also taught me that figures of speech are convenient literary tools. Such skills, once learned, are used automatically, almost without question.

Not everyone writes with ease. For those who are proficient writers, the skills the activity embodies are often used automatically, and are so various that attempts to define 'writing' become fraught with difficulty. A simplistic definition might be 'the symbolic representation of language', and reading 'the translation of said symbolic representation of language'. As Smith reminds us, 'Writing should not be isolated from other aspects of language and certainly cannot be separated from thought' (Smith 1982: 4).

The cognitive and metacognitive dimensions of writing have been researched comprehensively (e.g. Britton *et al.* 1975, Flower and Hayes 1981, Graves 1983, Wray 1994). Cognition refers to one's faculty of knowing, metacognition to the knowledge of one's cognitive process and products and the ability deliberately and consciously to control them. Of all the language processes, writing is possibly the one which makes most visible and self-evident the metacognitive dimension.

'Writing allows us to think about our thinking' (Calkins 1983: 139).

Writing however involves much more than a cognitive/metacognitive process and the acquisition of a set of psycholinguistic skills; entwined within these are social and cultural elements. Like other aspects of language, writing is a social process taking different forms in different contexts and between diverse cultural groups. Literacy by nature is a socially-constructed skill; views of literacy are socially orientated. How literacy, and thus writing, is defined and used changes over time and between cultural groups. Ethnographic studies such as that undertaken by Shirley Brice Heath (1983) would support this understanding, and in turn serve to highlight major implications for children's schooling when attitudes to literacy and thus perceived abilities may reflect diverse literate traditions.

Pam Czerniewska suggests:

> When children, with their different experiences of interacting with print enter school they will find that only some of their literacy practices are valued, and for some children the school literacy may seem very different from that found in their homes.
>
> (Czerniewska 1992: 15)

Eve Gregory (1993), researching difficulties experienced by a five-year-old Chinese boy learning to read on entering his British school, reached similar conclusions.

Hidden within the way texts are structured are implicit values and cultural assumptions. Not only will literacy practices differ, texts and the way in which they are constructed varies. Texts take different forms dependent upon social purpose and value, informed by cultural practices, modelled 'according to patterns of social interaction in a particular culture' (Cope and Kalantzis 1993: 7).

Literacy is imbued with ideologies relevant to situation and context. Among all the literacies practised, it is the one associated with school that is somehow seen as the defining type, that which sets the standard against which others are valued or not. Street tells us, 'Non school literacies have come to be seen as inferior attempts at the real thing, to be compensated for by enhanced schooling' (Street and Street 1991: 143). Research in the field of emergent literacy has shown that children enter school with well-formed literacy skills, with developed, if individual, perceptions of writing. 'Most children will arrive at school knowing something about what written language is, how it works and what it is used for' (Hall 1987: vi).

This study starts from the viewpoint that there is no single definition of literacy or what it means to be literate. It is seen as a constantly shifting description of a permanently changing state. However because I believe, as Barton suggests, that 'people's views of literacy are important in how and what they learn' (Barton 1991: 10), the knowledge of what children bring to school in terms of perceptions about writing and purpose for writing would seem to be of vital importance.

Purpose is such an intangible concept. It ebbs and flows; it effects a metamorphosis even as I work. An enforced break has caused chaos. I have lost the stream of what I am trying to say, lost sight of why I am trying to say it – my purpose? My neck aches, my side hurts, my fingers are sore and my mind is elsewhere. I cannot separate me and how I feel from my writing. I am not sure that I should try to, since who I am inevitably influences what and how I write; woven into my writing are images and ideas from my past and present. It concerns me that perhaps the reader will, like the writer, come to this part of the text in an unfavourable frame of mind, and this will affect the reading of it. Frank Hatt's words come to mind: 'One reader will read the same text differently on different occasions; indeed he will read different parts of the same text in different ways during the course of one reading act as his mood, his purpose and his knowledge change' (in Hunt 1991: 98). How is it that we expect children to write on demand, to order, to finish on time, to pick up where they left off, however they feel – and still deliver quality work?

The phone rings and I am interrupted once again – c'est la vie! This latest interruption comes just as I try to re-examine my perceptions, re-evaluate my purposes.

Purpose, it seems to me, is a compound term embodying a host of meanings dependent on context. Used in a literacy sense I suggest it might combine aspects of:

- motivation
- intention
- function
- audience

all interdependent aspects of process and product.

Motivation refers to 'that which induces a person to act', in this case to write. For children in school the motivation *(purpose)* for their writing may well be fuelled by many influences. Some children, able to write, may choose not to: 'Despite the years of effort which had been put into teaching these children to write, many, perhaps most, did not find it a satisfying task' (Davies 1989: 16). There are likely to be distinctly different motivators for each child, some of which may have little or nothing to do with the writing task itself. Cope and Kalantzis (1993) talk of 'immediate' and 'longer-term' motivation; the former belonging to the task itself and the latter coming with the demonstrable effects of the skill, usually in a wider social context.

Intention *(purpose),* would seem to carry a nuance quite distinct from motivation *(purpose)*. It relates to the ultimate aim of the action. Wilkinson, Barnsley and Hanna (1980) identify three models of communication which seem to relate to intention. The first is transmission. This is where one writer communicates information to another (or others) with no expectation of reply. Reciprocity is similar to transmission but it requires a response from the reader(s). Finally Wilkinson identifies reflection, where writers write for themselves with the express idea of reflecting, immediately or at a later date, on what has been written.

Function *(purpose)* is quite unlike the two previous '*purposes*' yet undeniably interconnected. It has to do with style, ways in which writing can be used to affect the reader(s), so that the function of the writing becomes to direct, inform, amuse, warn, move emotionally and so on. It concerns choices which are made with regard to linguistic structures, vocabulary and text layout in order to affect effectively. 'How a text works is a function of what it is for' (Cope and Kalantzis 1993: 7). Audience *(purpose)* for writing is almost self-explanatory. Elbow suggests: 'The essential act at the heart of writing is the act of giving' (Elbow 1981: 21). This implies that audience (self or others) is a quintessential part of the whole purpose of writing.

I have not yet defined my purposes for this writing. In all honesty it is difficult to be clear about them; they are multi-faceted. I suspect that though some of them are easy to pinpoint and define, there are other less tangible, indefinable purposes at work. Principally I write for myself, I seek to clarify issues that I find interesting, disturbing and difficult to understand. Writing about them allows me to gather my thoughts in one place, make them visible, reflect upon them, add new ideas (both my own and others'); then juggle them endlessly to create a new and better understanding of the issue under consideration. With this piece of work, necessarily, I have an audience in addition to myself. This affects my writing; for now I must also write to inform, interest and engage others. I am not seeking agreement with my ideas, but I do wish to cause the reader to become interested in, and also reflect on, the issues which interest me; and yes, I wish them to think well of me, to respect, even admire my writing. This awareness of my audiences and my desire to influence them has in turn determined the way in which I have deliberately manipulated the form of the writing, created, within certain imposed boundaries, a particular kind of text. It could be argued that I have no option; if I wish to complete my degree course successfully I must complete this writing assignment. I wonder would this alone offer me sufficient purpose for writing? What of children's perceptions of purpose for writing in school? The only way to discover these is to ask children.

The school attended by the children asked was a mixed, multi-ethnic, infant and junior school, with some 400 pupils, situated in Peterborough. The school follows a literacy policy which is underpinned by a belief in 'emergent literacy': that is, that children '*grow into*' reading and writing, a process which begins long before children enter school, through the activities and experiences of their everyday lives. Thus the policy articulates a determination to build upon children's existing literacy knowledge and skills. Not all the staff are totally committed to an emergent literacy philosophy, and thus to the policy, and views on writing contrast quite sharply throughout the school. Data were collected in different ways. Children and staff were informally interviewed using open-ended questions which drew heavily on studies in the same field (National Writing Project 1990, Wray 1994).

The interviews followed one of two formats. The first was a series of very general questions about writing, including such questions asked of whole class groups (twenty-five to thirty-five children, all of similar ages). Queries such as *What is writing? Why do people write? Who do you write for? How did you learn to write? What is a writer?* were posed to classes, in an effort to gather general information regarding children's perceptions of writing and writers, in both school and the community at large. These interviews were conducted in thirteen classrooms and involved children from four years to eleven years old. Second, individual and small group interviews were held, the object being to try to relate questions to specific writing tasks. Participant teachers were also interviewed about their attitudes to, and perceptions of, writing in their classes. These interviews were conducted with three different age groups from Year 6 (10–11 year olds), Year 3 (7–8 year olds) and Year 1 (children aged from 5–6 years).

I am sitting in a class full of children aged between five and six, notebook in hand, tape recorder ready, a host of questions in mind. The very fact that the research is in its infancy makes it difficult, I am not sure what I want to ask and how best to ask it. I think I know what I am looking for but I don't know how to find it. I feel rather foolish. It is something of an unfamiliar task in a very familiar setting, and I find it hard to remain detached. I am also afraid that my very presence will alter whatever data I am trying to collect. I feel rather like an eavesdropper but I don't feel confident that I will hear what I am here to hear when it is said! I also feel that I must appear to others a little like the businessman in The Little Prince *(Saint-Exupéry 1945) somehow removed from the realities and practicalities of life, interested only in 'matters of consequence'. That worries me. I try hard to recall a section from the same book when the railway switchman makes perceptive observations about the children and adults who are travelling on his trains.[1] It is the adults, it seems, who are always in a great hurry, never satisfied with where they are but not knowing what they are looking for. It is only the children who are 'flattening their noses against the window panes'. 'Only the children know what they are looking for', comments the Little Prince. I hope I can be seen to emulate 'the children' and adopt a fresh, honest, open and excited approach; not 'the businessman' with his unreal illusions of personal import and grandeur! By the time the class interview is completed it is playtime. The children are eager to go. I linger on in the classroom trying to collect my thoughts. Eventually and rather wearily, I gather together my notes and piles of collected data and I too leave the classroom.*

A considerable amount of data was collected, too much to work with comfortably. Interview tapes were listened to several times. The tapes which seemed most representative of the children's views or contained, for me, the most interesting data were transcribed. The transcribed tapes which included three 'teacher', three 'small group' and six 'class' interviews were scrutinised and reflected upon at length. Comments which reappeared frequently, but were made by different children, were noted. Answers which I found to be out of character with other children or my own ideas were recorded. Where I had expected comments which were not made, I observed their absence.

There was an extraordinary diversity of attitudes, yet areas of commonality. Few children could define writing, an eleven year old commenting, 'We know what it is but we can't say it in words'. Of those children whose interviews were transcribed, only three from the reception class stated that they could not write. The rest, some 200 pupils aged four to eleven, were confident that they could write. Asking whether writing was easy or difficult produced mixed reactions which appeared to change from year to year. Writing, it appeared, became more difficult for children in the 'middle primary years', those aged between seven and nine years old. ' I forget how to spell words.' 'I can't think of what to write.'

To the question 'Do you like writing at school?' responses were again

---

1 Also from *The Little Prince* (Saint Exupéry 1945: 72, 73. The switchman ends by saying the children are lucky.

mixed. While for the reception children (aged four and five) answers were almost unanimous – all but two said yes – the children aged around seven to nine had quite different responses. Ten out of the twenty-nine liked writing at school, while the other nineteen confessed that they did not. Interviewed pupils at the upper end of the school (ten and eleven years old) seemed even more disenchanted with writing at school; only seven out of thirty-five said they enjoyed it, and the remaining twenty-eight appeared not to: 'It's boring.' 'I never have time to finish it.' For many children and their teachers, presentational skills were paramount.

Asked how they would judge a good piece of work, children made comments like: 'Good spelling, nice neat work.' 'If it's neat.' Similar answers were given to the question 'What advice would you give to children coming into this class next year to help them with their writing?' 'You must have neat handwriting.' Few children appeared to have an understanding of different forms of writing beyond ideas of 'hieroglyphics', 'calligraphy', 'French'.

In terms of perceived audience, the younger children wrote mostly for parents and friends; the older children for their teachers. Some older children were conscious of themselves as audience. Although the children acknowledged that they did a lot of writing at school, the 'what for' was either unknown or formulated in vague terms of learning, education and future employment advantages.

Reasons given by the children for actually doing the set writing tasks proved, in a way, to be the most interesting. They divided into several discrete areas, one concerned with a kind of imposed motivation: 'Our teacher tells us to'. Another was to do with a sort of personal need to learn or to gain a good 'education'. A few children had quite different reasons for writing, reasons which did not fit comfortably into any of the other categories. For them motivation appeared to be socially orientated. I came to the conclusion that for some children, writing provided a convenient 'tool' which they used, somehow, to negotiate their social status within class. 'To keep up your reputation in school.' 'Sometimes I get three housepoints for writing and people in class feel jealous, so then I don't work so hard.'

For the three teachers interviewed, perceptions of purpose for the children's writing seemed only sometimes in line with the children's own perceptions. The teachers observed that for them, most writing tasks in school were multi-functional, that is, they served several different purposes, not all of which they felt filtered down to the children. None of the interviewed teachers ever wrote with the children, although two of them sometimes used examples of their own work prepared in advance. It was unclear whether the children were aware that these examples of writing were the teachers' own work: certainly the children never saw them being written. Interestingly enough, all three teachers interviewed expressed personal dislike or difficulty with writing.

My own writing task is almost complete, I feel rather like a tightly stretched, charred piece of elastic. It has not been easy for, like the interviewed teachers, I find writing difficult, almost tortuous. Curiously, at the same time I also find it highly addictive. This study has allowed me to reflect on children and their writing; my original idea was to do only that. However, I realised that it was important at the same time to investigate my own attitudes to, and perceptions of, writing; to reflect on my purposes for writing. I was also keen to put to the test the contention that if us teachers of writing we are to fully understand the role, then we must also become writers ourselves (Emig 1983): It is a view sincerely echoed by Donald Graves, that doyen of 'process' learning, and it is his metaphor that sticks in my mind. When we ask children to write sincerely, we ask them to undress. Children won't undress for long unless teachers 'undress' with them, by exposing their writing to children (Gilbert 1989). Metaphorically I have tried to 'undress', and in so doing feel I have deepened my own understanding of the 'writing act'. I also offer the reader a double perspective: children's perceptions of writing; teacher/researchers' process of writing. In some ways the latter of these two is a distorted perspective. I have covered my own footprints, papered over the cracks and hidden the seams. I have drafted and re-drafted, I have made copious notes, jiggled words and phrases endlessly and played with layouts. In short I have hidden from view my making process. I present, hopefully, a polished, finished product: ironic in a way that like the children, in the final analysis, the presentation of my writing assumes such a vital importance!

I have had fewer constraints, many more advantages, than the children writing at school. I did have a choice as to whether I wrote – do children? I could fashion my writing (up to a point) as I desired – can children? I had knowledge of acceptable and appropriate forms of writing – do children? I could choose when to write, when not to write – can children? I had free choice of subject for my writing – do children often?

With these questions in my mind I am sitting outside in the garden in one of my favourite spots. The sun is warm and comforting on my neck and the smell of honeysuckle and roses wafts over me on the gentle breeze. It is quiet and peaceful, for once, and I am in the enviable position of being able, at last, to sit and gently reflect . . . do children? I hope that I have caused you, the reader, to do so.

Conclusions and reflections

No real conclusions have resulted from this research, only observations and more questions.

Data collection was problematical and the research methods used could well have influenced the findings. Choosing tapes for transcription, however careful, is inevitably arbitrary, resulting possibly in some seemingly trivial, but actually vital, comments being wasted. Questions asked were not necessarily the 'best' or 'most appropriate' questions. What to ask and how to ask it in order best to research the subject of enquiry must (or should) be a question that besets all researchers. Some interviews were unsatisfactory; young children are notoriously difficult to interview, and there were occasions when answers seemed influenced by one another's replies. Within classes not every child had opportunity to speak, or indeed chose to comment. It is impossible to know whether answers given by one individual were representative of others. Children frequently 'lost voice', finding the close presence of both a member of staff and the tape recorder inhibiting. In the most successful technique a small group of pupils were left alone, tape recorder running, to discuss either a piece of written work or a series of questions related to writing.

It is difficult to decide whether findings made were a result of the way in which the research was conducted: whether perceptions highlighted were a product of the school or classroom 'writing curriculum', or whether they originated elsewhere. In retrospect I feel that the adopted 'interview technique' took the original research question out of context. It might have been better to interview children engaged in writing tasks, or to have conducted a series of field observations on children as they wrote: perhaps a combination of both.

Perceptions held by the children about writing were not always in line with one another, with teachers' perceptions or my own. It is clear, and perhaps we should be aware, that some children ascribe purposes to their writing tasks in school that are quite different from those that we as teachers ascribe to the same writing tasks. In fact this, for me, was one of the most interesting and surprising of my findings.

That there was, for at least some of the children interviewed, a social dimension to writing in school, was quite unexpected and very intriguing. (On reflection there was of course a social dimension to my own writing!) A proportion of the children appeared to use writing and writing tasks to manipulate social situations, even negotiate social status. Whether this was a learned facility or a by-product of the writing curriculum and the way in which it was delivered is unclear. What is clear is that it is an area that merits further research.

Many of the children had perceptions of writing that were centered around presentational and secretarial skills. This observation is in line with other related research (e.g. Wray 1994: 42–8) (It is interesting that for me too presentation was paramount.) The question is why, and does it matter? Is it as a result of schooling or something else? Do we as teachers emphasise certain aspects of writing above others, either knowingly or unknowingly?

In school the writing curriculum at present is largely influenced by the demands of the National Curriculum. Teachers may feel constrained by its demands. Does formal assessment and testing play a part in influencing perceptions? After all, the descriptor for each National Curriculum level makes reference to presentational skills. The knowledge that movement from one level to the next could theoretically rest or fall on such skills is salutary indeed.

Why is it that, in teaching and learning writing, the 'product' still seems to take precedence over the 'process' of writing? This in spite of current inclinations towards 'workshop style' pedagogies (e.g. Graves 1983), where emphasis shifts thinking away from the products of writing towards the process of writing, from the text to the writer, and emergent approaches (where teaching builds on existing literacy awareness). Are schools only paying lip-service to theories and research, which after all seek to inform, develop and improve our practice? Maybe it is social/cultural conventions themselves which inform our perceptions. The question is, whose conventions?

The absence of an awareness, by the children, of different writing forms is disturbing; the concept *is* difficult to grasp, and it may be that the question posed was misunderstood. In reality, perceptions of writing relating to form would seem to me to be of vital importance. (The success of this study relies on an appreciation of writing forms.) Do we as teachers focus sufficiently on different forms of writing? Do we make children aware of the different ways of arranging text for meaning? Might we be wise to give credence to the observations of Pam Gilbert (1989), who argues that unless children are exposed to different forms of writing and made aware of the power of certain arrangements of writing in particular contexts, they might be severely disadvantaged?

Christie suggests:

> To be literate in the contemporary world is to understand the very large range of written forms, to learn to recognise and create the various genres found in one's culture is to learn to exercise choices – choices in building and ordering different kinds of meaning and hence, potentially, choices in directing the course of one's life.
>
> (Christie 1990: 3)

Do we as teachers manage to equip children with knowledge of, and competence in, literacy practices both for school and for beyond school? How are children's perceptions of writing influenced by the way in which writing is taught at school?

It was interesting to note that the children of different ages seemed to have slightly differing attitudes to, and perceptions of, writing. Is this a feature of maturation or do schools somehow cause children to redefine writing? Do schools even disenchant children from the act of writing?

A longitudinal study recording children's attitudes to, perceptions of and exposure to literacy practices throughout primary school would be extraordinarily interesting.

Medwell, for me, sums up the whole situation perfectly:

The purposes of writing will be dictated by the culture that gives rise to them, and the processes of writing will be those processes for writing agreed as appropriate within that culture.

(Medwell 1994: 121)

It may be that only in a situation where young writers are able to negotiate tasks for purposes which they can recognise and have some say in, can the classroom culture, and the perceptions and context of the individuals within it, significantly increase young children's understandings about writing:

Thus the pen is calm
Words on paper etched in time
Still reflections now.

* * *

NARRATIVE SUMMARY 4

Issues arising from Tish's innovative research

When Tish was writing up her research on children's perceptions of purpose in their writing, she started with a conventional mode. In the process, however, she became reflective about her own experiences as a writer conducting this academic study. These self-reflections spilled over into her reflections about the children's writing, informing the way she thought about the research. The findings from her research, in turn, began to spill over into her reflections about her own writing experience. Thus, a conversation was born between her research and her own writing experience. It was this interactive conversation of ideas and feelings that gave rise to her desire to create an innovative text in two different fonts, in order to represent this internal conversation.

Tish experimented with the structure of the essay, but in such a way that she did not put her work at risk. One font represented her experiences; one represented the research. Thus, she developed a structure which was a mixture of the innovative and the traditional, so that the innovative could be taken out, if necessary, leaving the traditional to work effectively on its own. She had a clear eye on the formal assessment criteria in order to play safe, if necessary. Hers was something of a rather playful attempt at innovation, to see if it could be done as she was envisaging it.

Tish did not feel at odds with the academy with this study, and there was no strong sense that it had to be done in a particular way which was driven by strong inner feelings. The experiment was, however, reinforced and validated through supervision, and it was this reinforcement that persuaded her to persist with this more risky route.

Tish fell upon her approach 'almost by accident' in dealing with the question of how to put herself into the research. The study was emergently innovative as she dealt with this issue of self-exploration and self-understanding. 'I had to get inside myself,' she said. Thus, the experiment was really for herself and her own purposes, not for an external audience.

Some reading she had done on post-modernism provided a stimulus for thinking innovatively about how this might be done. Tish described a piece of writing in which the author had written in two different columns vertically 'one of which was a reflection on where she was at any particular moment, and the other was a reflection on her personal writing and theories of lecturing'. Tish found this fascinating but difficult to read, so in developing her own approach, she chose a format which would create a more flowing text.

The personal style of writing in which she represented her own experience in the second font was her preferred style. Thus, the innovative quality of the process and the text seemed to emerge quite naturally for her in confronting these research issues. It had to be her style and it had to have flow and unity.

The group member who had acted as a critical reader for this study felt that the interplay between the two dimensions of the research really added something. 'The parallel enhanced the overall message', she said, 'because it was like you were getting it twice but in different ways.'

Communicative practices in a classroom for children with severe and profound learning difficulties

A case study of methodologies of reflective practice

Linda Ferguson

Editorial note

When Linda carried out this research, she was working as a classroom teacher in a school for pupils with severe and profound learning difficulties. She was in the second year of her Masters' course, and this was her final piece of work, written in 1996. The chapter has been edited from a 15,000 word dissertation.

Introduction

It is commonplace now to claim that good teachers are (or ought to be) reflective practitioners, but what exactly does this phrase mean, and what are its practical implications? In this study, I set out to learn more about the processes of reflective practice and how I might learn through reflection on my practice, by carrying out a review and evaluation of one specific area of my teaching. I chose to consider my work within the area of communication, and to explore how the learning environment supports and promotes children's communication skills.

My interest in exploring the processes of reflective practice and in applying them specifically within the area of communication arose from a complex combination of personal circumstances, including significant influences from my Masters' studies. First, was contact with the literature on research methodology in general, and practitioner methodology in particular made me begin to question the sources of my own professional knowledge and ideas about 'good practice'. Although I constantly evaluated my own work intuitively, I did not consciously place much importance on my day to day experience as a source of new knowledge and understanding. I realised that I perceived my ideas to be derived mainly from literature, research and training. The literature on practitioner methodology drew my attention to the work of Stenhouse (1975), who argues that ideas derived from research must be regarded as provisional and open to question. Teachers must therefore see themselves as researchers in their own right, continually exploring and discovering what application such ideas might have in their own schools and classrooms.

Second, having encountered Ebbutt's (1983) notion of a 'performance gap', I had begun to question if there might be a mismatch between my stated philosophy of communication and that which I delivered in the classroom. In my former work as a speech and language therapist, I had been responsible for describing and recommending a model of 'good communicative practice' for adults who worked with children who had learning difficulties. I began to feel a pressing need to re-articulate and re-examine my beliefs and philosophy regarding communication, in the light of fifteen years as a speech and language therapist and my three years as a classroom teacher.

In particular, I wanted to re-consider work offered in a previous module of the course entitled *Language and Literacy in Contemporary Society*, part of which involved looking at language in the classroom. The work of Heath (1983), Tizard and Hughes (1984) and Wells (1986) was discussed along with others. At that time, I re-affirmed my commitment to multimodal (signs, symbols, objects and/or speech) communication, read the literature and then moved on. Subsequently, I began to question if such an environment might merely empower the adults rather than the children, in terms of communication. I reflected that rarely did I make explicit the nature of communication, how it was used in the classroom and the possibilities it might offer the children as individuals. Had I merely increased the language opportunities of the adults and disempowered the children?

I decided to organise the study in a way which would allow me to address simultaneously both sets of issues and concerns. Focusing on the communicative practices in my classroom would allow me to explore new insights and understandings which might result from applying the ideas of reflective practice to this specific area. It would also provide a context in which to learn more about the processes of reflective practice, and re-evaluate the ideas presented in the literature from the perspective of my own experience.

The class

Within my class group, there are eight children (five boys and three girls) aged between four and eight years. In my opinion, three of these children (two girls and one boy) have profound and multiple learning difficulties, in other words, they are working at a pre-intentional level, while five children (four boys and one girl) have severe learning difficulties, in other words they are able to demonstrate intentionality in their behaviours, but have limited cognitive skills. Of the group, one is registered deaf-blind, one is blind and three have visual impairments. Seven of the children have cerebral palsy, three have strict drug regimes and six suffer from epilepsy. Each is a unique individual, all enjoy fun and are sometimes reluctant to work, just like any child.

In terms of communicative skills, three are placed at the early (that is, pre-intentional) end of the continuum; two have recently begun to demonstrate intentionality, while the remaining three children use combinations of facial expression, gesture and eye pointing to communicate; one child has approximately seven spoken words. Two of these children understand a range of everyday phrases and sentences in contextually bound situations, while a third understands much of the conversational speech offered in the classroom and is beginning to demonstrate early concept development, for example big, hot, red, blue. He is unable to use speech owing to the severity of his physical disability. There are three adults routinely working with the class group, myself and two learning support assistants, and we have worked together for three years.

Concerns about communication: starting points for the study

One of the consequences of offering a total multimodal communication framework and viewing each child as a communicator is that the role of the adult in the interaction is heightened. I had encouraged learning support assistants to respond to children's behaviours as if they had both communicative intent and linguistic content. This gave opportunities for interaction, turn-taking, adult attention and positive feedback *vis à vis* behaviour and its possible meaning, for example, 'Good boy for closing your eyes to say "yes".' It also meant that virtually all of the language was directed and interpreted by adults. Tizard and Hughes (1984) and Wells (1986) had highlighted the differences in the language used by children in the home and in educational settings. Their work also considered the role of the parent and the teacher in creating and controlling opportunities for the children to talk. I began to wonder if the way that I utilised a total communication environment served to strengthen the divide between adult and child by increasing the role and the power of the adult communicator. Almost simultaneously, I reflected back upon some recent work that I had undertaken centred on the notion of inclusive schooling. This had been part of a particularly challenging module for me personally and professionally, and had caused me to examine my own practice and perspective. In a production entitled *A Nice Safe Place* (BBC 1995), the BBC Disability Programmes Unit highlighted criticisms made by adults with learning difficulties who had attended special schools. Many of their comments had focused on the power of the teacher and the low expectations that the teachers had of their pupils.

Our personal-professional definition of communication can lead us to exclude certain children from the communicative process. Newson states,

'It is only because he [the child] is treated as a communicator that he learns the essential art of communication' (Newson 1978: 42).

One of the consequences of accepting children's behaviours as potentially communicative is the need for the adult to place consistent linguistic interpretations on a range of behaviours. I began to reflect on the responsibility we had within this interpretative framework, and how we might be perceived by the children if we were mistaken in our interpretations – these children have no voice to correct or counsel us.

Investigating classroom communication

I decided that in my investigation of communication I wanted to go beyond the confines of my classroom. I remembered that Delamont (1992) spoke of using 'other stories' to illuminate the research undertaken. One year before, I had met with the deputy head teacher of our local mainstream primary school in an attempt to begin some joint technology sessions with my class and some Year 6 pupils. This had been highly successful, and we had witnessed some quality interactions among the children. We were amazed when Scott watched his new friend knit a scarf for our snowman. Usually he offered fleeting attention, but on this occasion he watched her for five minutes, altering his eye gaze as she moved. We had seen Alex tolerate his hands being moved in papier mâché in a way he would never allow us. We had celebrated these moments, aware that these children brought something to our classroom which, though difficult to define or quantify, was enabling and empowering.

As I considered how to use data from our integration work, I wondered if this might be supplemented by examining how children in a mainstream school use language to structure and support their own learning. I was aware that this would also afford me the opportunity to observe how a mainstream teacher uses language in response to the messages and questionings of pupils who are practised and confident in the use of spoken language. Hart (1995b) raises the possibility that the learning of mainstream pupils might benefit from our understanding of the struggles of pupils who have special educational needs. Reversing the directional gaze, I wanted to find out if the learning opportunities for children with severe learning difficulties could be enhanced by an appreciation of the mainstream language experience.

I made contact with a reception teacher at a local school who was interested in language and communication, and who had previously worked with children having moderate learning difficulties. I was able to join her class on three occasions. I wanted to observe how she used language with the children in a teaching context; how the children used language with her, and to support their own personal learning, but I did not want to be too focused in the direction of my interest lest I closed my eyes to important data. On the basis of these visits, I made field notes and videoed an art lesson.

I chose to parallel this data source with videotaped material from one of our integrated technology sessions. Each week eight Year 6 pupils from our neighbouring primary school spend fifty minutes partnering the children in my class in a technology lesson. The mainstream pupils help access the work, offer models of how tools are used and physically prompt my children to participate in the task at hand. Equally importantly, they have time to engage in social interactions, share conversations and learn about each other's strengths and areas of difficulty.

In order to look more closely at my own communication practices under 'normal' conditions, I decided to video two different teaching and learning sessions. I chose an early morning English lesson which offers opportunities for the children to acknowledge each other's presence, to take turns and to communicate with each other in a structured, routine session. This also offered a means by which I could reflect upon the way I respond to and interpret the communicative behaviours of the children. I also videoed a class art session in order to parallel the work filmed in the mainstream school and to reflect upon my own use of language during a teaching session.

Professional conversations

Owing to time constraints and work commitments, it had not been possible for me to work collaboratively or to share thoughts and concerns with colleagues in my work place on a regular basis. I therefore decided to talk to two teachers about their thoughts on language and communication, to see if their ideas and experience would help illuminate, extend or challenge my own.

I chose to interview the deputy head of my school because of his interest in communication and in building pupils' self-esteem. Soon after commencing the interview I realised that I had begun to use the opportunity to explore issues with him rather than eliciting only his opinions. In this way, the interview became a conversation and felt richer to me, because of the sharing of concerns and the opportunity it afforded me to hear how he reflected upon issues. It also offered me a chance to say my thoughts out loud, instead of within my own, sometimes fragmented internal monologues.

I was also able to have a shorter, but equally valuable conversation with the mainstream reception teacher who invited me into her classroom. This conversation centred around a review of her own philosophy of the use of language in the classroom environment and the features she considered important in her pupils' use of language.

Frameworks for analysis

From the literature on reflective practice, I drew three approaches to the task of data analysis, which I used to consider the communicative practices within my classroom and to explore my concerns regarding communication and empowerment.

Reflective conversations

I had read Schön's (1983) *The Reflective Practitioner* as part of the literature offered by the Masters' course and, at a time when I was struggling with theories of research and their potential application, this work offered an opportunity to name some of the processes I brought to the task of reviewing my own practice. I realised that I frequently held conversations with myself regarding my perceptions of my practice conversations, usually brought about by successes or misunderstandings in my work with the children: 'when intuitive performance leads to surprises, pleasing and promising or unwanted, we may respond by reflecting in action' (Schön 1983: 56).

As the practitioner tries to make sense of the situation, 'he reflects on the understandings which have been implicit in his actions understandings which he surfaces, criticises, restructures, and embodies in further action' (Schön 1983: 50).

Schön describes the practitioner's interaction with the situation as a 'reflective conversation' in which the practitioner shapes the situation, in accordance with his initial appreciation of it. The situation 'talks back' and the practitioner responds to the situation's back-talk. The professional shapes the situation through conversation with it, so that personal models and appreciations are also shaped by the situation. The professional is in the situation that he or she seeks to understand.

Having found parallels between my intuitive practice and Schön's 'reflective conversation', I wanted to explore how such conversation could aid my examination of the communicative practices in my classroom and, in particular, my concerns surrounding empowerment. I wanted to use the technique of reflective conversation to interrogate my thinking.

Critical incidents

I was aware that there were times in my everyday teaching when something 'stood out' from our routine interactions. What made some incidents stand out over others, and what potential was there in examining such incidents?

Tripp (1993) believes that critical incidents, like all data, are created, produced by the way that we look at a situation, and have implicit within them a value judgement, the basis of which is the significance we attach to the meaning of the incident. Tripp believes that teachers need constantly to monitor their routines with a view to changing them by asking questions such as, 'How am I going to decide what I ought to do, and how can I justify why I ought to do it?' (Tripp 1993: 10). He sees the development of a critical incident file as central to that process.

Tripp describes how teachers' critical incident files often begin with a wide-ranging exploratory phase generating a number of directions, many of which are never developed. Extending the number of critical incidents allows new ideas and connections to be made. This offers both breadth and depth to the file. He states that revision and re-analysis of the file, leading to categorisation and patterning, can also deepen a file.

Once more I felt that the literature had echoed and formalised an activity I had previously addressed intuitively. I decided to open a critical incident file by retrospectively detailing the incidents involving Scott and Alex, and adding to the file as a means of acquiring data through which to consider patterns within the context of communicative practice in my classroom. I chose to use critical incident analysis to interrogate my observations of key events.

Innovative thinking

I had previously read an article by Hart (1995a) entitled 'Action-in-reflection', which claims to build on, and then distance itself from, the work of Schön, 'to describe processes of classroom reflection in terms of five distinct interpretative moves' (Hart 1995a: 211).

These moves or modes include the 'interconnective mode', which explores possible links between the child and the learning context. The 'oppositional mode' challenges interpretations previously made by offering alternative interpretations of the same evidence. The 'decentred mode' invites us to attempt to appreciate the meaning and logic of the child's response from the child's point of view. The 'affective mode' examines the part that feelings play in leading us to arrive at our particular interpretation of a situation. The 'hypothetical mode' asks whether there might be a need to suspend judgement for a time, in order to learn more. Hart makes the point in her article that each of these modes should be recognisable to teachers as strategies which already exist within their interpretative repertoire.

This paper synthesised many issues of importance for me. It offered a structure on which to base analysis of my data; it acknowledged the importance of the role of the child in the classroom experience; it allowed me to consider my own investment in the research process; it had been used with children designated as having 'special educational needs', and it excited me. I decided to utilise the interpretative moves to interrogate my communicative interpretations of children's behaviours.

I also used it to help justify my highly selective use of data. Within traditional research methodologies, the data with which I have chosen to work in order to re-examine my practice could be viewed as scant. However, within a reflective practice methodology, the author argues,

> conventional notions of data collection and analysis give way to a research process in which observations, fieldnotes, samples of work are merely the occasion for the thinking that provides the starting point for the research. Our preliminary interpretations – or, more precisely, problems arising in making those interpretations – are our data.
>
> (Hart 1995a: 227)

I anticipated that the potential for developing new understanding about communication lay, not in the richness and volume of the data, but in the way that the methodology enabled me to manage the data. In particular, I wanted to find out whether the methods I had adopted could help me name, examine and understand the concerns I had around the issue of power and communication.

Reflective practice and the communicative process

In this section, I propose to outline the new insights that emerged from my internal conversations, stimulated by the various different data sources and approaches to data analysis outlined.

Participation in the communicative process

In Schön's (1983) terms, it was the work of Tizard and Hughes (1984) and Wells (1986) which provided the 'surprise' which troubled me and made me realise there was an issue to be addressed. Their works caused me to question whether the total communication environment which I was seeking to create was serving to empower the adults or the children in the classroom.

I found my 'reflective conversation' about these issues was aided most constructively by comments made by my deputy head. These helped me 'surface and criticise' the tacit assumptions implicit in my existing thinking and practice. They helped me achieve new insight into the 'problem', which in turn served to suggest a constructive way forward.

This is the first section of the taped conversation which caught my attention:

> It's making sure that what we're doing there, then, is for the right reasons. I think back to the thing about what we offer – it's interesting because of the reasons for it. And certainly in the system we work, too often the method being used to support youngsters' communication is

in place almost to utilise a system working rather than, is it what the youngster really needs?

What exactly did my colleague mean by this? I could identify with his concerns regarding systems which determine the shape and nature of the communication that take place. Sometimes the practicalities involved in setting up one system of communication meant there was a tendency to use that system to the exclusion of others, even though another approach might be more suited to the needs of one or two pupils in the class.

However, the next part of the conversation struck me even more forcefully. He said

> back to empowerment. It's giving it back to the youngsters . . . it was breaking a rule of mine, not to make the schedule too busy: but I gave the control to her (the pupil), we have to go with the youngsters. We have to see this as a joint enterprise, not, have we got something to offer you – aren't we wonderful?

Listening to this suddenly enabled me to see that I, too, had lost perspective on communication as a joint enterprise. The message hidden in the way I presented communication in the classroom – which now surfaced for examination – was indeed 'I have something to offer you'. I offered the children a range of communicative systems, such as signing, the use of symbols, natural gesture and speech, and encouraged them to use these systems through modelling and reinforcement. But systems such as these do not, in themselves, make explicit the process of communication.

I realised that my thinking and practice had to be restructured in accordance with this perception of communication as a genuinely two-way process and not something that I offer the children. I had to attempt to share the entire process with the children. I needed to share with them the way in which symbols, signs, speech and so on all represent language (perhaps by sharing how each of us in the class would communicate the concept 'yes' or 'drink' differently); the way in which communication offers power to everyone (perhaps by creating a shared situation where each child was given whatever they communicated irrespective of the means used); and how we can understand each other's use of communication (perhaps by restructuring the morning's timetable so that they all experienced what one member of the class had decided).

These were all strategies I had used previously, but never as whole group activities, and not in the context of sharing and understanding of the power of communication.

I now appreciated a new interpretation of empowerment (encapsulated within a sharing of the process) within a communicative context; an interpretation upon which I could act and then revisit to establish whether further reflection was necessary: Schön's (1983) spiral of 'appreciation, action and re-appreciation'.

Expectations in the communicative process

I utilised Tripp's (1993) 'critical incident' analysis to pursue my concerns surrounding a possible mismatch between my espoused values (including every pupil in the process of communication) and my practice (possibly underestimating their abilities within that process). The analysis opened up for me new insights into the dynamics of communication, the way in which they might operate to disempower, and what I might do to further create a genuinely empowering environment.

Determining the nature of the event is the first step towards understanding it; but in order to turn the event into a critical incident, something more than merely categorising it has to be done. We have to ask both what happened and what allowed it to happen, which means that we have to describe some of the deeper structures that produce that kind of incident (Tripp 1993: 9). Some of the 'thinking strategies' that Tripp proposes are identified in Table 6.1, and the manner in which I applied those strategies to two incidents in my file is detailed next.

Critical incident 1: communicating with Danielle

Danielle's head came forward on to her chest while I was feeding her. I said, 'Could you lift your head, Danielle?' (although not expecting her to do so). She lifted her head up, I praised her and turned to the rest of the staff and said, 'That was brilliant; not only did she lift her head, but she must have understood what I was saying.' Danielle looked at me and gave me a huge smile.

The systematic application of Tripp's thinking strategies (Table 6.1) raised some interesting issues and questions surrounding my expectations within the communicative process.

Table 6.1 Thinking strategies

- *Plus, minus and interesting*: a means of clarifying what we like or dislike about an incident, to evaluate it and gauge how we relate to it.
- *Alternatives, possibilities and choices*: thinking of other things that could have happened and devising ways to make them happen.
- *Other point of view*: seeking out other views, especially those of participants and informed non-participants.
- *Parts and qualities*: an examination of our attitudes, values and judgements.
- *Reversal*: turns a justification for inaction into questions about it.

Source: Tripp 1993.

When I initially documented this incident, I perceived it positively as a description of Danielle demonstrating skills which we had not previously seen. I was pleased to have stayed with the interaction long enough to have seen Danielle's smile, and to be able to share the incident with the other adults in the room, enabling us to celebrate her achievements together. The application of Tripp's strategies (*plus, minus* and *interesting*) led me into less comfortable territory. I realised that my initial position was one of negativity: I had not expected Danielle to understand my conversation with her, nor did I think she would be able to lift her head. I was also concerned that I had verbalised my limited expectations of Danielle to the staff within her hearing – and understanding. Subsequent reflection, however, allowed me to acknowledge that the sharing of difficulties should be as valid as the sharing of success, providing both are carried out in a supportive environment.

Further application of Tripp's strategies (*alternatives, possibilities* and *choices*) led me to a realisation that if Danielle had not been able to lift her head and smile at me, I would not have realised that she had understood my comment to her: her physical difficulties would have masked her level of language skills. Again, my position within the communicative process was not as open and positive as I chose to believe. I needed to find some way of enabling Danielle to communicate and demonstrate her linguistic skills, utilising a body movement already under her control, for example lifting her right hand, and to share conversations with her with an expectation that she would understand, structuring my language so there would be an opportunity for her to comment using her response of hand lifting.

Another question came to mind (Tripp's *other point of view*): what if, within the afore-mentioned scenario, Danielle's raising of her hand became an undifferentiated response to a range of questions, rather than a means of affirmation? Perhaps it is more important to give someone a 'voice' that can be heard and acknowledged, before negotiating how that voice or response might be used in a differentiated manner.

I believe my attitude to Danielle is positive (Tripp's *parts and qualities*). I value her as a person and had previously perceived my approach to her as enabling – and yet some of the judgements I was making served to underestimate her skills. It seemed that the values and attitudes I extolled were not always evident in my practice. Communication in the classroom offered Danielle the opportunity to share in a conversation, but I did not have the expectation of her being an active participant. Tripp's *reversal* strategy demonstrated that, for me, there is a tension between an open-mindedness about children's abilities and the inevitable limitations brought about by the extent of their learning disabilities.

Critical incident 2: the story of Noah's Ark

I was reading the story of Noah's Ark to the class and was beginning to worry that I had lost their interest. I tried to 'lighten' the story by telling a joke about the weather. As soon as I did this, Scott shouted and laughed.

The use of Tripp's critical incident analysis once more offered thinking strategies to describe some of the deeper structures underpinning the incident. Initially I was pleased that Scott had responded to the joke. Then (*plus, minus* and *interesting*) I realised that maybe he had been attending to the whole story and that I had underestimated his interest in and attention to the story.

The application of *alternatives, possibilities* and *choices*: made me acknowledge that my description of the incident itself was not sufficiently detailed. I had not documented why 'I thought I had lost their interest'. Further recollection of the incident was highly illuminating; I thought I had lost their interest because they were silent. I needed to reconsider the possible meanings of silence, and to ensure that I did not underestimate the abilities of the children to listen or to utilise silence.

In seeking the opinions of the two classroom assistants (Tripp's *other point of view),* we realised that we shared similar pleasure about Scott's response to the joke, while acknowledging that together, we needed to clarify our idea about our interpretation of silence within communication.

Just as with Danielle (*parts and qualities*), I realised that I must ensure my positive attitude to Scott is reflected in an open-mindedness about his skills. I need to make positive assumptions about his understanding until he shows me that something is too difficult for him.

Within the *reversal* strategy, both Scott and Danielle raised issues for me concerning the balance between my open-mindedness regarding the children's abilities and the inevitable limitations brought about by the extent of their learning difficulties.

The use of reflective conversation and critical incident analysis had led me to reconsider my position *vis-à-vis* power within the process of communication. I was beginning to see that my expectations within the communicative process needed to be focused more upon allowing the children open access to wide-ranging conversations (using all modalities of communication that would enable them to be participants) rather than assuming a particular level of understanding on their behalf. This position seemed to resonate with some of my earlier reflections around communication as a joint enterprise, and not just something I offered the children on a regular basis.

Interpretation in the communicative process

Prior to this study, I had considered my personal-professional philosophy to centre on the valuing of each child in my class as an individual whose skills and strengths were to be celebrated. I viewed them as communicators while being aware of the adults' responsibility to observe their behaviours, accept them as communication, report them to the children and act upon their message.

Within the context of this study, I began to question my role as interpreter as another way of exercising power which might in fact, disempower the children. What right have I to place meaning on their behaviours? What if I placed the wrong meaning on a behaviour?

I chose to utilise Hart's (1995a) interpretative moves to examine this issue through an analysis of my interpretation of the children's responses. Two examples are used to explain the new insights that were opened up, concentrating on the particular 'moves' which, in each case, proved to be the most illuminating.

Communicating with Scott

Scott has profound and multiple learning difficulties but we believe he understands some language. Due to his extreme physical disability, the only movement under his voluntary control is an eye blink. We have chosen to utilise this eye blink as a way for Scott to communicate 'yes'. It must be acknowledged that there would be little objective evidence to substantiate agreement among outsiders about the consistency of this eye blink response. There is usually, however, an intuitive consensus among classroom staff.

In considering the five interpretative modes in the context of our interpretation of Scott's eye blink, it was the decentred mode in particular which offered a new dimension. This asks, 'What meaning and purpose does this activity have for the child?' What is important to Scott about our response to his eye blink? Perhaps eye blinking is a very positive behaviour for Scott, irrespective of the correctness of our interpretation. It prolongs adult contact, offers opportunities for praise, signals that something else is about to happen, and usually more than one adult is there to be pleased about his response. Therefore it secures positive, quality interaction with adults and so has its own meaning independent of comprehension of the spoken word.

Communicating with Christopher

Christopher has profound and multiple learning difficulties as a result of a degenerative condition. He has the most beautiful smile but we are no longer sure that it signals pleasure in what he is doing (though it might accompany positive thoughts). He will often shake his head but again, the communication message 'no' does not always seem appropriate. He can be relaxed and accepting of his drink but then shake his head. It feels uncomfortable for me to place intent on this behaviour, assuming 'you don't want the drink', when such a message seems at odds with his general state of being.

Hart's (1995a) 'affective' mode examines the part that feelings play in leading us to arrive at a particular interpretation of a situation. I had to acknowledge that my concern and compassion for him was limiting the way in which I viewed his learning.

The 'oppositional' mode opened up opportunities for me to consider different readings of the situation. Christopher could be shaking his head because he is uncomfortable, to communicate 'no', or it could be an involuntary movement which has no communicative significance. I realised that the difficulty in placing meaning on Christopher's behaviours lies with us. We need to be more creative in our responses. It is our responsibility to judge the context and on that basis decide whether to say 'Christopher's smiling, do you like that?' or 'Christopher says "no"', or whether indeed our communication should be descriptive, 'You're shaking your head now.' Communication does not have to impute intentionality.

I followed the exploration of these two most potent interpretative modes with an examination of the others, to ensure all possibilities had been addressed. On this occasion, the hypothetical mode suggested that I should indeed suspend judgement. I needed time to reflect on these new thoughts that had occurred concerning my use of language with Christopher.

Silence in the communicative process

The issue of silence, which has already been raised, came up again during observation of how mainstream children use language to structure their learning, which alerted me to the fact that I no longer included silence in my communicative repertoire.

I was videoing a particular session with Alex and his mainstream partner and, as I observed through the lens, I became despondent. There was no doubt this was a quality interaction; they demonstrated joint attention to the task, they both seemed relaxed, Alex was allowing his partner to guide his hand and they were helping each other colour the apple – but there was no language. On reviewing the video, I detailed the following,

> Mainstream partner taking Alex's hand: 'Right, Alex, we're just going to do this . . .'
> 'We're just colouring the stalk green.' Lots of silence while colouring.
> 'Do you want to feel it now?'
> Alex: 'Yes.' (Partner helped Alex feel the paper.)
> Mainstream partner: 'I'll finish it off now.'
> 'Are your hands clean?'
> 'Yeah.'

Reflecting upon my habitual use of language in the classroom, I realised I invariably accompanied my actions and the actions of the children with a verbal commentary. I had forgotten there were other ways to be. I used the video of the mainstream art lesson to think further.

One boy talked constantly about what he was doing, the choices he was making and the reasons for those choices; one girl said nothing while choosing and applying the chalks to the paper; another girl in the group talked while she drew, but her conversations were not about the task. The teacher allowed this diversity of language in action by observing each child's work without censure or comment: 'To develop our professional judgement, we have to move beyond our everyday "working" way of looking at things' (Tripp 1993: 12).

Implications for practice

This study has caused me to re-examine my philosophical stance regarding communication. It has also occasioned reflection upon the way in which philosophy interfaces with practice in a classroom context. I now appreciate that a philosophy of empowerment will not, of itself, suffice to ensure its existence in practice. I have also begun to appreciate the concept of invisible power, and how this can operate within classroom interactions which are intended to be empowering.

The use of Schön's (1983) reflective conversation allowed me the opportunity to use data offered by the deputy to reshape the problem I was experiencing in naming my concerns surrounding empowerment. By reflecting upon 'this joint enterprise, not, have we got something to offer you, aren't we wonderful?' I was able to locate myself in the equation of empowerment and to make explicit some of the ways in which I maintained an imbalance. I focused on the pupils as recipients of my communicative practice, rather than on the communicative process in which we were all equally engaged. By making explicit the different ways in which we all communicate, and by working together with communication in order to demonstrate its power either by 'asking for' favourite activities (toys, drinks) or by using their communicative skills to organise other children in the class, and to practise these skills with their mainstream peers, I hope to move towards a shared understanding of the process of communication and the power it can offer.

I have come to realise that the way in which I frame my understanding of the children in terms of my expectations of them is another way in which invisible power can be evidenced. Using Tripp's (1993) critical incident analysis, I moved from a set of observations into an exploration of values of which I was unaware. This process enabled me to see the existence of a mismatch between my perceived stance (valuing the contribution made by each pupil) and the scheme I sometimes utilised within the classroom context (I did not think Danielle would understand when I said 'Lift your head'). I need to remove any restrictions which I place on the children within our interactions, and believe that many things are possible until there is evidenced a reason for saying 'She can't do this'. I have to further examine the assumptions I make about each of the children within the communicative process, and work towards correcting against 'self-fulfilling prophecies'. I need to make explicit the assumptions I hold and ensure there is evidence to support them.

One of the huge challenges of working with children with severe or profound learning difficulties in their lack of voice. This is not to suggest that their voice is not present, rather it is not always audible. It is possible to observe, with confidence, a pupil's positive response to a learning situation, and similarly to note when a communicative opportunity has been missed. There exists nevertheless a huge area of uncertainty, the middle ground. We develop our own repertoire on which to base our understandings and with which to inform our practice. Reflective practice has offered me the opportunity to acknowledge my existing skills, but also to discover ways in which my own repertoire could be extended and enhanced. Hart's (1995a) 'innovative thinking' offered me a structure on which to place my existing observations, and the opportunity to widen my perspective on the children's responses to learning. It offered me the possibility of using language to communicate without attributing assumed meaning and intentionality: communication can celebrate 'being together'.

Through observing children from a mainstream setting and by the process of reflective conversation, I have expanded my understanding of the communicative process to include silent communication. I am aware that I used to be familiar with this, but somehow over the years, I have settled into a way of working which appears to assume that the more verbally active, the better the environment for learning. It is important that I now begin to reflect upon any effects these changes might have and to re-examine their use in the communicative context of the classroom. Does silence enable the pupil to perform at a higher level? How can I ensure that silence has a comfortable feel rather than being perceived as bringing an extra pressure to the task?

Initially, I perceived my exploration of reflective practice to involve the use of three discrete processes, each of which could be utilised to examine practice. This study has altered that perception. I now understand reflective practice to represent a means of drawing together various strands of knowledge, experience and concerns, unique to the individual practitioner, to facilitate an exploration of possible interpretations based on that knowledge, experience and concern. Reflective practice allows, indeed recommends, regular reworking of the strands in a move towards increasing confidence in the representation. I perceive the process to be creative, emotive and challenging.

My perspective within this study has been to focus on the usefulness of the three chosen tools of reflective practice (reflective conversation, critical incident analysis and innovative thinking) rather than on the volume of data collected. I would now choose to add one additional tool to the process of reflective practice: the act of committing words to paper in a thoughtful manner, which has enabled me to refine my language and add rigour to the process of thinking.

I perceive this study to be the first step towards my development as a reflective practitioner. This paper has enabled me to reflect upon deeper structures underlying my practice and existing, but previously unacknowledged, gaps between my philosophy and practice. It has also offered opportunities to consider ways in which my practice might change. I propose to integrate these changes into my repertoire of classroom practice, and to use the aforementioned tools of reflection (reflective conversation, critical incident analysis, innovative thinking and writing) to re-appraise their usefulness in moving forward my understanding of the communicative process.

* * *

NARRATIVE SUMMARY 5

Issues arising from Linda's innovative research

Linda's decision to structure her study in the form of a conversation between two distinct sets of research purposes emerged as a way of resolving her dilemma whether the principal focus of the research was to be the processes of reflective practice or issues of classroom communication. She resolved this dilemma by creating a research process in which she was able to learn about reflective practice by exploring this in the context of a study of classroom communication, and to learn about classroom communication by applying to it specific techniques of reflective practice.

Part of what is unconventional about Linda's study is her selective use of the various data collected. One of the Darers, in responding to her study, was surprised initially that so little data was used. She was prompted to ask 'Where is all the data?' although, as she read on, the minimal use of data seemed not to matter. What was important for Linda, in this study, was the *thinking prompted* by her engagement with data, not an exhaustive examination of what might be learned from all the data collected. Her approach to analysis was to use the data to generate a series of reflective dialogues with her existing understandings. The focus was her own thinking – and the use of techniques of reflective practice to develop her thinking – and so her *interpretations* were really the data for her study, they were the raw material out of which new understandings emerged.

This is very different from how material gathered through observation and interview is traditionally handled. In writing her study up, Linda needed to be able to justify her use and interpretation of data, but found that she could not appeal to authoritative sources in the traditional literature on methodology to give weight to her arguments. This created considerable pressure at the writing-up stage, because it seemed that her written text would need to be extra-good in order to convince examiners of the acceptability of a non-conventional approach. Support and encouragement from supervisors was important here in reinforcing her belief in the validity of her chosen approach.

Linda found herself torn between what she felt was expected by the academy and the kind of approach that she felt drawn towards for her own personal and professional purposes. On the one hand, she wanted the security of working within the clearly defined rules and guidelines of traditional research methodology. On the other hand, the experience of the course on research methodology had not left her feeling empowered to use traditional research methods to investigate her practice. She said, 'I kept going to books about research methodology . . . but not engaging with it at any level other than thinking, this doesn't sit comfortably with me.'

Although she was not someone who felt confident about taking risks, it was important to Linda that her study should be personally meaningful and contribute significantly to the development of her work with children. This personal drive provided the impetus to take the risks needed to develop a methodological approach that fitted what she wanted to know and that she would find comfortable and empowering. Nevertheless, she continued to experience a tension between what she felt that she needed to do for her own personal and professional purposes and what she felt that she ought to do in order to satisfy the requirements of the academy.

Linda drew courage to stay with her deeply personal approach from a growing sense that the work 'lost quality' when she tried to make her research or writing 'fit the rules'. There came a point when her investment in the work was such, she said, that 'even if I failed I had to carry on . . . I mean, it would have devastated me if I had failed but it came to the point that it was more important to move my practice on and reflect on my practice by doing this piece of work than fulfilling any criteria.'

Linda found that this was a rewarding as well as a high-risk strategy. The focus on herself and her practice made the study an intensely personal experience. She felt that she was 'living it' at every stage. More than any previous study, this piece of work allowed her to find her voice, and this voice comes through strongly in her writing. Linda insists that she was 'writing for herself and her practice', not for an external audience. When she re-reads the work now, she recognises that it has become a part of her. She says, 'It does not feel like something separate from what I do every day.'

Part 3

Fictional writing as a method of enquiry and reporting

Chapter 7

Imaginary gardens – enigmatic encounters

Tish Crotty

Editorial note

When Tish carried out this study, she was in the second year of her Masters' degree. She was still working for the Multicultural Education Service in the same school as when she carried out the earlier study. The chapter has been edited from an 8,000 word assignment in which the fable was presented as an in-text appendix. The fable itself is presented in edited and shortened form.

The aim of this study was to explore possible sources of bias in the assessment of bilingual and ethnic minority pupils as a precursor for defining action that might be taken to minimise its negative effects. Part of my unwillingness to investigate in depth, before now, questions surrounding the topic of assessment has been an awareness that it is a highly complex area and that I find studies dealing with issues of assessment make dry and rather difficult reading. I decided to experiment with an alternative format to that of the 'traditional essay'. I felt that if I could submit a few of the more complex and possibly emotive ideas under examination in an different style, I might succeed in making the study informative yet engaging and accessible.

At the same time I was interested to see what value there might be in trying to step outside the normal boundaries of academic orthodoxy, in terms of the style of investigation I undertook and the form of work I finally presented. I wanted to try to capture the essence of what it might feel like to be assessed from the standpoint of a different set of cultural norms. In effect I wanted to try to mirror and experience for myself what I felt might unwittingly be the experience of many bilingual or ethnic minority pupils. After some consideration I chose to use a 'fable' in the knowledge that this was a genre seldom used in research, and yet it was one which I found particularly well suited to the presentation and consideration of difficult ideas.

When I embarked on writing the fable initially, I thought that my methodology was clearly established. I intended to research the available literature so as to discover possible sources of bias. I would then use the fable as a means of representing my findings. To check I had comprehensively covered and included all possible sources of bias that I had been able to identify through the literature, I felt it would be important to write a comprehensive exposé of the draft fable and then edit all or parts of the tale. As an additional check, a sort of 'validity triangulation', I decided to solicit the help and opinions of some of my colleagues. I asked six of them to read the draft version of the fable and to make comments. I would take these into account as I edited the fable.

In the event my original methodology was set aside. I did not go back and edit the fable, as I had firmly intended to do. The actual process of constructing and writing it, then attempting to analyse it, became for me a journey of discovery. I believe it was a process that actually helped significantly to change my thinking. It initiated a considerable re-examination and an eventual re-structuring of my ideas regarding the whole issue I was researching. The comments made by my colleagues served only to augment my fresh thinking.

I was unprepared for and rather taken aback by this situation. The fable became far more than a simple vehicle which conveyed my research findings. My method of presenting the study had become part of the research, the fable part of my data.

I have since found out that I am not alone in recognising that writing can be a powerful aid to reflective thought. A growing body of researchers have begun to recognise writing *per se*, and narrative writing in particular, not only as a tool for reflective research but as a powerful device, capable of existing on its own as a research methodology, an idea I shall return to in my conclusion.

Thus the study begins with the presentation of my fable, *Imaginary gardens – enigmatic encounters*. The fable itself is followed by an 'exposé' of the fable, in which I hope to be able to make visible, not just the concepts it attempted to embrace, but also how the focus of my own original concerns about bias in assessment were changed as a result of writing it.

> *What is an 'imaginary garden'?*
> *It is a place more wondrous than any actually beheld garden –*
> *There are no limits to the flowers or trees grown there*
> > *or*
> *the possibilities of behaviour there.*
>
> (Graham 1973: 1)

Phoebe turned once, briefly, and waved to her mother. Then somewhat impatiently she hurried on towards the gate in the high brick wall. She walked positively, head held high, eyes firmly fixed on her goal. She was a beautiful child; skin the colour of burnished mahogany, hair a mass of jet black curls, eyes like bright gems and a smile which would brighten the bleakest of winter nights. In her hand she held a gift, a flower gathered from her own garden in such haste that it had the root still attached. It was an exquisite flower; small but delicately formed, petals the colour of deepest red-brown and scented with an unbelievable fragrance of chocolate!

Confidently Phoebe pushed open the big wrought-iron gate and stepped into the garden, The Garden of Intent.

A wonderful sight met her eyes. The garden itself was bounded by high walls stretching far out into the distance. A slender rill snaked across the path in front of her spanned by a small but ornate bridge. Beyond the rill through the trees she could see paths leading off in every direction, inviting exploration. The silence was total, the colours and perfumes gorgeous. Excitedly she stepped onto the bridge, pausing only to seek her reflection in the water of the rill. Her own face smiled back at her from the clear water and she laughed delightedly.

Once across the bridge she was startled to hear a deep voice:

'What is your name, child?'

Phoebe stopped still in her tracks listening, looking around her. She saw no one. She was about to continue on down the path when once again the voice boomed out. 'Stop! What is your name?'

Phoebe made no answer. In truth she was now a little uncertain and rather frightened.

'Your name child, what are you called?'

'What no tongue?' continued the deep voice authoritatively.

Phoebe intended to answer, really, but the voice just went on and on asking more and more questions. After a while Phoebe stopped listening. Most of the questions made no sense to her, didn't he realise that? Anyway she had questions of her own to ask, things she wanted to learn. She began to move away across the grass, slowly at first but gradually quickening her pace until finally she was running. Still the voice pursued her: 'I am Enilesab, you must answer my questions. You can't go on until I have found out where you've come from and where you're going.'

Phoebe ran on until she could run no further. Exhausted she sank to the ground.

Suddenly before her appeared an extraordinary dragon-like creature; on its back a figure ethereal and shimmering, whose form seemed to change even as she looked at it. For some strange reason she wasn't frightened; only curious.

'Who are you?' she whispered.

'I am Iodah,' replied the figure in a soft, kind voice, 'and this – pointing to the Dragon creature – 'is Tiamat. Why were you running, where are you going to?'

I don't know,' murmured Phoebe in a faint voice, 'I was frightened.'

'Phoebe, here is my advice. Start with what you know. Follow the well-trodden path.'

Iodah reached down and plucked a scale from the dragon's back. He handed it to Phoebe. 'Take this, part of the answer lies here.' So saying, the curious creature with the strange figure on its back faded from her eyes.

Phoebe gazed at the dragon-scale in her hand. On it were some lines. She thrust the scale deep in her pocket.

Looking up, Phoebe found herself in a small open glade criss-crossed with paths. She tried each path in turn, all were overgrown and quite impassable except the last she came to. It was this one she followed. It was well trodden but it did not feel inviting. She passed through what she imagined must be the old part of the garden, for the path was bounded by high ancient brick walls crumbling in places, with weeds beginning to flourish in the gaps. Here and there she saw gates but when she tried to open them they were always locked. Eventually she came to an archway. It led to a small enclosed garden encircled by a high hedge.

The garden was set on a slight hill and was beautifully ordered; neat and tidy, with small rectangular beds filled with flowers. Each bed ran in the same direction, from the base of the incline to the rise. In the far corner of the garden was a statue, in the centre of the garden was a small pool and in the middle of one of the flower beds was an old man, bent nearly double, tending the garden. He didn't appear to see Phoebe.

She wandered quietly through the garden, stopping every so often to peer into one of the flower beds. In them the flowers were planted in straight rows across the hill, crowded in the middle, sparse at either end. All were carefully labelled. She was disappointed to find that none of the plants in the garden looked like hers, in fact all the flowers were blue and the plants very alike; or were they? On closer inspection she realised that in each bed the plants at the top end were tall and handsome with huge bright flowers, while at the bottom they seemed much smaller, slightly sickly-looking, bearing few if any flowers. At this end was a pile of dead or dying plants.

She passed the statue she had seen from the archway. It was the head of a man and had written below it in very bold letters BINET 1905. She walked on slowly still searching for her flower, until she came to the bed where the old man was working. She stopped and as she did so, the old man looked up. Phoebe held up her plant which was looking rather wilted and said to him,' Do you grow this here in your garden?'

The old man shook his head. 'No, it didn't do well when I tried it here. I don't know why some of them don't.'

'Oh,' said Phoebe, close to tears.

'You might find it in one of the other gardens,' continued the old man, and then turned back to his work.

Disappointed, Phoebe made her way slowly towards the gate she could see at the far end of the garden. She passed the pool in the middle of the garden and glanced into it. Sadly she saw that the water, although motionless, was murky, and her reflection was indistinct and blurred.

The gate led back out into the forest. Phoebe had no idea which way to go next. She wished she had asked the gardener which path she should follow. If only there were some signposts or someone to help her. She thought of the strange creature she had seen and absently she fingered the dragon-scale in her pocket. A sound on the path behind her made her spin around. There stood the creature Tiamet. On its back, as before was Iodah. 'Oh Iodah' cried Phoebe, 'I did as you said but I found only bewilderment.'

'Ah,' said Iodah gently, 'perhaps you were in the wrong garden asking the wrong questions. Perhaps the gardener did not understand what it is you seek and why you look for it. Did he ask you? . . . No. . . . Well, do not give up, for there are other gardens, with gardeners who will understand'.

'How will I find them?' said Phoebe.

'They will find you,' came the answer. 'Those who know how to look and ask will find you. To learn you must also discover what others know, and be aware of what you don't know.' So saying, Iodah plucked a second scale from the back of the dragon, handed it to Phoebe and disappeared, dragon and all! Phoebe once more was alone.

Tired and dispirited she sat down, took the second dragon-scale from her pocket and stared at it. It too had lines on it. She carried on down the path, sniffing at the flower in her hand to keep her spirits up. Eventually ahead of her the trees thinned and she saw a high stone wall. By following the wall she found a small gap through which she squeezed.

She found herself in a huge garden full of gardeners. Each had a paper and pen in his hand and was walking through the flower beds. Every so often one stopped and make a mark on the paper he held. Every flower bed was a different size and shape, although the plants and flowers that grew in them looked alike.

Just as there had been in the last garden, in the middle of this garden was a pool, and in the corner of the garden, not a statue, but a tall round tower built of stone without windows or door. The tower cast a thin long shadow over the length of the garden, and where it fell the garden was gloomy and quite dark.

Phoebe approached the nearest gardener. 'What are you doing?' she asked. 'We ask the questions here,' was the abrupt reply, and he turned back to what he had been doing. Undeterred Phoebe went up to the next gardener and asked him the same question. He looked up slowly and replied, 'We are checking.' Checking, what does that mean, thought Phoebe. As if in reply the gardener continued, 'I am checking to see if the plants are a good shape. He (pointing to the next gardener) is checking to see if the flowers are the right colour; he (pointing right across the garden) is checking to see if the plants grow well, and so on. Every one is checking something from the list.'

'What list?' quizzed Phoebe.

'Our list,' was the response, 'We decide what we are looking for and then we look for it!'

Phoebe moved away. Nowhere could she see her flower, she didn't know where to start to look for it. Why did it not grow here? She found herself near the tall tower, and seated at its foot was yet another gardener. 'What is this?' she asked, curious to know what purpose the strange building served.

'Folly, it's a folly,' came the riposte. 'The Folly of Tick.'

Phoebe sighed. Everything seemed so strange, so unfamiliar. She passed the centre of the garden where the pool lay; it was shaded by the folly and although the water was dark her reflection showed her face looking pale almost white. In her hand her flower also looked pale and it had lost two of its precious petals. She ran out of the garden through the first gap she found in the high wall back into the woodland.

Once back in the trees she realised how gloomy it was. She hadn't noticed the mist before, now it seemed to cloak everything so that shapes and colours were blurred and unclear. The garden seemed to have lost a little of its magic and become confusing and slightly treacherous. Still she held tightly to her flower as if it were some sort of bond between her and home. 'Where am I going to go next?' She couldn't help voicing her thoughts. An echo returned:

–– That is for us to know and you to find out ––

On she stumbled through the mist, everything in the forest suddenly seeming to conspire against her. The tree roots tripped her; she was cut by wild sharp-leafed plants and stung by insects with venomous intentions. She tried to wrap herself up tightly to protect herself, but the wild plants and insects had a way of finding those parts she had left exposed and vulnerable. Almost in desperation she shouted out, 'Iodah, Iodah, where are you? Help me, please, or I shall be lost forever.'

As if by magic there in front of Phoebe stood Tiamet, the Dragon-creature; on its back was Iodah. 'Do not be afraid,' came the soft, reassuring voice. 'There is a way forward through the trees, you just have to look for it. Trust your instincts; often when things become complicated, the simple paths are forgotten or scorned. Original intentions get distorted. Take this, it will help you and others like you who are lost.' He handed Phoebe a third scale from Tiamat's back and disappeared in a cloud of dust.

Phoebe ran after him, but he moved at such a speed that she gave up almost immediately. She started to cry, soft silent tears that ran down her face in rivulets. On she stumbled along the path until it ended abruptly in a large wooden gate. Either side of the gate there was a stout wooden fence which seemed to go on forever. Holding her breath she slowly opened the gate.

A splendid park lay in front of her, set on a steep hill. It was divided neatly into two by a fast flowing stream. There was a waterfall gushing from a rocky outcrop high on the hill which fell into a deep swirling pool. It was this pool which fed the stream. Numerous bridges crossed the stream at points up the hill. On one side of the stream the land was terraced, while on the other side it was further divided into small gardens enclosed by high wattle fences.

At the top of the garden above the waterfall was an impressive looking open-fronted stone arbour, its roof supported by three giant stone columns. Inside the arbour Phoebe could just see a table, seated at which was one man. She couldn't see his face. Several more people stood around the table. Running up through the terraces were flights of steps, and everywhere there were people.

She stared transfixed at the incredible spectacle in front of her eyes, before climbing slowly up the hill through the terraces. Each terrace had a number, except the first: it was simply labelled 'W'. None of the people looked up, they were obviously very busy, although Phoebe wasn't sure what they were doing. Some looked to be weeding or hoeing, while others were moving plants from one level to the next. Phoebe peered into each terrace in turn looking, as always, for her plant. There were many more varieties than in the other gardens certainly, but nowhere could she find her 'chocolate' plant.

Each garden enclosure had its own gardener working in it. She walked past several before she plucked up enough courage to speak to one. 'Hallo,' said Phoebe and, holding up her plant, continued, 'Do you grow my plant here?'

The gardener looked at it carefully, then said, 'Yes, I believe I do have one of those. Let me look at my notes. Yes, I have, but mine has never flowered, I didn't think it could. It's here, look, in the corner of the garden.' Sure enough, there in the corner was a plant like Phoebe's, but small and unhappy looking.

'But it needs sun,' said Phoebe, 'and a rich soil with not too much water in summer, then it would grow flowers. You must move it!'

'Can't do that; everything's decided and laid down by the Director. We just do our best,' the gardener said regretfully, and went back to his work.

Feeling herself dismissed, Phoebe left the gardener and climbed high up the hill, intending to wash her face in the waterfall pool. When she got there she found to her dismay that the water in the pool was far too turbulent. Indeed she could not even see her reflection, just an agitated surface, frothy and disturbed. In her fright she dropped her plant into the pool, watching helplessly as it disappeared.

Without thinking she raced to a small hole she had seen in the corner of the fence, intending to make her escape. Instead she found her way barred by a giant of a man. 'You cannot leave, you have not yet given an account of yourself!' He thrust towards her a sheaf of papers. Phoebe dodged his outstretched arm, dived through his legs and wriggled with great agility through the hole in the fence, escaping out into the forest.

On she raced through the trees, until so scratched and bruised she felt as though her body might break. Without warning, like a mirage in the desert, she saw in front of her Iodah, astride not Tiamet as before, but a magnificent bird, body of scarlet and wings like shimmering rainbows. Phoebe moved towards the image but as she moved so it moved away. Alarmed, she followed it until finally it came to rest.

Approaching slowly for fear that it might once more flee, she came upon a rough clearing brimming with plants of every description, flowers of every hue. Small bushes grew alongside tall grasses, gaudy coloured flowers against soft pastel shades. Where one would expect discord there was unexpected harmony. No fence or wall surrounded the glade, and the stream that ran along the side was fresh and clear. Phoebe was overcome by the beauty she saw, the peace and tranquillity she felt. Who could have created such a paradise, how and why?

'It is the Garden of Hope, an "imaginary" garden,' came a soft voice, Iodah's voice. There in front of her was Iodah (still astride the magnificent bird), his formless shape somehow now more tangible, more real. 'Here all things grow and *mature in harmony. Even those elements which might conflict elsewhere, here have a place. Together we work to create the conditions in which each will flourish; we try to understand their needs, to foster and appreciate their unique qualities; their own success nourishes them.'*

Phoebe stood transfixed. Finally she stammered, 'I lost my gift; I couldn't learn; I did not understand; they asked me to account for myself and all I saw was failure.'

Iodah replied softly, 'Phoebe, you have not failed, it is they that have failed you. Only the foolish judge others before they judge themselves rightly. Now you must go. Follow this path until you reach the twin towers and the gate which leads to freedom. Here, this is for you.' He handed her a flower, a deep red-brown chocolate scented flower, her flower; beautiful and perfect.

Overjoyed she moved towards him, but he had gone. In his place a fourth dragon-scale lay. Slowly she picked it up and made her way down the path. In the distance she could see the twin towers just as he had promised she would, between them a small rusty gate. As she approached the gate a man came out of one of the towers shouting at her, 'You cannot leave until I have checked you have taken nothing from the garden!'

Phoebe felt the four dragon-scales in her pocket digging into her side. Taking them from her pocket she said, 'I have only these.' She opened her hand to show the man, and the scales fell to the ground. They landed in such a way that the lines on them formed writing.

The man bent to look at them, and as he did so Phoebe, holding tightly to her flower which she had hidden beneath the folds in her dress, ran to the gate, opened it and stepped through to freedom. A faint echo followed her:

'Wait what does this mean? I cannot understand, I cannot read this, I do not speak this language. Help me.'

Phoebe turned once, briefly, but she did not wave.

Towards an understanding of bias

According to Greek mythology the name Phoibe (Phoebe) stands for, symbolically, 'the bright one'. In the fable Phoebe is black, overtly typical of the minority ethnic child, and depicts both the children from minority groups and bilingual children. She is full of self-esteem, respectful of her background, proud of her culture, bright and eager to learn. The flower she carries (her gift) represents her and all those like her. It is a peculiarly unusual plant with a unique flower. It is of African origin, 'shy' of rooting, and requires specific conditions to thrive. It has particular qualities, not easily recognisable or necessarily appreciated, and certainly not evidenced unless the growing conditions are appropriate.

Thus Phoebe enters the garden – the child enters school – to come face to face with, among other things, a battery of assessment procedures: procedures which encompass evidence collection and judgement making.

The fable recounts the gradual process through which Phoebe's flower progressively wilts and fades as a result of the encounters she has in the garden. Each of these experiences attempts to portray a particular source of possible bias in the assessment process. Those directed at her flower are analogous to assessment procedures to which she herself could be subject. Many, though not all of them, seem to be hostile experiences which in some way militate against her.

Bourne (1994: 220) suggests that particular assessment styles, and the cultural norms they work within, are likely to be discriminatory against certain groups of children. Certainly it is true that many assessment techniques work from within parameters that are defined and guided by cultural values set or influenced by the dominant cultural group. It is therefore likely that they are slanted, albeit inadvertently, against those children whose cultural background differs significantly from the culture of those devising, administering and marking the tests: 'The choice of questions, the design of the test and the process of setting norms and standardising the tests are all ways of differentiating between social groups, by validating the knowledge and experience of some and denying those of others' (Bourne 1994: 215).

Heath (1983) clearly revealed that knowledge is culturally situated; that modes of expression, styles of learning and values accorded to particular skills are also culturally based. In a major ethnographic study, based in North Carolina and spanning ten years, Heath collected data about two communities living only miles apart. Her analysis highlighted the differences between the language and literacy practices of these communities, and how they were bound up with the culture and ways of life of the communities themselves. It also revealed the cultural bias operating in teachers' assessments of children's abilities and cooperativeness on arrival at school, resulting from teachers' lack of awareness of the impact of cultural norms on their own perceptions and interpretations. The data showed, Heath argued, that the way events are narrated, even what counts as 'acceptable' in terms of 'knowledge', is culturally situated.

> *After a while Phoebe stopped listening.*
> *Most of the questions made no sense to her, didn't he realise that?*
>
> (Fable)

In fact Phoebe's responses to Enilesab are judged by him to be evidence of 'poor' performance or 'troublesome' behaviour, although they are not a reflection of either at all but a result of circumstance and situation. Phoebe's disinclination to answer the questions fired at her by Enilesab were in truth due to her becoming 'uncertain and rather frightened'.

I used Phoebe's numerous encounters in the fable to illustrate other such ways in which such a cultural bias might operate negatively for pupils from minority groups. In 'Binet's Garden', set on the classic 'bell curve' hill, the psychometric, standardised, norm-referenced tests hold court. Difficulties with this mode of assessment include 'item bias' where a significant proportion of the items used in the test may be outside the cultural experience, customs or values of a particular group. (Phoebe's chocolate plant had no place here: its qualities were not among those recognised or measured.)

Other possibly contentious cultural issues arise with the use of any assessment which is reputed to be norm-referenced. Gregory and Kelly maintain that: 'By definition, the standardisation of a test on a representative sample means that the bulk of the sample will come from the dominant group' (Gregory and Kelly 1994: 204).

> *it didn't do well when I tried it, I don't know why some of them don't.*
>
> (Fable)

Even the few tests which have been standardised on a bilingual, multi-ethnic population tend to ignore issues of heterogeneity within the bilingual population itself.

'Item bias' is not simply a feature of norm-referenced tests, it is as likely to occur in any criteria-referenced test. It is in situations in the fable where tests are criterion-referenced that Phoebe experiences additional plight. Irrespective of what is actually being assessed in such tests, the questions themselves tend to relate to particular experiences and values, ones which frequently lie outside those experienced by the minority child, whose experiences are often summarily dismissed. Indeed not only the questions can be culturally derived, but commonly the criteria themselves chosen for assessment are also culturally determined, and are frequently idiosyncratic or anomalous: 'One "Record of achievement" for nursery aged children requires educators to record whether each child "Puts coat on hook", "Combs or brushes hair at home", "Blows nose when reminded"' (Drummond 1994b: 4).

> *'We decide what we're looking for and we look for it.'*
>
> (Fable)

The penultimate garden Phoebe encounters in the fable is inspired by the National Curriculum and curriculum-related assessment; it is here that she faces further puzzling and, for her, quite distressing situations.

Curriculum-related assessment is currently a highly topical issue, and is often presented as a fairer, more relevant and advantageous form of assessment for pupils of ethnic minority backgrounds. The National Curriculum is reputed to be a curriculum model which promotes equal opportunities. However it could be argued that it is, in a highly subtle and hidden fashion, skewed against children like Phoebe. In effect what it conceivably may do is legitimise specific subject content and learning objectives, applaud certain forms of knowledge and particular kinds of ability; all of which reflect and promote both overt and hidden ethnocentric assumptions. This promotion of one set of values tends to marginalise and devalue the worth of other ideals: 'On the issue of course content it is clear that CRA [curriculum related assessment] can only be a non discriminatory approach if the curriculum on which the assessment is based is non-discriminatory' (Cline and Frederickson 1996: 6).

This apart, there are further problems associated with any assessment that is curriculum-related. Cummins (1984) suggests that, where behavioural objectives are used in curriculum planning, only the pre-specified behaviour patterns are permissible as evidence of a child's 'understanding'. Other behaviour patterns are dismissed by omission, even though they may in fact offer evidence of the same 'understanding'.

Second, it is possible that if a child approaches a task from an angle different to that which is expected, she may emerge with a quite different, equally valid 'understanding', which may be discounted or misinterpreted as evidence of mis-understanding rather than accepted of proof of a 'new-understanding'.

Task analysis, or the breaking down of skills or assessment tasks into small units, can cause difficulties for both the learner and for the assessed child, in that such analysis has the tendency to divorce learning, skills and knowledge from its context. Cummins (1984) argues that one of the best ways of enabling children who are bilingual or from an ethnic minority background to learn is to embed the knowledge to be acquired and thus assessed as comprehensively as possible within a context meaningful to the child.

Assessment of course involves not only the assessed, but also the assessor. The way in which children's responses may be interpreted may be open to question. Cline and Frederickson cite a study which showed teachers to be: 'Biased in their judgements about children's attainment of teaching objectives in a way that underestimated the achievements of children from black and ethnic minority communities' (Cline and Frederickson 1991: 4).

For Phoebe this presents real problems as she journeys through the garden. Not only is her lack of response to Enilesab's questions misinterpreted, the questions she asks in other parts of the garden are also considered inappropriate:

> *'What are you doing?' she asked....*
> *'We ask the questions here,' was the abrupt reply.*
>
> (Fable)

It is not only in a cultural dimension that Phoebe and her flower encounter assessment situations that may be biased against them. A little like the bilingual child in school, Phoebe's flower has a 'language' which differs from that which is used throughout the garden. Possibly a little like the bilingual child in school, this is interpreted as an absence of language. Phoebe is accused of having no tongue when she fails to answer a question put to her by Enilesab.

Any but the fluent bilingual student, it seems, begins from a disadvantageous position. So Phoebe, who entered the garden with such enthusiasm and such high expectations, leaves with quite different emotions. She becomes confused and frightened. As she moves through the gardens there is a gradual but obvious decline in her faith and a loss of self-esteem. From the very first moment when she catches sight of her true reflection in the 'slender rill' (Fable) her self-image deteriorates to such an extent that as she peers into the troubled waters of the 'National Curriculum' pool (Fable), she sees no reflection of herself at all and her flower is lost completely. Phoebe as she was has all but disappeared. She leaves the garden with nothing apart from her flower, returned to her by Iodah, but hidden now beneath the folds of her dress.

Beyond bias

'Ah.... Perhaps you were in the wrong garden asking the wrong questions.'
(Fable)

Perhaps I had been in the wrong grounds – asking the wrong questions!

I began this study with the aim of investigating sources of bias within assessment for bilingual and ethnic minority children, my assumption being that such bias may cause these children to be disadvantaged by assessment. My investigation was intended to be a precursor for defining action that may be taken by teachers to eliminate or, at least, minimise such disadvantage. My proposal was to use an allegorical narrative, a 'fable' as a method of illuminating and presenting my findings.

In the event, writing the fable proved to have quite different consequences. As I analysed the fable in an effort to re-experience the thinking that had created it, a different picture emerged surrounding the enigmas of assessment and ethnic minority/bilingual children. With it came a new understanding of the concerns I had set out to investigate, and fresh concerns regarding the whole process of assessment for children. 'There is no such thing as a fair test, nor could there be: the situation is too complex and the notion simplistic' (Gipps 1995: 279).

It was through my reading of the relevant literature that I came to understand exactly that: there was no such thing as neutral assessment. Any assessment process will of necessity embody historically-situated and culturally-specific norms and values with respect to what counts as knowledge and/or achievement. It is not possible to construct a neutral assessment, nor is it necessarily advisable to seek after absolute equality of outcomes across diverse groups. 'Manipulating test items and procedures in order to produce equal opportunities may be doing violence to the construct or skill being assessed and camouflaging genuine group differences' (Gipps 1995: 272).

The orchestration of test items, and the creation of assessment situations which avoided any context more favourable to one group of pupils than to another, would be virtually impossible. It would also be rather pointless: diluting any assessment down to such an extent would render it virtually meaningless. Equally, to expect assessors to be completely neutral or totally objective would be unrealistic. Inevitably when people make judgements they bring their own values and experiences into play; judgements after all are subjective constructs.

It seems to me that it was through the writing of the fable that I became aware of a set of quite different concerns regarding assessment. To concentrate solely on the sources of, the circumstances surrounding and the consequences of bias, seemed in retrospect to be somehow missing the point; quite literally in fact, 'asking the wrong questions'. Much of what Phoebe experienced may have been intensified by a bias, but was not necessarily a direct result of that bias; some of her distress was clearly a result of other factors.

Assessment is a highly complex procedure. It is a process which can have far-reaching, sometimes quite unintended, consequences for the child who lies at the heart of the process. Indeed it can serve, as Cummins (1984) points out, everybody's interest within the educational system except the child's, as Phoebe discovered to her cost as she journeyed through the garden. She became increasingly confused and unhappy, the garden became unfriendly and capricious.

The garden seemed to have lost a little of its magic and become confusing and slightly treacherous.

(Fable)

I came to understand that what Phoebe had experienced in the garden could equally well have been experienced by many children other than those she was intended to represent; in fact by any child whose skills, abilities, knowledge or styles of presentation lay outside the boundaries of those that were measured or those that were expected. It was, I believe, through the experience of writing the fable that I found my interests switching from a concern about bias to concerns more generally about what assessment does to children's identities and their sense of themselves as learners. As I found out through Phoebe's eyes, and other children are likely to find regardless of ethnicity or cultural background, assessment can seem unnecessary and somewhat threatening. It was perhaps limitations in my own thinking about assessment that caused me originally to formulate my concerns in terms of bias; writing the fable, I believe, enabled me to think beyond some of those limitations.

It could be suggested that all children are disadvantaged by assessment situations, regardless of what is being tested or how. The assessed tend to be in the dark: they work with a blindfold and it is thus they are hindered. They find themselves in an unfamiliar situation, without a comprehensive 'knowledge' or 'understanding' of what is taking place, where they are going, what is expected of them, or what the possible outcomes of their actions are likely to involve.

> *Phoebe had no idea which way to go next. She wished she had asked the gardener which path she should follow. If only there were signposts or someone to help her.*
>
> (Fable)

For the child in school it seems that it is the teacher who holds all the meanings that matter, all the questions and the answers. This situation is likely to be both stressful and intimidating to the child, and inevitably leads to great feelings of anxiety, loss of self-confidence and with it motivation.

> *On she stumbled through the mist, everything in the forest suddenly seeming to conspire against her. The tree roots tripped her; she was cut by wild, sharp-leafed plants and stung by insects with venomous intentions. She tried to wrap herself up tightly to protect herself, but the wild plants and insects had a way of finding those parts she had left exposed and vulnerable.*
>
> (Fable)

Children are vulnerable emotionally, and it is perhaps both dangerous and short-sighted to underestimate the effect that affective factors play in assessment. Self-confidence and motivation are crucially related to all successful learning, thus to all assessment (if we accept assessment as intrinsic to learning), thus to all pupils.

> *I lost my gift; I couldn't learn; I did not understand; they asked me to account for myself and all I saw was failure.*
>
> (Fable)

The impossibility of separating the cognitive from the affective in students' responses has to be considered if interpretations of assessment outcomes are to be valid and therefore just.

> (Murphy 1995: 257)

Phoebe's journey through the Garden of Intent, her search for her flower, somehow illustrated for me far more than confusion. There was confusion, but for Phoebe there was also a more intense feeling. What I began with was a distanced 'adult' concern about bias; what I emerged with was a 'child's eye' view of confusion leading to alienation as a result of the assessment process. Somehow Phoebe was not a 'part' of what was happening, she became a prisoner within a process over which she had no control. From her beginnings as a self confident, happy child with much to give and a strong desire to learn:

> *She walked positively, head held high, eyes firmly fixed on her goal.*
>
> (Fable)

> *She became a frightened, confused, wounded, alienated creature.*
> *On she raced through the trees until so scratched and bruised she felt as though her body might break.*
>
> (Fable)

The garden frankly did not provide the educative, enjoyable experience it could or should have done. Instead of understanding and learning Phoebe was antagonised and estranged.

As I wrote the fable a new understanding of 'bias' did emerge, but it was superseded by a fresh concern, one about the experience of assessment and of what it may do, if we are not careful, to children, and especially to bilingual and ethnic minority children who are particularly vulnerable. It seems to me that we have to address the possibility that assessment could be an alienating experience for children. With these concerns in mind grew a conviction about the kind of assessment that is perhaps needed, one that positively endorses children's developing identities and sense of themselves as learners. Perhaps as teachers we need to be able to see assessment not simply as a measuring device or one to aid comparison. We need to see it as an active learning process: a learning process that places the emphasis on individuals rather than differences between individuals. A learning process not just for the pupil but equally for the teacher; one in which both are active participants rather than passive recipients. In the fable this was clearly not the case. Phoebe did not take an active part in what was happening any more than any of the plants in the garden did.

In the fable, it is Iodah who values Phoebe's unique qualities, who reassures and guides her through the garden. It is Iodah who eventually gives her back her identity and self-esteem.

> *He handed her a flower, a deep red-brown chocolate scented flower, her flower; beautiful and perfect.*
>
> (Fable)

Iodah provides Phoebe with nourishment and hope. Each time she meets Iodah she actually gains from him something positive and worthwhile to her. It is through him that she is able to build up and upon her personal resources, each time she receives something from him they grow.

Iodah in the fable seemed to possess qualities which perhaps could be seen to be essential to the 'positive' view of assessment I have come to believe is possible. It is one which would seem to recognise the value of differences within children; to note and take account of the part emotions might play in assessment situations, and how circumstances might actually influence such situations. It is also a view of assessment which I feel perhaps may go beyond the present formative/summative distinction, for it is one which embodies a two-way process. Certainly formative assessment is a model of assessment which may inform the teacher's teaching, but it does not necessarily at the same time illuminate the child's understanding or guard against the child's possible alienation. It seems to me that assessment presents an opportunity which needs to be seized, for the teacher and the pupil to learn positively and constructively from one another, and with one another, so that each one, teacher and child, develops new understanding as a result of the assessment.

It is with this new view of assessment in mind that it would then seem appropriate to return to the original question; reopen the issue of bias and reformulate concerns regarding bias within the assessment process. One way of doing this might be to use the fable itself as a starting point for discussion with teachers and children.

To begin Phoebe saw 'paths leading off in every direction inviting exploration'; when she came to explore them she found them 'overgrown and quite impassable'. She discovered gates which 'when she tried to open them they were always locked'. One wonders which paths were impassable, to whom? One wonders if the gates were locked only to certain people? It was not just that Phoebe was confused and alienated by what happened. It also became apparent that what she and her flower had to offer had little if any value. Equally it became clear that the obverse was also true. Apart from her restored identity 'now hidden beneath the folds in her dress', Phoebe takes nothing from the garden except the memory of an experience with all the qualities of a bad nightmare:

> *Indeed she could not even see her reflection, just an agitated surface, frothy and disturbed.*
>
> (Fable)

and a vision of what might be:

> *Where one would expect discord there was unexpected harmony.*
>
> (Fable)

The garden, it seemed, had little of value to offer Phoebe.

This suggestion has serious implications and raises significant questions about learning and assessment; about knowledge, ability, achievements. Who and what defines and validates these things? What constitutes evidence on which judgements are made, who makes those judgements and according to whose beliefs? Perhaps some of these are questions that we as teachers should constantly be asking ourselves as we assess our children. If we develop the capacity for open-minded questioning; if we are prepared constantly to challenge our own beliefs, to examine norms, to ask difficult questions of ourselves; we may then, and only then, be in a position to have confidence in the judgements we make with and about others.

The value of fictional writing

At this point in the study it seems appropriate to return to the actual writing of it. The fable had actually acted as some sort of catalyst for my own reflection. It became, in effect, part of my research data. I have no doubt that had I chosen to use a different form of literary presentation my findings would have been essentially different from those I finally emerged with; as valid maybe, but possibly not as 'thought provoking'. May maintains that: 'All forms of literature are, in a large sense fantasy. . . . The material is selected, manipulated, enhanced. . . . They come from the same source, they share the same goals: to help us discover who we are and what we are' (May 1995: 90).

Presenting ideas in such a fictional form allowed me to view the topic of assessment in an unusually distanced way. It was written from the view point of the child, 'assessment through Phoebe's eyes', and it enabled me to experience assessment from a perspective to which I was not usually party. It was not curtailed by what actually happened in a particular situation or number of situations, rather I could introduce as many possible scenarios as I felt inclined to do.

It is beyond the scope of this study to pursue in depth the links between my 'discovered' methodology and other contemporary developments in the use of fictional writing as a research method. There is however a growing interest in, and a developing understanding of, both its value and its potential. As a direct comparison to this study, Winter (1989: 177) uses an example of 'fable' writing within an action research process, to highlight a situation where the act of writing the fable appeared to create circumstances which resulted in particularly reflective thought on the part of the writer.

Analysing and researching issues concerned with education through narrative is perhaps one way of tapping the resources that lie within the field itself; that is using lives, experiences or personally created fictional images, and the subsequent reflections on these, as relevant data in itself, which while essentially personal, taken as a body may serve to inform a greater understanding of educational questions.

Critically speaking, the danger of this form of writing as opposed to pure reflective writing, the danger of using it as a research methodology in its own right, might be that it becomes, as Convery (1993: 147) critiquing his own fictional research writing, suggests, 'intellectual escapism'. Like Convery, I would dispute this suggestion, and like him maintain that 'fictional writing did not lead to my avoidance of real situations, but rather the redefinition of a situation encouraged more productive problem solving' (ibid.).

Having written the fable I was tempted initially to return to it, to re-write the parts which seemed to have grown from the fable itself, for it did assume an identity of its own and move in directions I neither intended or foresaw. I resisted the temptation because I felt that to have changed it subsequently would have been to impose my understandings and values as a professional teacher on the storytelling, the characters and the events as they occur within the fable. I would effectively narrow the distance I had created, which had allowed me such productive reflection.

In terms of attempting to step outside my own frame of reference for academic work, I have found the experience immensely challenging, incredibly daunting but extraordinarily rewarding. Writing this study has provided an unusual but deeply satisfying learning experience.

Conclusions

What then are the implications arising from this study for the assessment of the study itself? In writing it I have ironically, to all intents and purposes, traded places with Phoebe! Inevitably, as an assessed student, I am subject to similar pressures to those to which children are exposed at school, and of which Phoebe is a victim in the fable.

There is of course a substantial difference. I do have a choice about whether I lay myself open to a process of assessment (unlike many children), although it would be against my better interests and my long-term aims if I were to withdraw from this particular assessment.

I have preferred to follow a different path and adopted a form of presentation that is plainly unusual within the accepted orthodoxy of research and research writing. There are thus real challenges here. Education has to do with comprehension, with learning, and with evidence of that learning being judged by and through assessment. It has been interesting to try to adopt a broad open-minded approach, to critically examine present criteria and values; to ask questions of myself and to look for an appropriate way to 'judge the evidence'.

My assessment will clearly involve an acceptance of the method I have chosen to best evaluate the counter arguments of this particular debate.

The insight and passage of understanding about this issue, through which I have passed, challenge more conventional approaches. I hope that this path will challenge other readers, but also provide insight into the central strands of the debate. The use of a narrative of representational images to reveal the argument has enabled knowledge and learning to take place for me, and I have tried to make it explicit in a thoughtful and thought-provoking, if unconventional, manner.

Thus praxis, if not making perfect, has provided illumination!

> Underlying the very act of seeing for each of us is a whole set of beliefs and values about the world and the people in it, values that we rarely make explicit, still rarely explore and critically examine.
>
> (Drummond 1993: 9)

* * *

NARRATIVE SUMMARY 6

Issues arising from Tish's further innovative research

For Tish, as well as her supervisor and examiners, this was the most controversial of the Darers' studies.

From the beginning, Tish made a conscious decision to adopt a genre that was deliberately innovative, deliberately radical and deliberately challenging to the assessment norms of the course. She did this in order to raise, through her written text, the very issues about bias in assessment that were the substance of the study; to place herself in a position at risk and susceptibility to bias and rejection in line with the main arguments of her work. She wanted to provoke the academy, through her own form of presentation, into thinking about its own assessment philosophy and practices. In addition, she wanted a genre that could generate multiple readings and interpretations. A multi-layered fable form fulfilled, for her, these demands. It was just what was needed, she felt, and she was passionately driven to pursue it to the point where there seemed to be no choice. She would have done it, no matter what. Thus, the medium became, for Tish, part of her message, and for this reason she counted it as the best of her studies. The fable genre enabled her to do what she wanted to do.

Tish was prepared to take such a high risk not just because she strongly felt she had to but also in order to see what would happen. Tish was, in this sense, putting the academy to the test. This strategy matched well the view she had of herself as a radical. It possessed and excited her at one and the same time, just as a 'dare' is supposed to do.

When she discussed her plans in supervision, her supervisor looked somewhat aghast! While being supportive of the overall concept of what Tish was trying to do, her supervisor was concerned that trying to do it all through a fable might be *too* risky. Tish was counselled into a different approach. The fable became data upon which to reflect in order further to explore issues of bias in assessment. In this new process, the 'compromise' genre became, in itself, innovative at the level of methodology. Fable as data is distinctly unconventional: deconstruction of fable as reflective methodology, equally so. Tish went along with this in order to play safer with her degree but she definitely saw this as a compromise, even though she admitted that the new reflective process developed her thinking. In this compromise, she also turned her eye towards the criteria and academic expectations such as literature references. Although she had read much conventional literature on assessment to underpin her fable, this had not been made visible in the fable genre. It became visible in the 'compromise' genre.

There had been some difficulty, for the supervisor, in accessing the issues Tish intended in the fable form. The multi-layered meanings of the fable, in which everything had a double meaning for Tish, were not equally accessible to the supervisor as audience, although Tish declared, paradoxically, that she was not concerned about an audience accessing all her allusions. So although her authorial intentions had been strong in the sense of expressing her own thinking through the fable, they were not as strongly matched by commitment to her audience. In the event, her authorial intentions were not realised adequately for the reader.

In the examination process, Tish achieved her purposes but in a negative and painful way. She did, indeed, put herself at risk, and experienced the rejection she sought to theorise in her fable (although the work did receive a pass grade). Her examiners expressed appreciation of the freshness of her writing and the innovative qualities in her work, but they felt she had not adequately come to grips with assessment issues. One also resisted the persuasive quality of the genre, seeing this as a form of manipulation and therefore not appropriate for the academic mode. Tish saw such responses as a negation of her purposes. They had, she felt, missed the point of what she was trying to do. And because she had invested so much of herself in the venture, the examiner feedback was seen, by her, as a negation of herself. The ensuing hurt, anger and pain were great: they were in proportion to the scale of her personal emotional investment in the work. And they reverberated for a long time.

For Tish, the assessment system had demonstrated that it could not bend sufficiently to value the innovative and radical work of one who stepped outside the academic norm in such an experimental way. Despite this, Tish still adhered to her own judgement that this was her best piece of work because it had been so experimental and because, for her, it had achieved what it had set out to do in a complete and satisfying way.

Chapter 8

Not a perfect offering

Liz Waterland

> **Editorial note**
>
> When Liz carried out this study, she was working as headteacher of a city infant school with 210 children from three to seven years old. She was in the second year of her Masters' course in Applied Research in Education, accredited by the University of East Anglia and based at the Cambridge Institute of Education. The chapter has been edited from a 18,000 word dissertation, which has been published in complete form by Thimble Press. The accreditation process also included an oral examination, for which candidates prepared a 2,000 word paper addressing methodological issues.

Preface

Not a perfect offering is an imaginative reconstruction of several months in the life of our school. I wanted to understand better the experiences the school offers its children, parents and staff as they approach and begin the new school year. This is always a difficult transition, and it is important, especially with the four year olds, to make it as successful as possible.

I spent three months observing, and recording what I saw in words and pictures; listening, and recording what I heard on tape, paper and in memory. I then re-created my research as a story unfolding month by month. So this is a work of fiction. That is to say, none of the characters, except, I think, myself, actually exists (and I have certainly re-created myself for the purpose). The people who became the characters are real enough, and so are the things that happened and became the beginning, middle and end of the story (although not necessarily in that order).

June

You would know a good deal about the school and its area if you looked at the local paper's city map and noticed the names of the streets round the school: Jubilee Street, George Street, Palmerston Road. Rows of Victorian terraced houses with some seventies council building and, further up, towards the new townships, some very recent private building, raw new bricks and what the agents call town houses . . . today's terraces.

The road goes under the railway bridge at one point. It becomes darker and there is often a puddle in the road which sometimes floods enough to stop traffic on really wet days. There isn't a pavement under the bridge and you have to step carefully into the road and round the puddle; cars and lorries don't expect people to be walking under the bridge and so they are an extra hazard; not many pedestrians walk along there. Except when the Fair is held on Fair Meadow three times a year, then the traffic and the puddle have to give way to the crowds.

When Rebecca came under the bridge for the first time it seemed like a tunnel of huge dimensions. She stopped and looked up to its dripping walls and the strange green bricks; the noise of her feet was trembling among the wet spaces and tumbling back down to her, a long way away and yet still her own. Pulled along, she felt her mother's distrust of the bridge and the wetness. Her mother thought she was frightened of the traffic sweeping round the roundabout to mow them down, but Rebecca knew it was the bridge. She knew, after all, what cars could do; like strangers, they took you away to a place where you were dead, but what did wet bridges threaten?

That bridge was the start of school for her. Even when they walked out of it onto the pavement again, past the Co-op and up the little road, it had begun the new thing and not well.

'You go through the bridge and then out on to the straight bit. Rebecca. Listen.'

Her hand was shaken but so was she, and she felt only the tug of the familiar hand and the arm which ended in the face that was her mum.

'One day you can do this on your own. Listen because of the traffic. Will you listen? Listen to me.'

When? Mum? When? But it was too late for the answer or even to listen to the question any more. Sometimes they could stop and look in the paper shop for a comic or a bag of crisps (but not sweets) or sometimes it was possible for them to go round by the church path to stop and see the children playing at the place where they played called a school. Today it was the school path. Rebecca watched and saw . . .

. . . Paul, who was crouched down with his head close to the brick wall at the end of the playground.

If you bend down very low and look by the corner of the wall there is a hole. It has a little little head in it with little little sticks that wave about and then the head comes out and it is an ANT. Does it live in the hole or does the hole lead to the ant's house? This time it has a bit of dust that stuck to its sticks and it waves and waves to get it off. If an ant sits still it can clean them with its front paws and then the dust drops off. The little hole is for putting a twig in that will pick the ant up and then it can walk along the twig and if you stand up it wobbles and falls off. Bend down again and put the stick there again and then it gets on. It falls off again. But if you put the stick in the hole it . . . it can get bigger. I can dig it and the dust falls out of the hole in a little pile. The twig breaks. Get a better one. Dig it out and see the sandy bits that fall out of the brick with a bloodsucker on it. I saw a bloodsucker! The bloodsucker is red that is how you know it is a bloodsucker and it is round and it has little legs all round it and if you get it on you it will suck your blood and then you die. The stick touches it and the bloodsucker has gone down the hole. The ants will look out because that's how it lives by sucking ants' blood so it has to be very small.

If you sit on the wall you can stop people running along it and then they get cross and push you and you tell them you got a bloodsucker and it will suck them dead.

Perhaps the ant is frightened when it goes in and then it meets the bloodsucker in the long tunnel and it is dead. Dead like Fluffy. Fluffy was dead because the car hit her and she didn't know not to run out in the road. Let that be a lesson to you.

On the front door it says,

HEADTEACHER: MRS E. WATERLAND

I am watching through the window of the cloakroom.

There they are down by that corner again. If they go on digging away much more, the bottom brick will probably fall out. Still, when the playground is tarmacked, the hole will probably be filled in anyway. I do hope they will agree to put in the hills we wanted; the old humpy bit where long-ago concrete set in a strange half-moon shape, perhaps from spilling out of a broken and rained-on cement bag, gives the children so much pleasure just jumping and running. But will it compensate for the loss of the little hole in the wall? Perhaps I'd better specify some hole to be left, just big enough for a twig to go in. Well, the chances of the resurfacing are fairly low so we can worry about that when the time comes. I am told that we can have the mobile re-roofed or the playground made safe, but not both. Flooding or falling over; a difficult choice.

Every day that little girl and her mother have been here looking down the steps towards the playground. A potential customer, no doubt, about four-ish, and getting used to seeing the school first. Well, I shall meet them soon enough.

The parent at the top of the steps has a very anxious look. I wonder about her, about her name, her child and her anxiety.

Her name is Carol, Rebecca's mother.

Rebecca watched the child by the wall. What was he doing? Would she have to do it? 'What is he doing, Mum?' but Carol hadn't seen him . . . or at least had seen him but not noticed him. No answer. She was looking, rather, for the adult. There was a teacher out there every day and some-times the children came up to her. They seemed to like her, the faces turned up to talk and even sometimes, listen. Sometimes the lady bent down and talked right to their faces. Sometimes the finger pointed or shook. She remembered when a finger like that made her shake.

'I hated school, me. No good at it, you see, and always in trouble for something. One teacher, he had a pneumatic finger we called it. Drove it straight into your chest so you had to walk backwards to the wall and then he had you. *Don't. You. Ever. Do. That. Again.* And you bite your lip, don't you, to stop the tears.'

'Look, Rebecca, you see the lady? That's the teacher in Big School. You mind her or you'll get it.' Oh, God. No. Not to frighten her so soon. 'She looks nice, though, doesn't she? We'll see her soon maybe.'

Carol took her small daughter's hand again and pulled gently. The little girl liked to stop and see the children playing when they came past. It took her mind off the bridge. Every time she hung back at the bridge, frightened of the traffic. Well, her mother thought, so she should be frightened of the traffic.

'We'll go down today, Rebecca, and see about you starting. Hold the rail down the steps and mind and behave.' The steps were steep. When the baby came there would be a tussle with the buggy. But it'll all be a tussle then.

Rebecca concentrated hard on the steps. They were difficult. She held on to her mother's hand and the rail with the other hand, watching her feet and feeling the cold brass rail running smoothly under her fingers as she went. Because she wasn't looking at the playground, she missed seeing Sarah. Before, when they had come sometimes, Sarah had caught her eye. A square little girl with dark hair and eyes, Sarah wore a wonderful coat, a recent birthday present. Her friends admired her coat and so did her teachers. What was it like? Cherry red, new, and with a full skirt and gold buttons. Only I can't do the top ones, Mrs Cruickshank. I can't do my buttons. They're real gold and the coat is red. If you stroke it it's all cold and smooth.

Rebecca saw the coat first and the child afterwards.

This time, though, because of the steps she missed seeing the sorrow. It was a puddle and the rough edge of the playground. The letter to Sarah's parents apologised and explained that the school was waiting for the play-ground to be resurfaced. The fall was an accident and the general assistant had done her best with the coat. It was Sarah we couldn't do our best with.

'The poor child's inconsolable. I told her the coat would clean but she just goes on about how she's not allowed to get it dirty and her mum will be cross. Can you see Mum after school and explain what happened? Is it Mum that comes?'

My coat, my coat, my coat, my coat. And then, suddenly, there's blood, hurting somewhere. I fell over and hurt my knee and my coat is all hurt, too. Coats hurt with dirt on red; people hurt with red on dirt. I'm not to get dirty, I'm not to get dirty.

The lady has a jumper with a picture of a cat on it. When you sit on her knee you can put your face against the cat. Look! It's all furry, like a real one.

'Feeling better, pet? Don't worry. We'll put some magic cream on that knee and then Mrs Waterland will write to Mummy and tell her it was an accident. Do you like my pussy cat? I knitted it specially to cheer up little girls who'd had a fall over.'

Sarah showed off her plaster when she got back to the classroom. Mrs Waterland had been in the office with a lady and a little girl. It was the first time Sarah had seen Rebecca but Rebecca remembered Sarah.

'That's the coat girl,' she told her mother urgently.

'What, what do you mean? She does talk nonsense sometimes.'

Desperately, Carol wished she was less easily embarrassed. It was the school and all the feelings she hardly recognised except for the effects they had on her, the blushing, the talking and, oh, worst of all, the tension over what her daughter might say. It made her unfair, she knew it did, and hated the voice that emerged from her tight, dry throat, the nagging, fractious voice that made Rebecca look at her with fear and uncertainty and tightened the health visitor's mouth.

Carol came to the door and saw the notice, handwritten in bold school writing. WELCOME. The door was on a spring but it closed slowly enough for you to get in without hurrying. Several doors, one with a notice on it: PLEASE COME IN.

There were two ladies in the room, obviously an office; computer, telephones and filing drawers. One, smiling, said 'Can I help you?'

It was just that feeling of shyness, of not being allowed to be there and having to explain yourself to the lady. She pulled Rebecca forward, more roughly than she meant to, and the other lady bent down, 'Hello, have you come to look at our school? What's your name?' Carol waited tensely, for the inevitable. Rebecca hid behind her and put her thumb in . . . again. She did show you up when she did that.

The first lady looked at Carol. 'Do you want to register her? Is it for school or nursery?'

For a moment, Carol panicked . . . a different difficulty; something else to worry about. You could see the fear flit across her face.

'How old is your little girl? We'll know from that. It is rather complicated, it all depends on her birthday, you see.'

'She's four, four in April.' Please, Rebecca, come out from behind me. Look at least half intelligent.

'School, then, in September. Do you live in our area?'

'Just on Victoria Road. The other side of the bridge, is that all right?' Was that the right thing to say? Was that the right answer?

'Oh yes, that's right. Would you like a look round the school while you're here? See if you like the look of us?'

The lady was smiling again. Carol wondered what to say. Was the lady busy or did she mean it? It would be nice to look at the place but who was the lady? She hadn't said anything about her name. Rude, I'd call it, not to introduce herself.

'Yes, please, but not now if you're busy . . . we could come back . . .'

You could hear a lot of children coming along the corridor; not noisy but rumbling and twittering. A teacher calls out, 'Rosey, don't push, please. Quietly, children, or we'll turn round and go straight back.' The noise stopped at once. That was good. Discipline. That was what Rebecca needed. Make her talk when she was spoken to.

Rebecca was looking round now. Not quite so close to Mum but still holding on to Mum's coat. The noises were strange. And the feet and a door banged. There was a bird singing. Did they have a bird? Mum's coat is blue and there is a little tear.

Sure enough the child, Rebecca (another one), is edging out to look at us properly. The tear or tear is not so interesting as the shaggy toy dog in the corner.

'That's Pudge. He looks after the children and they look after him.'

'Can I hold him?' she says and for a moment I wonder what Mum's reaction will be. She is scandalised at the child's boldness.

'Rebecca! That's the lady's. Put it down.'

I have to smile. Does she think it is my own personal cuddly for when life gets too much for me? I pick Pudge up and reassure her that it's all right. 'He's for the children.' The lady isn't so bad after all, that's what I hope she's thinking. She'll go home and say to Rebecca's father (there is one, is there?), 'She was a nice lady. Had a big toy dog for the kiddies and let Rebecca hold it. Ever so nice.' Still being ever so nice, I prepare to take the two of them round school if they would like a look.

'Well, no, not now. We can come again, another time, but it's dinner time and Rebecca's dad gets home for dinner while he's on shifts.' Yes, yes, of course. No problem. In fact, better really since I can be prepared and have the tour script ready. Here's the library and our lovely big hall. Will your little girl/boy (delete as applicable) be having cooked dinner, have you decided yet?

Carol signed the form and left it on the desk. She took the big floppy dog out of Rebecca's arms; not roughly, just certainly, and took her hand again.

'Thank you, thanks. I'll come in again and see round. Thank you.'

Rebecca trotted beside her, looking up at her mother. Well, that was done. At least she hadn't disgraced herself and all the form was easy to fill in. Rebecca hadn't even cried. Relieved, Carol looked down at her daughter. 'Shall we have some crisps on the way home?'

Rebecca bent her head suddenly. Crisps, yes. But then it was the bridge again. And every day. Bridges are far, when you are going under or over them.

July

She never had gone back for a look round.

Still, in the end it hadn't mattered, after all. The school sent a letter and it told you when to bring Rebecca to see the school and for parents to have a cup of tea with other parents and meet the Headteacher, Mrs E. Waterland. Was that the lady they met?

'You're going to school today. To see the lady again. And some other children.'

Please Rebecca, be good. Don't let me down. Talk to the lady and do as you're told. What if she doesn't like it, what if she runs away? There was a boy who did a runner from a school in the local paper, knocked down just outside the gates. Did they lock the gates? Did they lock the doors? How did they stop the children running away?

'Listen, Rebecca, you're to stay when you go to school till Mum comes for you. You're not to go out on your own or the cars will get you under the bridge, do you hear?' Frighten her. That'll stop her running off.

Rebecca looked up, bewildered, at her mother. For a moment Carol cursed herself. There, now she'd put the idea of running off into the kiddy's head. She shook her arm, gently. 'Do you hear, only with Mum. Or Dad.' She added the afterthought without much conviction. Still, after the baby came he might just have to take or fetch sometimes. Suppose the baby wanted feeding at home time? Surely he'd see that?

If only starting Rebecca at school was going to make things easier.

After dinner, the little girl, self-aware in her yellow dress and white summer sandals, stood waiting. She had come in the door and there was a lady that Mummy said she had seen before but there had been a fluffy dog then and he wasn't there now. She couldn't remember the lady but she remembered the door and the way it closed behind her very slowly as if a person you couldn't see was shutting it with a click behind you. It had made her jump again, that little, secret click. She walked along a long carpet with little squares, one foot in each square until she bumped into a table. Mummy tapped her head and said, 'Look where you're going.' How did she know where she was going? Blindly she followed, unaware that her mother was following the lady until they came to another door. Near the door was a toy cooker and a saucepan, like the one at playschool.

Tentatively, Rebecca opened the oven door and looked in. There was a dolly inside. Why was the dolly in the oven?

'Mummy, there's a dolly in the oven, Mummy. Look.'

She reached in and took the doll out. It was old, with strange, harsh hair sticking straight up and no clothes on. There was felt pen on her tummy. Rebecca pulled her mother's skirt. 'Mummy. Look.'

Something hurt me! Something hurt me!

The child staggered under the thump of her mother's hand to the side of her head. There was a roaring voice that said something.

The yellow dress was spotted with crying.

Ashamed, Carol looked down at her daughter. She had wanted to do it right with the lady there and now it was all spoilt. Rebecca had been naughty and now she had lost her temper in front of everybody. What would they all think of her and of the child?

Slowly, so as not to stand up too soon and show her face, Carol bent down and picked up the doll. Gently the lady took it from her. She said it didn't matter.

The lady bent to Rebecca and turned her face up to her. While Carol was fumbling in her pocket, the lady produced a tissue and wiped Rebecca's eyes. Appalled at such an invasion of her privacy, Rebecca recoiled from the pink paper and buried her head in her mother's skirt, the familiar smell better than this strange place and the doll that hurt your head when you touched it.

'I'm ever so sorry,' Mummy was saying, 'she isn't usually so naughty.' Had she convinced the teacher? Holding the doll awkwardly, the teacher opened the door.

'Come on in and meet your friends, Rebecca, and your new teacher. A bit of an upset, I'm afraid, Jean, but this is Rebecca and her mummy.'

Another lady bent down to see the little wet face and the fright. Her eyes flicked up to see the parent standing just behind as she nearly laughed at the similarity of expression. Both ashamed, bewildered, out of their depth. An experienced teacher, she recognised equal need.

'Why not just come in and watch for a while before Rebecca joins in?' she said gently, indicating a small chair at the side of the room. Thankfully, Carol sat down and pulled Rebecca to her knee. She buried her face in the shining hair, smelling of Vosene, and the other smell, Comfort, came from the clean yellow dress.

Rebecca looked up at her mother and felt the tension drain away a little. It wasn't so frightening for her mummy now. Sniffing still, she peeped at the big room.

School, not playschool, something different, but still some children and some tables and some chairs and some grown-ups. There was a table with painting. Rebecca enjoyed painting. Did she dare to go and see? She touched her mother's face, twisting round to see her reaction. 'Can I paint?'

As she came up to the table one of the ladies smiled at her and held out a papery sort of coat. 'You'll need an apron, Rebecca. I'll help you put it on.' The coat thing seemed to be the apron, and Rebecca turned round and held her arm backwards towards the sleeves. The red apron was very strange. It went on and you had to put your arms in front of you to put it on. At playschool you put one, blindly, over your head. Rebecca looked down at herself and felt the lady pulling the neck firmly and doing the apron up behind her. Shyly, Rebecca said thank you. She glanced towards her mother, who smiled at her. That was all right, then.

You pick up the brush. Red first. Hold the brush up and the paint runs off it in a thin stream of colour, back in the pot but you have to wipe the brush on the pot to stop the drips on the table. The playschool lady told you that. Wipe, carefully, once, twice. Paper is white and clean. Put your brush on it and pull it, it goes over the paper. The little brushy bits stick out like a fan and the red comes in a thick smooth line with hairy edges. Slowly down the paper, watch the line coming and the hairy edges spread down. Stop. Pick up the brush and drip it again. Wipe. Once. Twice. Just a little drip from the end on the paper. Drop. Touch it with the brush and the drop joins the brush again. If you push the brush straight down it spreads out like a hand with fingers and then you get a round bit. Swirly round and swirly round. The two rounds and a line. You put the brush back in the pot and then another colour. Yellow. Pick the brush up and wipe. Once. Twice. Put the yellow line exactly over the red one and it goes another colour, not red any more and not yellow but there is still red on the edges and the thick bit of yellow is sitting on top of the red and you can see the brush has gone red and the new colour, called . . . called oranges. An oranges line with red and yellow bits. If you wiggle your hand the brush wiggles and the line wiggles. More paint. Blue. Wipe. Once. Twice. Dots. Dot. Dot. Dot.

The voice surprised the child as she bent over her paper. 'What a lovely painting. Can you tell me about it?' Rebecca didn't look up. Stopping making dots she whispered, 'I done oranges.' The adult bent lower. 'Sorry, I couldn't hear you.' Defeated, Rebecca shook her head and stood back. Pulling ineffectually on the sleeves of her apron, she tried to take it off. The hands which belonged to the voice helped her and, freed, she went back to her mother.

For a while Rebecca stood and watched until, enticed by the jigsaws, she ventured to another table. 'Mum, come and do this one.' Carol got up and followed her. They sat side by side and, once again, Jean was struck by how alike they looked as they bent over a Postman Pat puzzle. Neither spoke. Jean waited until the puzzle was finished and then came over.

'Mrs Adamson. Would Rebecca stay here while you go to the hall for coffee and the meeting? We'd come and fetch you if she was upset.'

Carol looked uncertain. Rebecca was started on a Mickey Mouse.

'She stays at playschool now,' she said doubtfully.

Going up that corridor on your own without Rebecca to be the reason and then that big hall and there were some chairs she'd seen. Where did you have to sit? Who did you have to talk to? Could she bridge the gap with whoever sat next to her?

Rebecca was pleased with the jigsaw. You put the bit with Mickey Mouse's ear in and then it's finished. Run your hand over the picture and you can feel the pieces all fitted together and rough but no spaces so you know it's done. Tell mum.

The trouble is that when you are doing a jigsaw you have to concentrate and you might even hum a tune called 'Postman Pat' so you don't hear what grown-ups are saying to each other. They never told her, just each other, and she didn't know that Mum had gone and that was why she had said be good. She meant be good while I'm gone like she used to say at playschool but then she always left at playschool. You didn't know she had gone this time. Or where. Or why.

'I want to go home. I want to go home.'

Recalled from the hall, in front of everybody, Carol was mortified by her daughter's screams. 'I'm ever so sorry. She isn't usually like this. Do stop it, you silly girl.'

'It doesn't matter, Mrs Adamson. Honestly. Lots of children find it hard when they first visit. Just stay with her for the rest of the time and she'll be fine. Won't you, Rebecca, now Mummy's here again?'

Exhausted, the child sat and sucked her thumb on her mother's lap while Carol rocked her daughter slowly to calm herself and to let her embarrassment ebb away. What they must think of her! All the other children playing so nicely and the mums in the hall looking at her when the teacher came to fetch her out because Rebecca was being such a baby.

Well, she was just a baby, anyway. Only four. Carol's expression of tension and blame softened as she thought how little her daughter was. Her own baby and the new one on the way. No wonder, poor little toad. Well, September was a long way off yet and that headmistress said that the kiddies would start for just two hours at first until they were happy. Not so bad, maybe. She stroked Rebecca's hair.

'We'll go home soon, Baby Bunting, and you can take your picture to show Daddy, shall you?' Baby Bunting meant forgiveness. The child relaxed.

On the way home they stopped for some sweets. 'Don't expect these every day you go to school, though, will you?'

September

The holiday has bridged the gap between old and new. The school is clean, scrubbed from the top of the walls to bottom of the urinals. The cobwebs on the high windows are gone, the drips behind the sink where the paintpots are washed have nearly vanished, only a faint pink stain shows that red pigment is particularly difficult to shift.

The great pleasure of teaching is this fresh start each year. Clean school, new children, new plans and ideas. This time all will be well; this term will be straight-forward, clean of illness, oil leaks, vandals and staffroom grumbles. Hope is what teachers have a real talent for.

That first day was dreadful, for a start off. Rebecca got up all right and put on her new uniform. It was nice that the school had a uniform, making it a bit special for the kiddies. She didn't want any breakfast, though, and was ever so quiet. Even when Dave got out the new rucksack he'd bought for her she wasn't what you'd call thrilled, said thank you nicely, though. Carol was afraid that Dave would be cross with Rebecca for not being thrilled enough but he was all right about it. Said that she'd be bound to be a bit nervous, first day, and she was to have a lovely morning and tell him all about it when he got home.

Dave had seemed more interested in Rebecca starting school since the teacher had come to the house and he'd been home off shift. Talking about it, he'd thought it was good that the teacher had come for a visit, and he'd liked the chance to explain that they'd been a bit worried about Rebecca's ears because of all the infections she'd had. Carol was sorry that she hadn't thought to say that herself but she'd been so anxious that Rebecca should behave properly and that the teacher would think her nicely brought up and good. It was always the same; something got in the way of her thoughts when she was faced with the teachers and school.

Dave managed much better. He was plain and straightforward, she'd always liked that about him. When the new baby had been born he'd been wonderful about the things you had to do, registering and all that, and now he was helping and so proud of the little boy. They called him Mark. A good baby, thank heavens, and Rebecca seemed to like him. It was bad timing, Carol knew, with Rebecca starting school, but you couldn't think of everything.

For now, it was enough to worry about getting the child to school on this first morning.

On the way it got worse. Rebecca started dragging back, which made walking so tiring and difficult. Then the tears had started. By the time they got to the bridge the little girl was crying uncontrollably and Carol was virtually dragging her along. Thank God that Dave had stopped at home to look after Mark for her, else she wouldn't have been able to manage at all. Taking Rebecca by the shoulders, Carol bent down and shook her daughter.

'Listen, Rebecca, you got to go to school. You'll like it ever so much when you get there and you're just playing up.' As always, anxiety made her voice shrill and disagreeable, but at least the shaking made Rebecca stop shrieking. She settled down to a steady and irritating sobbing as they went into the dark shadow under the bridge, the child held firmly by the wrist, dragging her feet, and the mother, tight-lipped and harsh, hating herself and the morning.

At the beginning of the path by the church the little girl in the bright red coat that Rebecca talked about was standing patiently while her mother adjusted the straps on a pushchair in which sat a chubby toddler, the image of her sister. Carol couldn't get past so she waited just behind. Rebecca, tear-sodden and exhausted, recognised the coat too, and put her thumb in while she watched.

Sarah's mother straightened up and then realised that she had been holding up the traffic. 'Oh, I am sorry,' she said cheerfully to Carol as she wriggled the pushchair aside. 'Do you want to get by?' Carol smiled uncertainly. 'New, are you?' the other mother asked and the two began to walk on, keeping pace with each other.

The little girl's mother seemed very unsure of herself, and the little girl had been crying, that was obvious. Her mum looked as if she'd be crying, too, in another minute. 'Sarah, say hello to the little girl. What's your name pet? Rebecca. That's nice. Say hello to Rebecca, Sarah. Sarah'll look after Rebecca, won't you? She's ever so motherly. Lovely with Jade, that's our youngest. We've had such a terrible holiday. Jade's had chickenpox and Sarah was sick all last night. Her dad had her this weekend and it's always sickness after that. Too much junk food and late nights. It's all right for him; she never starts till she gets home. I thought I'd keep her at home today but she wanted to come. You should have heard the fuss! It's good isn't it? My mum always says that we used to batter on the doors to get out; nowadays they're battering to get in!'

The steady, friendly voice chattering on calmed Carol and took her attention from Rebecca. The tension eased and she found herself nodding and smiling in reply. Beside her, Rebecca had stopped dragging and was walking alongside plump little Sarah. After the first 'Hello', obedient to her mother's commands, neither Sarah nor Rebecca had spoken but both were eyeing each other and Sarah was noticing with interest the new patent leather shoes the other wore. 'Your shoes're shiny,' she remarked kindly.

The steps gave Carol her chance to be friendly. 'Let me take your little girl's hand while you do the pushchair,' she said and felt pleased when Sarah took her free hand and, both feet together, jumped down the steps beside her. Rebecca, more uncertain, held the rail as they went. At the bottom Carol felt even more pleasure that Sarah did not immediately let go but continued to hold her hand as they crossed the playground between the crowds of children and parents to wait by the cloakroom door for it to be opened.

Sarah does not wait to say goodbye to Rebecca. She and her mother, who gives a quick reassurance as she goes, 'Don't worry, she'll be fine,' disappear to tell a less than thrilled class teacher about the sickness in the night. Carol and Rebecca wait for Jean to show them Rebecca's peg. There is a curious feeling of calm about them both now as they stand among the other newcomers. Close together and united by both fears and, for the first time, anticipation, some sort of bridge has been crossed.

I know Sarah and Paul already, of course. It is no surprise that Sarah is beaming up at me as she bustles the dinner register importantly up the corridor. We chat about her holiday and her sister for a moment or two before she says, in a perfect imitation of her mother, 'Well, I'd better be getting on', and continues on her errand. A good, competent child. What a treasure!

Paul I am less happy about. He has come back fractious and withdrawn from us in a worrying way. Such a self-contained little boy last year, this year he seems to be brooding and sullen. I watch him at playtime. He stands by the wall, just in front of his interesting hole, but he makes no attempt to see if his beloved ants are still there. He watches the others and doesn't move. In class his teacher is concerned about him, too. He hasn't settled and is a source of constant ripples and unease.

Gradually, Paul began to shuffle, still sitting cross-legged, you'd be hard put to say how, still watching his teacher, until he'd moved several feet across the carpet from the isolated spot he had chosen first. Now he was just behind Hannah. Pat watched him out of the corner of her eye while she went on reading the story. This one she hadn't got to grips with yet. Jean had said he was a lovely lad but so far he had only been a pain. A new class was always an upheaval for the children but she was puzzled by the difference between what she had heard about the child and what she had met.

Paul sat upright and apparently innocent as Hannah suddenly squealed, turned and punched him. 'Mrs Dane, Hannah hit me for nothing!' Outraged, Hannah began to cry. 'He pinched me, Mrs Dane, he pinched me.' 'I never!' Pat, with infinite patience shushed them both. 'Not another word from either of you till I ask you,' and she began the tedious business of trying to get the truth out of small children. Claim and counter-claim, accusations, mainly from those who couldn't possibly have any idea of what had happened, who were the other side of the group, tears and lies. All of the class were relying on her for justice; if she could not offer it, there would be another reason not to trust the grown-up world.

Eventually, with a leap of faith that she had got it right, Pat pronounced the verdict. Hannah had indeed punched Paul; that was obvious, but she had been provoked. Paul, on balance of probability, had pinched the little girl. Therefore, he was to be sat on his own on the naughty chair, a social outcast far from the storytelling. Hannah was told, yet again, that it was not right to take the law into her own hands.

The formula came fluently. 'If you had told me that Paul had pinched you, you would have been good and he would have got told off; now you are in trouble, too, because you hit him. You must not fight back, Hannah. Do you understand?' Pat looked at the children and wondered again what the point was of the determined efforts they made to prevent retaliation.

Half the children had been told to fight back by their parents and the rest got the same message from the TV anyway.

'Now, can we get back to the story, please? Where were we?' A mental note made to discuss Paul with Jean and Liz at playtime.

His mother came to tell me that he hadn't wanted to come back to school and still said he didn't want to. She couldn't get anything out of him at home. Could I try? Perhaps he was being bullied and was frightened to tell. I promised to have a word with Paul and see what I could find out. Sometimes a child will talk to a teacher because the emotional investment is less and the teacher can keep calmer than a parent. It is never easy, though. How much they rely on our ability to imagine it better. I am not prepared for this one, though.

'It's the man in my head. He won't go away. He's there all the time and he's going to get my mummy. He said he would and he's got the key and it's my fault because I told and I told Mummy and it was Mummy and he . . . he was . . . and he hit her and he. And he said he would it's because of me and the locks and they can't get him and he's in my head. It hurts my head. He hurts my head. He hurts and it's Mummy. They don't know where he is and he's here. Please tell them.'

The little boy is inconsolable. His nose running ribbons, and crying in great gulps and frantically gasping for air, he sits on my lap and judders out some dreadful story that I can make no sense of. All I can do is wait until the terror has passed far enough for me to question him.

'Paul, who is the man? Tell me about him. No one is going to hurt you.' (Oh, the certainties we lie with.) 'Tell me about him and we can help you.' (Oh, the certainties we lie with.) It takes a long time but slowly I find out about the parts of Paul's life that are unimaginable to me and that no one had told me about. I find out that Paul and his brother had told their mother that her last boyfriend had treated them with great cruelty whenever they had been alone with him. She, in a new relationship, had at once told the police. Paul had spent much of the summer holiday, when my imagination had pictured him at the seaside or playing happily in the garden, giving evidence on video for the abuse proceedings to begin. In the meantime, the man had disappeared, no one knew where he was and the police, Paul knew, had been unable to find him. Kindly, his mother had promised him that, if he told the police all about it, they would catch the man and put him in prison so that he could never hurt the boys again. But they hadn't had they? And somewhere out there was a man who had promised, in God knows what demonic circumstances, that, if Paul told, he would come back and get his mother. The man had a key to enter the house but he hardly needed to. He was already deep inside, in Paul's head. Every night he crept around in there, every day he put his hand over Paul's eyes and said 'Guess who?' Unable to sleep or work or play, the child was possessed by the fear of his secret visitor.

'Why didn't you tell Mummy about the man in your head, Paul? She wouldn't let anyone hurt you, would she?' It is hard not to let the tears well up when a five year old answers a question like that by saying, 'I didn't want to worry her.'

I ask to see Mum and her new boyfriend. They are nice people, and both have come to school often to see Paul in the concerts or talk about his work. They are genuinely upset when I tell them what Paul has told me and the reasons why he kept quiet about it all.

Mum shakes her head. 'I really thought he had got over it and had coped with it all,' she says, and I believe she really did think that. The idea that children get over things easily is very strong. A dead pet? Get another and they'll soon get over it. A stay in hospital? Buy some sweets and they'll soon get over it. Divorcing parents? See daddy once a week and they'll soon get over it. The road to hell is paved with a lack of imagination.

I can't tell you how the story of Paul ends, even in my imagining. He went for family therapy for a little while but then the council rehoused them after the new baby was born and they moved away. Perhaps I could pretend to know what has happened to him since but, paradoxically, while it was lack of imagination that I blame for his misery, I can't bring myself to construct him any further now. I would insult the truth of his bravery. I do sometimes wonder if he has ever found another ant hole to crouch in front of and study. If you know a better hole, go to it. The joke being, of course, that there is no better hole; this is all we have.

Later on that day Sarah's teacher stopped by my filing cabinet where I was trying to guess what I had filed something under so that I could find it again. She was carrying a pile of children's work and picked one out. 'Look at this,' she said, delightedly. 'What a joy the child is!'

STORY BY SARAH age 5 and a hrf.

DRAGON ISLAND

can you spot the giaant's Bird's In my picture? Now I will start the story one day me and my brthe and my sisder and my fend when to dragon island the giant Bird's Brort us there and we killed the dragon's seesd the giant kild the pirates and us and the salu's floow home on the giant Bird's.

Rebecca enjoys writing too. She always did like to scribble and draw; any bit of old paper and a pencil keep her happy. It was a blessing during the long waits at the antenatal clinic before the baby was born and Carol always kept something she could draw on in her handbag. Once, Rebecca had drawn a picture of the nurse and given it to her. The nurse had been really pleased. She was a good girl, really, kind and very good with the baby now. Settled into school as well, thank goodness. Sarah was her friend in the other class and Carol got on well with Sandra, Sarah's mum.

The only worry now was the way Rebecca still cried every morning as they set out from home and at the end of the day. The teacher said it wasn't unusual. 'Lots of children find the first leaving each day hard and most are a little tired and cross after their first few days of full time. And there's the new baby.' Ever so nice when she said it but it still seemed a worry. Why did Rebecca do it? She was fine in school all day, the teacher said, and she seemed to enjoy it. Lots to tell her dad about in the evening anyway. Carol was secretly rather proud that her small daughter chattered so happily about her doings. Not like some. She'd heard mothers say they couldn't get a word about school out of theirs. Dave and she knew all about the new teddy bear in the book corner and the lady who cooks the dinners. It was just the crying at each end of the day. Not frantic anymore, just steady sobs. Tore you up it did.

Getting cross hadn't helped. Dave had lost his temper at first, thinking Rebecca was being a baby and baffled that she wouldn't tell. Then Carol had tried wheedling it out of her but she just shook her head and dropped her eyes in that way that meant you might as well save your breath. Even teacher had tried (what was her name?) but couldn't get anywhere. Well, at least Rebecca is good at school; nothing to be ashamed of there.

One day was a highlight for Rebecca. You had to line up first. You line up for coats and dinner and to come in from play but one day it was another lining up. When she asked the lady where they were going she said 'Music'. Music is on the radio and telly. Where is the telly? 'Where is the telly?' But the lady stood at the end of the line and then the teacher came and said they were all ready. You had to stand up very straight and not talk and then you go along the long bit past the playhouse and the dolly that got writing on its tummy and went in the oven. (Rebecca turned her eyes away. Jean wondered why the child never wanted her turn in the playhouse.) You went past lots of other children in rooms. The big hall, not with a front door, is for dinner but now there wasn't any tables. Teacher took you to a corner place with a carpet and sat you down. Then another lady came and said 'Hello, children.' Rebecca, shyly, said hello and the lady smiled at her.

That was the day that Rebecca discovered she could play the triangle. It isn't an easy instrument for small children, having an annoying habit of swinging round when you hit it. Trying to solve the problem by holding it still results in a curious donging noise that drops dead at your feet instead of the flying bell notes that ring so satisfyingly. Her wrists still braceleted with baby fat, dimples twinkle in and out on her hands as she holds the beater clutched in her fist. Jerkily at first she brings her hand down and up all in line with her arm, stiff as a drumstick. As she gets the idea, though, her wrist relaxes and the sweetening of the tone of the instrument rewards her efforts.

Watching, I wonder if she will remember this afternoon, the September sun flooding through the huge windows of the hall, and the singing and the triangle?

May

We are still here, except for Paul. All still working together, doing our best, children, parents and staff. The lovely weather of that September has moved on through a cool and damp winter to a showery, sunny May. The school grounds, which are the great surprise of our city school, are foaming with wild flowers, meadowsweet, May blossom, cow parsley, campion, dog daisies. The white season.

Nearly a year after this story began Sarah is still laughing her way through the days; a golden child, good at everything. She has grown out of the red coat and in any case would scorn its babyishness now. Buttons are no mystery any more; these days she offers to tie boys' shoelaces after PE.

It took us a long time to discover Rebecca's fear, which you will have realised at once, of the darkness under the bridge. It was the Billy Goats Gruff that finally got it out of her one evening when Dave was reading it to her; her own troll came out of the shadows then and was butted under a lorry by her daddy. The silly thing was, as Carol said, there was another way they could have come to the school all along. It was a bit longer but the baby enjoyed the airing and Rebecca could walk with Emma, her second best friend (Sarah was the first). It just goes to show that you never know with kiddies. Rebecca still enjoys music and is reading a bit, too. Carol is very proud of her.

Carol and Sandra are good friends. Sometimes they spend the afternoon together while the two little ones play before they set out to collect the girls from school. Sandra tried to get Carol to come on the PTA committee but so far she hasn't got the courage. The baby is a good excuse, anyway.

I often wonder about Paul. We heard from another school that he had been admitted and I passed on all the information I had but that was the last contact. I hope he came through it all and, like so many children, survives. Perhaps they do get over things; how else could most grow up sane?

As for the school, well, we carry on. At this stage in the year the children all know each other and the staff, they walk confidently and have secret jokes. The community has been called into existence by our combined wills; children, staff and parents linked by some vision that we share.

Looking back, I think how far we have come since September and the beginning of this story. The summer term is half-way over and already we are planning for our new intake; the list is finalised, the booklets printed, the visits planned. It seems neat and tidy, all systems up and running. We have planned for the children's beginning to be as good as it can be. Now we can only imagine what they will make of the first days and weeks of the new year when they move to new classes or visit for the first time.

It is our imagination that will make all well or all ill; we cannot ask small children to make sense of the world of school unless we have stepped into it with them. We need to bend our backs to their eye level and wonder what it is that we see. We need to listen to the voices and words that children hear as if they are a foreign language. We need to feel fears and joys that are long lost to us, or that we may never have known.

We watch and listen and think and wonder, taking our notes and our photos but, in the end, it is only by constructing the world the child experiences within our own imaginations that we can make that world better. I owe a debt to Rebecca and Sarah and Paul, their parents and their teachers, although they are fiction, which will be repaid to their real heirs who will join my school in many futures.

* * *

NARRATIVE SUMMARY 7

Issues arising from Liz's innovative research

Liz was strongly at odds with the traditional academic approach to the point of rejection. She felt that traditional research, as she understood it, was not illuminating of human experience. Statistics tell us little of significance about people.

She brought to her research a long-term autobiographical interest in, and love of, words, stories, narrative. 'I think in words,' she said. Stories can illuminate where statistics do not or cannot. She knew herself, her loves and interests in these areas well enough to harness her own strengths to her research purpose. Because of this, there was a strong sense for Liz that the fictional story format was the only way she could have done her research. The institution only had validity for Liz if it could accommodate these strong personal, autobiographical purposes and predilections. Liz did not yield her purposes to the academy and it was only when the institution and the supervisor validated and accommodated these purposes that Liz felt able, in turn, to validate the academy. With this institutional support and validation, the study came into being.

The work took on a motivation of its own so that it would have developed whatever the institutional response had been. The motivation was such that Liz was prepared to risk her degree, though had she failed, she felt she would have failed herself for not writing it to a good enough standard. Her literary talents would have been brought into question, she felt, not the validity of the innovative form of her research text.

One key purpose of the research had to be about improving her own and others' understanding of parents' and children's experiences. Only particular research approaches and research texts could do that, Liz felt. She needed a research text for creating empathy. So, there was a strong sense of moral purpose behind her research.

Also, she wanted to create a text that not only engaged the reader's emotions but also created space for interpretation. Data are nothing in themselves, Liz believed. Interpretation is what matters in research. There is no one 'truth'. There is only the individual's truth, 'my truth'. She had a sense of a 'popular' audience for whom she wanted to write, so that her story could render many truths for different people.

Memory was seen as a valid form of data for her story. Her own remembered professional experiences down the years became the database for her research. She set her own validity criterion for this : 'The only rule I made was that it had to have happened'. She decided that the fictional story form would became a way of collapsing this mass of remembered experience, as data, into the generalisable form of character and plot. Thus, she used generalisation as a literary concept.

Throughout the work, therefore, Liz implicitly set her own validity criteria for her research: understanding; interpretation; reflection upon real life events; 'my truth' and others' truths.

Part 4

Reflecting on innovation and quality in practitioner research

Chapter 9

Innovation and quality in practitioner research

In this chapter, we look across all the individual studies and narrative summaries to explore what they have to contribute collectively to an understanding of the processes of innovation in practitioner research. For this analysis, we draw not just upon the commentaries themselves, but upon the original conversations and discussions around each piece of work upon which the summaries themselves were based. We examine the driving forces that lie behind innovative work, the forces that support and sustain innovation, and the relationship between the *processes* leading to innovation and *quality* in practitioner research.

The driving forces behind innovation

One point of agreement among the authors of all seven studies was that being innovative did not figure in their conscious plans as they embarked on the research. Innovation was not valued for its own sake. Indeed, it became increasingly clear that the descriptor 'innovative' came from us, the research tutors, not from the members of the project group. It was *our* word, used to encapsulate distinctive features of each piece of work (conceptualisation, methodology, styles of reporting) that had impressed *us*.

While group members were certainly conscious of having made a choice at a particular point to do things differently from what they perceived to be the conventional modes for academic work, they did so for specific reasons which were organically linked to their particular purposes and aspirations as well as their preferred cognitive and artistic styles. It became evident, as they explained and justified their chosen approaches, that the distinctive features of the work emerged as they strove to find ways of achieving their purposes that were satisfying and empowering for them personally, academically and professionally.

At some point in their research, group members had found themselves experiencing a tension between the models of research that they were encountering in their studies and what they felt that they *needed* to do, intellectually, emotionally and professionally, as they developed and wrote up their research in the interests of their professional practice. In different ways, and for different reasons, they felt impelled to step outside what they perceived to be conventional approaches to research if they were to be satisfied with their work, and if they were to achieve the purposes that they had set themselves.

What stood out for us, as we looked across the individual accounts, was the complex interplay of different factors: personal, academic and professional, that explained what brought about this tension, how it was resolved, and why the innovative work which resulted took a particular form. Consequently, we present our analysis of the processes helping to create and sustain innovation in a way which attempts to preserve and portray this interplay of factors, showing how innovation arises from the chemistry between them.

Individual perspectives on 'research'

The particular views of 'academic' work and what counts as 'research' that individuals brought to their studies provided the backcloth against which tensions were experienced and individuals formulated a sense of wanting or needing to do things 'differently'. These views were derived from a variety of sources, including individuals' previous experience of academic study, their professional training, experience and reading, and their knowledge of research methods and methodology derived (in part) from their current courses of study. As a result of these different personal histories, individuals drew different meanings and messages about institutional expectations and requirements, and about the scope for experimentation allowed within existing criteria.[1]

For some members of the group, the experience of tension was bound up with questions about the relevance of 'academic' modes of research to professional practice. Research was not worthwhile (and hence valid) unless it made a difference to the world of schools and classrooms. Liz Waterland (Chapter 8) said that she could not have done a 'formal' piece of research, because this did not correspond to what she saw as worthwhile and productive personal and professional learning. She felt that the

---

1 Because the courses followed by individual members of the group were so different in nature and subject to constant change, it is not easy to provide a straightforward account of the criteria by which the various studies in this book were assessed. Jacqui's and Liz's studies were assessed on a pass/fail basis, and assessment included a viva voce examination for which a methodological paper was prepared. The work of Joe, Tish and Linda was assessed against graded criteria (A, B, F), for which 'best fit' descriptions were provided. When Ros carried out her study, the B grade had been subdivided into B and B+. As a rough guide to the interpretation of these grades, we have included a copy of the grade descriptions in operation for Masters' work at the time of writing (Spring 2000) in the Appendix.

'conventional forms' and 'jargons' of academia turned educational research into something very alien to the sort of enquiry that teachers do every day when they reflect over things that have happened in their classroom and try to make sense of them.

> The problem with academia is that it has suggested to people that research is . . . something that you have to do in a library with a lot of books and it has to have footnotes and bibliography and publication dates and all these rules for the presentation of your dissertation and whatnot, and people think that it can't be research unless it has got all that. . . . I believe that any teacher or any person who sits and thinks about their experience because they want to understand it better in order to move on is researching.

For Liz, it was vital that the meaning of 'research' should be extended to encompass the kind of reflective enquiry that she felt would be able to challenge and develop her thinking, as well as being accessible, engaging and useful to others. She felt uncomfortable, initially, on her Masters' course, until she had negotiated with tutors that there was indeed scope within the academy for her to pursue work in accordance with her own perception of what constitutes worthwhile and valid research: 'When that was acceptable, I thought right, well now we can get somewhere and I can think about what I want to know about through story.'

Linda Ferguson (Chapter 6) felt somewhat similarly about the content of the reading on research methodology that she encountered when following the first of her two modular research courses on the Masters' programme. She said, 'I kept reading it and not engaging with it at any level other than thinking, this doesn't sit comfortably with me.' Linda realised that if research was genuinely to work for her and help to move her practice on, she needed to find an approach which sat more comfortably with her ways of thinking and being as a teacher.

Both Liz and Linda believed that they would do their most incisive and worthwhile professional thinking if they built their research methodology upon the reflective practices that they already engaged in as teachers, rather than trying to borrow the methods of enquiry of social science and apply them to their work.

The exigencies of the topic

For some members of the group, the impetus to pursue an innovative path was bound up with their chosen topic or question which seemed to *demand* a form of treatment that was different from, what they perceived to be, traditional approaches to research and reporting. For instance, Ros Frost (Chapter 2) felt that she needed a methodology capable of embracing the emotional dimension of experience and learning in order to pursue some profoundly painful issues arising in her professional life. The topic required a personal style of investigation and reporting to match the deeply personal nature of the purposes she had set herself. Unlike Liz, Ros was not taking up a particular philosophical stance towards research in general, but rather searching for a methodology that fitted her particular purposes on this occasion. A later study carried out in her second year was approached much more conventionally because, she explained, the topic (assessment) had much less of the 'personal' invested in it.

Similarly, Joe Geraci's commitment to trying to understand autism 'from the inside' (Chapter 4) required, he insisted, a text which did not leave the *reader* on the outside; it required a text which encouraged the reader to empathise with people with autism and come to care for them, as he had done through his research.

> I couldn't allow my research to be 'vacuumized', to have the life sucked out of it, to not have the human response affect the reader response. Why was this important? Because I cared about the people I was learning about during my research and I wanted to help the reader care too.

In Joe's case, it was not just the exigencies of the particular topic but the profound personal impact which the research had upon him which he wanted to try and capture in his style of reporting. What he was seeking for his own study was a literary style of writing that was the antithesis of the 'impersonal' style that he associated with academic texts.

Tish Crotty's chosen theme of bias in the assessment of bilingual pupils (Chapter 7) could have been carried out through a conventional 'literature review'. However, Tish thought it would be more interesting and potentially more enlightening to explore the parallel between her topic and the procedures for the assessment of the study itself by the university. By presenting her work in an unorthodox form, she created for herself and for her study the same kinds of risk and potential for rejection that (according to her analysis) bilingual children are subject to in the context of formal assessment. Tish was keen to ask what the consequences might be for the learner if the qualities and characteristics of the learning being assessed do not correspond to the norms implicit in the criteria being used. Do we question the criteria or conclude that what is being judged is deficient in partic-ular respects? In this way, Tish used the *form* of her study, as well as the content, as a way of raising the fundamental questions about bias in assess-ment that she wished to address. It was a means of enabling the examiner assessing her work to experience and grapple directly with the dilemmas that were at the heart of the concerns which had prompted the study in the first place.

Personal ways of thinking and learning

The impetus to try something different also arose from individuals' attempts to find modes of inquiry and reporting that were congruent with their personal ways of thinking and learning. The views of worthwhile 'research' which shaped the approaches adopted by Liz Waterland and Linda Ferguson discussed earlier were also intimately bound up with their knowledge of themselves as people and their personal strengths as learners. Linda felt that, given the kind of person she was, only a deeply personal approach, centred around her own thoughts and perceptions, would be genuinely satisfying as a learning experience for her. Liz described herself as a 'literary person', someone who enjoys words and books and stories, who thinks in words. Fiction could be as much a source of 'truth' as non-fiction. Words and stories, she claimed, are 'how I think about the world, and that is the way I like to learn about the world'.

Coming from a very different professional background, Jacqui Potter (Chapter 3) found herself, in general, stimulated rather than inhibited by her engagement with formal research methodology. Nevertheless, there came a moment in her study, during the early stages of data analysis, when she felt very dissatisfied with her attempts to apply the approaches suggested by her course and gleaned from books. Trying to code the data in her research by means of conventional category analysis, she suddenly found herself thinking, 'This is crazy. I'm not going to do this.' She felt that she was 'missing the whole story' by following this approach. Aware of her preference for thinking visually, she developed the idea of using a visual model as a tool for data analysis. As well as a method of analysis which she felt more satisfied and comfortable with, Jacqui's visual model also proved to offer a powerful tool for raising questions and enabling her to engage in a dynamic way with her data. It provided a means of overcoming the problems associated with the fragmentation of data, while using and building on her preferred style of learning.

More powerful methods of enquiry

Jacqui's preparedness to follow her hunches enabled her to discover a powerful method of data analysis that satisfied her purposes more fully. Other members of the group were also drawn to experimentation because of a sense that their invented methods might be capable of yielding more powerful insights into their chosen topics than the approaches that were more routinely used. In her first study, Tish Crotty (Chapter 5) chose to try out an experimental approach to her investigation of children's purposes for writing because she had a hunch that researching her own experience of writing a Masters' degree essay might shed important additional light on children's experience of writing. Her experiment with trying to develop and interweave these two parallel inquiries into a single continuous text proved to be a powerful tool for learning, opening up angles on the topic that otherwise would almost certainly have been left unexplored.

Ros Frost drew together a disparate collection of data sources which, she felt intuitively, had relevance to her questions (memories, school reports, analyses of classroom observations, literature and previous research), using these to generate new insights and understandings into her chosen topic. It was the juxtaposition of these different data sources, and her reflections upon them, as much as the understandings generated by each in isolation, that helped to free up her thinking and gain new perspectives upon her particular area of concern.

Similarly, once Linda Ferguson had summoned up the courage to pursue an experimental methodology based on the reflective conversations which she ordinarily had with herself in her day to day teaching, she found herself able to make use of other approaches to practitioner reflection described in the literature. Weaving these together into a personally tailored approach, she provided herself with some powerful alternative ways of engaging in reflective practice and interrogating her spontaneous interpretations.

Working from a position of strength

At some point in their research, then, and for reasons that were bound up with their purposes and aspirations, each member of the group made a decision to pursue their particular study in their own way rather than in accordance with what they perceived to be the accepted norms for academic research. The confidence to take this step was often, paradoxically, linked to feelings of insecurity and lack of confidence about working in the ways which they perceived to be characteristic of 'academic' work. Both Liz and Tish confessed that they were 'not very good' with more formal styles of writing. Linda felt disempowered by the theories of research introduced on her research methods course. Ros's idea of using a metaphor of a train to provide a structure for her writing came to her when she was worrying about how to begin because she had 'never been taught how to write an essay'. The metaphor acted as a tool for weaving together her ideas into a coherent whole and maintaining control over her writing.

For these practitioners, claiming for themselves the right to pursue the research in their own way was important as a means of re-establishing their sense of their own power and efficacy as learners. Their chosen topics were so important to them, and so complex, that they needed to be pursued from a position of strength rather than one of weakness and lack of confidence. The choice to do it their way was made in order to create for themselves what seemed to be the most empowering conditions for learning.

Once the decision had been made to define their own path, they were able to re-align and capitalise upon their own personal resources for learning. Liz Waterland drew on her love of words and stories for crafting her fictional text, while the sum of her experiences as a teacher over twenty years provided the 'data base' for reflecting on parents' and children's experience on starting school. Joe Geraci drew on his background in literary theory to work out how to write his text in a way that would engage his audience empathetically with his story.

Linda Ferguson based her methodology on her established ways of reflecting on her experience, through conversations with herself, and chose to focus on an area of her work where she could draw on her prior experience as a speech therapist. Tish Crotty's choice of a fable form to explore issues of bias in assessment was made knowing that she would be able to draw on her existing skills in literary writing. Ros Frost knew from her experience as an artist, that shifting from a visual to a verbal medium (or vice versa) could help to free up and stimulate thinking. Just as she used words to help stimulate her work in a visual medium, so she used a visual medium (her metaphor of a train) to assist the process of formulating ideas in words.

With the exception of Jacqui, all sensed that there was an element of risk in their choice of approach. Jacqui felt no qualms because, in her mind, she was simply doing what she had been advised to do all along on the course, to match the method to the question. She was convinced by the ethos of the course that, in her words, 'As long as you could justify what you had done, it would be all right.' All the others felt some degree of uncertainty. However justified their reasons for choosing to do things differently, the work would be judged by existing criteria so there was an implicit, and common, concern about what might happen if they did it their way and failed their Masters' degree.

At the point, then, where the various decisions were made which started them down an innovative path, all but Jacqui did so in the knowledge that their finished work would (in one or more respects) raise questions for their examiners in terms of whether it came within the bounds of what was acceptable and legitimate as sound, scholarly work. There was no way of knowing, at that stage, if they would actually be successful in achieving the purposes that they had set themselves for their particular study through the experimental means adopted. And, if they were, would their examiners be flexible in their interpretation of the assessment criteria? Tish did not know if her experiment with the 'fable' form would succeed; Ros did not know if her 'train' metaphor would be effective as a vehicle for structuring her ideas. If the experimental approaches were in the end found to be wanting, it might be too late to take action to remedy the situation, or to pursue the work through more conventional means.

Supporting and sustaining innovative work

Members of the group described various forms of support they received which encouraged them to pursue their chosen paths, in spite of these additional pressures and uncertainties. Some mentioned ways in which the specific courses that they had been following had communicated to them the implicit or explicit message that their thinking and individuality were valued, that it was acceptable to adopt more personal and informal styles of writing than perhaps were generally reflected in the research literature to which they had previously had access.

Joe, Tish and Linda had been part of a core group of people who found themselves together on several course modules and who provided support and encouragement for one another's experimentation. This group also requested specifically that course tutors provide some input on the use of autobiography in research. This was an area about which they knew there was a burgeoning tradition in the research literature, but which had not been specifically addressed on their research methods courses. In this way, they created an opportunity to test out the boundaries of what was acceptable, to check out if an area of work which had more immediate appeal would receive institutional sanction.

There was unanimity, however, that the key determining influence was the reaction of the supervisor to whatever was proposed. If the supervisor was positive, this institutional legitimation helped to provide courage to proceed. Everyone agreed that if support had not been forthcoming from supervisors, they might well not have taken the risk of going ahead with an unconventional approach, whatever their own pressing reasons for doing so. But some also acknowledged that to have compromised would have been profoundly disappointing. They would have been disappointed, not only in the outcomes of their work which fell short of their original vision, but also in an institution unable to embrace, and legitimate, forms of research which were felt by individuals themselves to be most useful and empowering. Indeed, one person, Liz, felt so strongly about it that she would not have been prepared to make such a compromise.

> What reconciled me, I think, to the course, in the end, was the idea that we may be able to think about research in [my] terms and that would be acceptable on this course, otherwise I am sure I would have left it.

The point of no return

The group members' own sense of the importance and value of what they were doing was also an important sustaining factor. A recurring theme running through the accounts was that once individuals had committed themselves to a particular approach, the work itself became more important than success in the examination process. Joe wrote:

> I was at a point when I realized that earning a Master in Education degree from Cambridge University was secondary to my wanting to share my odyssey of the exploration of autism. I wanted to share the thoughts and feelings I encountered during my exploration with a group of people who I knew would have an impact upon the rest of my life.

The more strongly individuals were convinced of the necessity of their chosen approach for the validity and worthwhileness of the research outcomes, the more important it became for them to complete the study as they desired it to be, irrespective of whether or not they eventually satisfied the criteria for accreditation. Linda described her feelings about this as follows:

> There was definitely a point at which I knew that even if I failed I had to carry on. . . . I mean it would have devastated me if I had failed but it came to the point that it was more important to move my practice on and reflect upon my practice by doing this piece of work than fulfilling the criteria.

If the choice was between compromising their work and failing to satisfy the official criteria, then they were prepared to risk their degree if necessary in order to see the work through to completion. However, this did not mean that group members ceased to give active thought to the criteria by which their work would be assessed. Indeed, in some cases, knowledge of these criteria played an important formative role in the development of the work. Ros, for instance, welcomed the discipline imposed by the criteria to make sure that all her ideas were thought through as rigorously as possible: 'It (the study) had to stand up to a rigorous justification and I suppose if there hadn't been the criteria then I would have given myself my own criteria.' Solving the crisis in her professional life was of such crucial importance to her that she needed to be sure she could have full confidence in whatever new understandings and solutions were generated. If academic criteria helped her to achieve that, then this increased her faith in the values of the institution.

The pressure created by the criteria that she knew would be used to assess her work also played a formative role in the development of Tish's second study, even though the experience was an uncomfortable one. Before Tish had reached 'the point of no return', her supervisor advised her that it probably would not be wise to submit the fable alone, without any sort of analytical commentary to explain the sophisticated thinking which lay behind it. At first, Tish was very much against the idea of including an analytical section; this, she felt at first, would be a compromise that defeated the whole object of what she had set out to do. However, recognising that her thinking about the issues of bias in assessment had actually changed in the process of writing, she gradually grew reconciled to the idea of using the fable differently (yet also in an innovative way) as *data* for reflective analysis, as a stimulus to the development of her own thinking, rather than purely as a means of encouraging others to engage reflectively with the issues of assessment which she had embodied in it. The pressures and limits imposed by the criteria thus acted as both a constraining and enabling force: on the one hand, they prevented her from pursuing her original path through to its conclusion; and on the other hand, they encouraged her to explore and develop her understanding of fictional writing as a *research method*, rather than purely as a means of representing her ideas.

Tish was never entirely reconciled to the compromise she made, in response to the criteria, with her original intentions for her fable. She found writing the analytical commentary enormously demanding, especially as she was only partly committed to it. Nevertheless, the process of making explicit how her thinking had changed in the course of writing the fable was beneficial. It did, she acknowledged, lead her to engage in more depth and complexity with the issues than she might have been prompted to do, as long as the insights remained in a less explicit form. In spite of her reservations, this was the study which she found most exciting and satisfying, and which she continued to feel proud of in retrospect, even though (while receiving a pass grade) it was the one that received the least favourable feedback from the examiners.

Taking control

What seemed to happen to Tish, and to the others in the group, was that in the process of coming to define and determine their own path, they took control of the process of research and their own learning. This happened to such a degree that they generated their *own* criteria for the work. Their strong sense of what they were trying to achieve with their work – which prompted them to develop it in a particular way, and if necessary to step outside what were perceived to be the accepted conventions for practitioner research – provided them with their own set of criteria *inherent* in their particular projects which, they felt, *had* to be achieved in order for them to achieve their purposes. For example, Joe describes the personal criteria he used for the construction of his writing as follows:

> I chose the narrative form because I wanted my writing style to be enjoyable to read and informative. Most good novels are dialogic, that is they speak to the reader, they have voices that the reader can respond to. I believed I could help the reader of my thesis understand better my thoughts if they could relate to the voices of my research. This is not to

say I think my research to be a work of fiction but rather [it should] have the engaging characteristics of fiction so that the reader is better able to respond to my writing and continue the dialogue I hoped to have begun with my writing.

In the detailed written communication from which this extract is drawn, Joe acknowledges that these decisions were not entirely conscious. In retrospect, he provides a more explicit and rational analysis than he was aware of making at the time. It seems that, because these practitioner researchers were operating with criteria that were inextricably linked with their purposes, they developed an inherent *sense* of what needed to be done to achieve them and whether or not they had been achieved. Moreover, because individuals were deeply committed to their purposes, and because the outcomes of the work mattered so much to them, they were prepared to keep working at what they were doing until the work measured up to the standards which they themselves had determined.

The processes which prompted and enabled them to define their own paths were the means by which they took control over their own research and learning to the point where criteria for judging the quality of the work were internal to their own thinking. These personalised criteria were different from the 'standards' established by academia in order to promote rigour and scholarship; they were particularised 'standards' rooted in what they themselves knew they wished to achieve with the work. There were consequently not the same problems of interpretation that can be associated with externally located academic criteria. The practitioners 'owned' the criteria and pressurised themselves to improve their work, because the awareness of their importance came *from the inside.*

In deciding to pursue their own path, or break with convention in specific respects, group members were thus in no sense giving themselves a licence to develop their work free from conventional 'research' concerns about methodological soundness and appropriateness, about ethical procedures, or about what counts as valid knowledge and trustworthy learning. On the contrary, where they found that existing rules and conventions did not fit or were experienced as unduly constraining, they invented new rules for themselves that corresponded to what they knew they were trying to achieve. One new rule, for instance, that was of critical importance in at least three of the studies was the text's power to engage the audience at an affective and an intellectual level.

I wanted to have . . . clarity for the reader and to present it as something readable. . . . Even though it wasn't fiction, I wanted to write something with that kind of accessibility to make the main academic points. . . . It had to be enjoyable as well.

(Ros)

I try and involve the reader in the reflectiveness as well because I don't want to say 'this is what the child has done and what you ought to understand from it is this' because maybe someone else has had different experiences of children behaving like that and will have other understandings. So I wanted the reader also to draw their own inferences based on their own experiences, and they may be as equally true.

(Liz)

Potential reader response was an important aspect of validation of the outcomes of the study; part of the authors' intention was to engage and move an audience, and criteria were therefore needed to judge whether or not the final text possessed the qualities required for audience engagement. Moreover, these self-generated criteria were not just bound up with surface features of the text. They were equally concerned with the depth and quality of the thinking that individuals pressed themselves to engage in, while working with their data in pursuit of their particular questions and concerns.

Once established, these self-imposed criteria took precedence over the institutionally defined assessment criteria, which was why Tish was able to remain convinced that her second study (Chapter 7) was her 'best' piece of work, even though it received a lower grade and less positive feedback than her work on perceptions of purpose for children's writing. It was because they were so convinced of their own power to define 'quality' for these particular pieces of work that members of the group would have been prepared to go ahead anyway, and complete the work to their *own* satisfaction, even if it had failed to satisfy institutional requirements.

Yet, as we have seen, the official criteria did also act as a stimulus to rigorous thinking and to the development of new approaches. At least some of the practitioners felt that the messages received from the academy were encouraging a belief in the significance of their own thinking and judgements, and an understanding that defining one's own path (provided you could justify it) came within the scope of what was generally accepted to be legitimate scholarly activity. As Joe Geraci explained:

The institution for which one writes must have an impact on what is written and how it is written. At the [School of Education], for the first time in my higher education experience, I was allowed to feel that *I* was the establishment I was writing for.

Innovation and quality in practitioner research

The interplay of factors

We have now identified the many factors influencing these practitioners' decision to take an innovative route in their research and how this route came to take its distinctive form. We have seen that innovative work arises from the interaction between many different elements, some exerting an enabling, and some a constraining, force on the processes of innovation.

When, independently, we examined the nature of these influences during our research, as explained in Chapter 1, we both found ourselves categorising them in terms of three major areas of influence: the personal, the academic (or institutional) and the professional (see Figure 9.1). We also

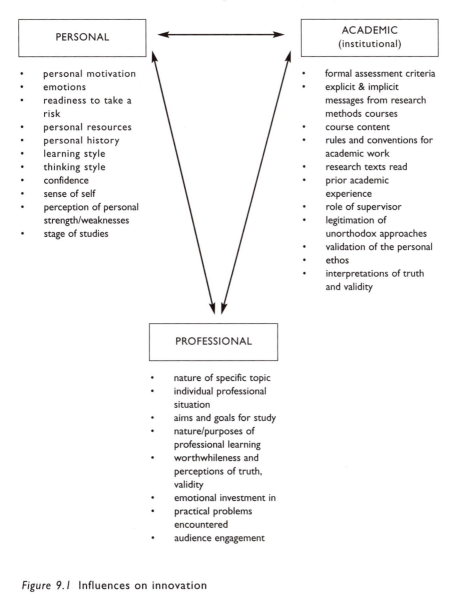

Figure 9.1 Influences on innovation

recognised that no single area of influence alone is sufficient to explain why practitioner researchers adopt an innovative approach, nor how they experience the innovative process within the academy. It is the sophisticated interplay of these three areas of influence – 'academic', 'personal' and 'professional' – that helps to explain both *why* innovation happens and also *how* it is experienced by practitioner researchers. The interplay of these three influences operates differently in each of the cases we have examined, yet in each case, the three influences were significant.

The constraints imposed by the perceived expectations, rules and conventions associated with 'academic' work were frequently at the heart of the tensions experienced by the practitioner researchers although it was by no means the case that these operated mainly as constraining forces. The discipline imposed by the official criteria for quality research also played an active, formative role in the development of the studies in at least two cases. 'Academic' influences, in various significant ways, exerted a positive, legitimating force without which some of the practitioner researchers might well not have taken the risk to go ahead and develop the research in their own way. The views of legitimate research of the tutors and supervisors within the academy, as well as their support practices, also had a significant influence on the choices the practitioners made about their research.

The 'academic' is not, of course, a single, simple, consensual or unchanging context. An academic institution is made of individual academics, in all their differences, and it may also be in a state of dynamic change for one reason or another. The 'institution' within which the members of our project group pursued their research, for example, was a rapidly changing one, as was noted in Chapter 1. We need to problematise the notion of the 'academic' or 'institutional' as we seek to understand how practitioner research is influenced, and what the implications might be for our own practices as Masters' degree tutors and supervisors.

Most people working in higher education would probably agree that, despite the modern trends towards standardisation of practices in accountability systems, the styles, knowledge and passions of individual tutors will have a profound effect on the learning experiences and choices of students coming to award-bearing courses. The tutors' own knowledge and background of research generally, and practitioner research in particular, will lead to different emphases, values and beliefs within their teaching, and thus impact differentially on students' learning. In addition, tutors within any academic context may place different interpretations on standard criteria and requirements, and this in turn will have a bearing on the support, encouragement and judgements offered to practitioners' research.

The impact of the 'academic' also takes an unpredictable variety of forms because it is mediated through the many *personal* qualities that individual practitioner researchers bring to their courses of study. The individual learning paths chosen by the group members were influenced by many distinctively individual factors, including personal learning styles and preferences, self-knowledge and understanding; individual strengths and resources, literary and artistic talents; individual biographies, psychology and personal crises; individuals' expectations of self and of academic study, and feelings of confidence (or otherwise), related (in some cases) to the particular point they had reached in their current studies.

Just as 'academic' influences functioned in ways that could be both enabling and constraining, so too – and somewhat paradoxically – 'personal' influences could function to constrain individuals from defining their own research path, or, in contrast, be one of the main driving forces. Linda Ferguson, for example, knew that she was the kind of person who felt better when she could refer to some external authority to give legitimacy to what she was doing. Although she chose, ultimately, to develop the study in her own way, Linda found that she had to 'fight all the time' her desire to legitimate her work by fitting it into existing conventions. In contrast, Liz Waterland knew from the outset that her own literary background, for her, took precedence over any perceived set expectations that the academy might impose (even though, in reality, there was no such imposition). Liz would have done it her way at all costs. She felt she had to do so.

Professional drives and interests were significantly influential in all cases. Each study grew from concerns, questions, tensions or conflicts that were embedded in, and emerged from, the professional working context, even though each study was different in nature. In turn, the learning which the research studies created was channelled back into the growth of professional understanding and practice, in both the short and, in some cases, the longer term. In this sense, professional drive, curiosity, concern and commitment fuelled all the studies and were influential in causing the practitioner researchers to adopt a personally developed innovative approach that helped them to achieve their professional ends or purposes in the research. Without such professional drive, the practitioners might not have cared as deeply as they did about doing their research in their own way in order to achieve these professional purposes.

The function of innovation

We suggest, then, on the basis of these researchers' experiences and testimonies, that innovation emerges from the chemistry between these three major areas of influence. Its purpose, for practitioners, is to create what are perceived to be more appropriate, enabling and supportive conditions for learning through research, and for communicating their learning to others in support of the development of professional understanding and practice.

We have suggested that the impetus to take an innovative route arises from the experience of tension between what practitioners believe is expected of them and what they feel that they need to do in order to develop their work in ways which are worthwhile and empowering. Yet, as we have also seen, to experience such a tension is not necessarily to embark on an innovative path. Practitioners weigh up the degree of risk that there may be if they choose an innovative route, taking into account the nature and degree of support forthcoming from the institution, their own personal confidence and resources for carrying it through, and how important it seems to pursue the study in a particular way. The various interacting influences outlined in the analysis and summarised in Figure 9.1 have the potential, thus, to explain both how this creative tension is brought about in individual cases and whether or not it is resolved in a way that enables practitioners to pursue an innovative route.

The tension is a creative one because it can generate the inner drive and commitment needed to sustain innovative work. Through the decision-making needed in order to resolve this tension, practitioner researchers can take control of their learning in such as way that they themselves become the severest judge and assessor of its quality. It is through these processes that the project group members were able to put a personal stamp on their work and to write with such a strong personal voice. It is through these processes of taking control that innovation has the potential to operate as a force for quality in practitioner research.

Re-thinking 'quality' in practitioner research

Each of the practitioner research studies discussed here represents, we feel, quality work. They were chosen by us initially because we had an intuitive feel that there was something not just different, but special about their quality, although we did not attempt to articulate fully what that was at the outset. Each was also validated as worthy of an award at Masters' degree level.

On the basis of this analysis, however, and the insights it has raised about practitioner research, we are now able to conceptualise the notion of quality much more clearly than we did at the beginning. We recognise that, in the case of the studies presented in this book, quality resided as much in the processes of doing and reporting research as in the end products themselves. Process and product were intimately related in the pursuit of quality practitioner research. Quality resided in the individuals' willingness to consider, critique, and adapt conventional views of research to match better the needs and demands of their own research projects. Where conventional approaches were not appropriate to the demands of their own research, then they had the courage to reject them in favour of individually tailored and innovative approaches. Furthermore, quality also resided in the practitioner researchers' capacities and willingness to recognise their own personal and professional strengths, and to draw upon these wisely and effectively in doing and reporting their research. In using their strengths in this way, their research benefited.

Quality was enriched by virtue of these practitioners being sensitive to the contextual influences, academic, personal and professional, that had the potential for both constraining and liberating their work. With a situational sensitivity and understanding, they worked with these contextual influences where it was advantageous to do so and were prepared to take risks when it was not.

Ultimately, then, quality has emerged where these forces have come together to create something unique over which the practitioner had a strong sense of ownership, commitment and self-critique. The *processes* which contributed to quality thus became the bedrock upon which the research '*product*' was created. The two could not be separated.

Chapter 10

New thinking for new practices

We now turn to the question of possible implications for practice arising from our research. Considerable caution needs to be exercised in making the shift from the new insights and understandings generated by the study to a discussion of their possible implications for practice. We need to be clear about what kinds of practical implications *can* legitimately be drawn from the experiences and ideas of six practitioner researchers working in a specific institutional context, that may be of interest and relevance not just to the development of our own professional work but to other practitioners and tutors working in other situations.

Given the small scale of our study, we consider that the outcomes are most appropriately used in ways that are illuminative, shedding light on issues that might help ourselves and others to think about practitioner research in new ways. For practitioner researchers, seeking to develop their understanding and professional actions in an academic context, the insights arising from the research might, for example, provide:

- a *stimulus to creative thinking*, suggesting possibilities for inquiry and writing that might not otherwise be considered and that might help others to create approaches on similar lines
- *encouragement* to pursue an innovative path, in appropriate circumstances, by illustrating what other practitioners gained from experimenting with unorthodox approaches for particular purposes in particular situations
- *support* in weighing up the risks that may be involved and in making an informed decision about their chances of success, drawing on these practitioners' experiences of what helped to maximise benefits and minimise risks
- *insight into the process of learning*, to help other practitioners create the best possible conditions for their own learning.

We have, indeed, accumulated a small amount of evidence since the project finished which suggests that the Darers' work can serve these purposes for other practitioner researchers on Masters' courses. Extracts from this evidence are presented in Chapter 11.

From our perspective as tutors, the insights yielded by the research have provided the means to revisit, revise, refine and reformulate the thinking about practitioner research which prompted us to embark on the study in the first place, and consequently to consider the implications for practice in the light of those developing understandings. We present this analysis in the second part of this chapter.

The practitioner researchers' perspective

Two further project meetings were held in order to help identify key issues and practical implications from the point of view of practitioners carrying out research in an award-bearing context. Some of these insights may be relevant to practitioners researching in other professional contexts. The key points are presented as responses to three questions that might be in the minds of those who find themselves drawn towards taking an innovative approach in their research:

- Why take the risk of trying something innovative?
- What can be done to maximise the opportunities and minimise the risks?
- What tensions and uncertainties nevertheless remain?

We will examine each of these questions in turn.

Question One: Why take the risk of trying something innovative?

Although not all members of the group felt themselves to be taking risks, those who did felt that they would have found it really helpful to have access to the experience of others who had tried something innovative (and been successful), if a book such as this had been available at the time. Courage to take risks needs to be underpinned by a sense that the risk is worth taking. The narrative commentaries explain why individuals chose to do what they did, why they felt that the risks were worth taking, and what they felt with hindsight they had gained as a consequence of adopting their particular approach.

To summarise, their reasons included:

- wanting to develop styles of writing capable of engaging the interest/empathy of a practitioner audience, and encourage active reflection and interrogation of the ideas presented
- wanting to overcome perceived limitations of conventional methodologies, such as approaches to data collection and analysis

- wanting to develop approaches that would build on personal and professional strengths, or feel more closely akin to practitioners' existing ways of thinking and learning
- perceiving a need to create approaches that were tailor-made for particular research purposes and topics
- interest in pursuing intriguing possibilities relating to a particular topic of study, for which there were no pre-existing models.

Among the beneficial outcomes identified, individuals described the experience of developing their own personal approach as exhilarating and deeply rewarding. They spoke of 'living the research, not just doing it'. This, coupled with a very strong personal investment, helped to sustain and motivate them through difficult patches. They also reported a strong sense of satisfaction with the outcomes of their research: not just with the written products, but with the impact of the work on their thinking and practice and, in some cases, with its impact on their lives more generally.

Question Two: What can be done to the maximise opportunities and minimise risks?

The group's experience also provides insight into what practitioner researchers can do to minimise risks and maximise their chances of success. Two broad areas were identified. One was to maximise uses made of the range of *resources for learning* provided by an award-bearing course, including supervision opportunities, peer support and critical friendships, course input on methods and methodologies, and individuals' own personal resources for learning. The second was to take very seriously their responsibility to *account for the research;* to accept the need to work doubly hard to explain and justify whatever approaches had been chosen.

Exploiting resources for learning

There was general agreement in the group that the supervisor's affirmation of the legitimacy and value of what they were doing was critical. Without that, it would be foolhardy to embark down an innovative path. But supervisors differ in their interpretations of what is legitimate research activity, even within an institution with an ostensibly common set of values. The group felt that it was important for practitioner researchers to develop the confidence to negotiate who will supervise the work. But they recognised, too, that it is important to have a supervisor who is more than just sympathetic to one's ideas; supervisors need to ask awkward questions, challenge practitioner researchers to justify their approaches, and help to take their thinking further. However committed one might be to a chosen approach, it is important to be open-minded enough 'to allow your supervisor in'.

Support from a group of like-minded or supportive peers may also be a critical factor. There were some in the group who would have been prepared to go it alone; but for others, the presence of a supportive group was as important as the encouragement and guidance of the supervisor in maintaining resolve to persist with an innovative route. Such a group can provide a safe context in which to rehearse ideas that individuals want to take to supervision, or to explore ways of responding to difficult questions already raised in supervision. Individuals said that they 'used each other as a catalyst' for developing their own ideas and approaches: never simply transplanting an idea from one context to another, but using it as a springboard for stimulating their own thinking about possibilities.

Awareness of a variety of methodologies derived from reading, from formal course sessions and from direct experience of trying out particular methods was also acknowledged, by most of the group, as an important prerequisite for successfully defining their own path. Familiarity with a range of methods and methodological issues meant that they could pick and mix from existing approaches, or create their own approaches for their own purposes. Even if they eventually chose to evolve or invent their own methods, they were not doing so in a vacuum; they had some understanding of the territory within which they were operating. This was very important, they said, because 'it gave us a benchmark'. It created an awareness of the need to ensure the rigorousness of their thinking, even though aspects of their work might take an unconventional form.

The group also highlighted the importance for practitioner researchers to optimise the use of their *own* resources for learning, by knowing themselves and developing methodologies that would build on their particular strengths. The choice of topic was of crucial significance for some in engaging their interest and commitment. For everyone the *choice of process* played a key role in firing their energy, imagination and shaping their sense of satisfaction with the outcomes. Liz, for example, said:

> What mattered to me was the way I did it. That's what I cared about more than the actual subject. I could have approached many subjects in the same way that I did and they could have been equally interesting and valuable. But I could have done that same topic in a way that I did not like, and it would have ruined the whole thing.

Most important of all, perhaps, was to sustain and reinforce a strong sense of 'self' driving the research. Ros said, 'You are the central thinking force, or guide . . . you are keeping a central thread through what you are doing', but at the same time 'you are always open, welcoming other people's contributions'.

Accounting for one's research

A further area where positive action can be taken to reduce risks and maximise chances of success is to accept the need to work extra hard to explain and justify whatever methods have been chosen, recognising that examiners and other audiences may well start from a position of doubt and/or scepticism about the acceptability of the approaches adopted. This is a far more demanding task than justifying conventional approaches, partly because the legitimacy of conventional approaches is unlikely to be questioned, and partly because there is a readily available literature to draw upon in order to facilitate critical discussion of the strengths and limitations of conventional approaches.

Nevertheless, the group felt that this was a vital task, not just for the purposes of satisfying formal assessment criteria but to satisfy their own sense of professional responsibility. Practitioners need to be confident in the grounds that support developments in their thinking if they are to use these to inform the development of practice. In stepping outside established rules and pathways, they were not freeing themselves from the encumbrance of rules, but rather taking responsibility themselves for working out what rules were appropriate to, and ought to apply in, their new context. Issues of quality and validity still needed to be addressed, though they were aware that there would be a need to reconsider what might count as 'quality' and 'validity' in relation to the particular approaches adopted.

Although it felt daunting at the time, the group did find themselves able to tackle this task. Once they had cut themselves loose, in one or more respects, from conventional rules and approaches, they were thrown back on their own resources in ways which encouraged the development of a stronger sense of agency in, or control over, their own learning as researchers. Their commitment to, and ownership of, the work was such that it generated an inner awareness of what they were striving to achieve, so that the drive to achieve the highest quality work came from within themselves, rather than being something that was felt to be imposed from outside. They could not rest until they had satisfied *themselves* that they had achieved their purposes for the work. Ultimately, they became their own severest judges because they knew better than anyone else what they were trying to do and whether or not it had been achieved.

Question Three: What tensions and uncertainties nevertheless remain?

The group's experience suggests that, while taking an innovative route can be empowering, exhilarating and deeply satisfying, it is never a comfortable or easy option. When practitioner researchers consciously take risks, they have to be prepared to live with the uncertainty of not knowing how their work will be received and validated by the academy for quite lengthy periods. The support of supervisors and peers can do much to bolster confidence, but individuals ultimately have to take responsibility for their own work, and live with the consequences.

How to interpret feedback, advice and questions raised by supervisors, particularly when innovative projects meet with doubt or resistance, can present complex dilemmas which are not easily resolved. On the one hand, there is the need to be open to question and challenge, as has already been noted; supervisors are expected to advise on methodology and help to establish 'where the bottom line is' in terms of scope for originality and innovation – without placing individuals at risk. But, on the other hand, members of the group felt that there ought to be freedom to experiment with carefully thought-out, innovative ideas: this is a dimension of intellectual and professional growth that, they feel, ought surely to be nurtured and validated within the academy. What counts as legitimate research is not set in stone; if practitioners always modify plans in deference to the academy's existing definition of legitimate research, this will curb not only their own possibilities for learning and development, but those of the academy too. If everyone plays safe, no growth will occur as a result of challenging and stretching existing boundaries. The summary at the end of Chapter 7 shows Tish Crotty and her supervisor grappling with these issues, and the compromise that was eventually reached.

However, as this case also illustrates, it is unwise to assume that the scope for negotiation and mutual learning that exists in supervision will be similarly operational in the examination process. Although supervisors may eventually be convinced about the value of an innovative approach, unseen examiners who have had no part in the conversations in which its value was negotiated may be less readily persuaded, in spite of care taken to explain and justify the approach.[1] Should there be scope for practitioner researchers to challenge institutional judgements, where work stretches the boundaries of what has, up to now, been considered acceptable and where it is honestly felt that the criteria have been inflexibly applied? There are inevitable tensions between the academy's gate keeping role, in safeguarding academic standards and the need to apply criteria in a creative yet fair manner. These tensions need to be acknowledged and handled with caution and delicacy by both practitioner researchers and their tutors.

It is important, though, to emphasise that, for the most part, the studies presented in this book were very favourably received by examiners. Indeed, this was part of the reason for their selection: to illustrate and emphasise the scope and flexibility that exists, *within* the existing criteria,

---

1 In the Cambridge Modular M.Ed., each study is marked independently by two internal examiners, who have had no involvement in the supervision process.

for methodological innovation and inventiveness. Moreover, the project members had no doubts whatsoever, with hindsight, that any risks had been worth taking. The excitement, exhilaration and belief in the value of what they were doing by far outweighed the tensions and uncertainties. In every case, their satisfaction with, and practical uses made of, their research have been long-lasting.

The tutors' perspective

Many of the issues raised in the first part of this chapter, and in Chapter 9, clearly also have implications for the work of tutors. There are implications for the way we design and teach research courses; for the spirit and ethos of innovation and creativity we foster; for the variety of methodological and textual types we offer and encourage; for the degree of risk and experimentation we accept, and the ways in which we facilitate and scaffold that risk for the students; for the knowledge we need of students' preferred learning and representational styles if we are to support their research effectively; for the criteria and systems of validation we develop and employ.

These implications for our practice are intimately bound up with changes in our thinking that have been brought about by our involvement in the project. We shall begin, then, by identifying what has been, for us, the most important new insight arising from the research and then go on to draw out in more detail the implications for our work supporting practitioner researchers in carrying out their studies.

The importance of methodological inventiveness

Perhaps the most important new insight for both of us has been awareness that, for some practitioner researchers, creating their own unique way through their research may be as important as their self-chosen research focus. We had understood for many years that *substantive choice* was fundamental to the motivation and effectiveness of practitioner research (Dadds 1995); that *what* practitioners chose to research was important to their sense of engagement and purpose. But we had understood far less well that *how* practitioners chose to research, and their sense of control over this, could be equally important to their motivation, their sense of identity within the research and their research outcomes.

We now realise that, for some practitioners, methodological choice could be a fundamentally important aspect of the quality of their research and, by implication, the quality of the outcomes. Without the freedom to innovate beyond the range of models provided by traditional social science research or action research, the practitioners in our group may have been less effective than they ultimately were in serving the growth of professional thought, subsequent professional actions or the resolution of professional conflicts through their research. In this, we find ourselves sympathetic to Elliott's claim (1990: 5) that 'One of the biggest constraints on one's development as a researcher, is the presumption that there is a right method or set of techniques for doing educational research'.

We both continue to value traditional empirical action research as a practice development methodology. The project has not changed that, and we recognise that action research will probably continue to be seen as the most prominent practice improvement methodology. Indeed, we have seen enough evidence over the years of its usefulness in developing professional thought and practice to continue to place confidence in its validity. This confidence is reinforced by the many accounts there now are of its effectiveness in a variety of contexts. But we now see traditional empirical action research as just one of the viable and valid methodologies available to practitioners, alongside many others which have already been created and others which will, inevitably, be created. Such alternatives have equal status and potential in their ability to help practitioners gain new insight into their field of practice, with a view to applying their new knowledge to the improvement of that practice.

Innovation in methodology and the creation of diverse but effective alternatives have, thus, come to assume a far greater significance within our new understanding of practitioner research methodology. We now ask ourselves whether methodological innovation, far from transgressing the norm, ought perhaps to be accepted as a more natural, necessary and legitimate part of any open-minded research culture that is seeking to enhance quality (see also Mellor 1999). In relation to forms of reporting in particular, the research has led us to a similar view to that of Lomax and Parker (1995: 302) who urge that 'Educational forms of representation should be pluralistic, rather than monolithic, and diverse, rather than constrained, so that they can celebrate the unique, personal, and subjective strengths of individual action research and help researchers display their own personal signatures.'

Indeed, so strong has been the shift in focus and the bringing centre stage of creative research alternatives as a result of our learning from the project, that we wonder whether we might actually be putting practice improvement at risk if we do not encourage, support and legitimate methodological creativity more prominently in the academy. The project has raised a genuine concern that we may actually be inhibiting quality and validity if we do not liberate people to be methodologically inventive in the light of their own questions, contexts, predispositions and talents. Quality, the research suggests, may depend in part upon the ways in which the awarding academic institution allows the talents, inspirations and artistry of innovative practitioner researchers to surface and be utilised in pursuit of self-identified professional purposes and drives.

Re-thinking emphases in research courses

The project has helped us to clarify this new position on methodological choice by providing confirmation of the necessary and enabling role that knowledge of a variety of approaches has played in the development of innovative work. Some of the studies included here show how established traditions can be drawn upon, adapted, moulded, to suit new purposes and research questions. Not all were completely innovative, or a unique departure from the methodologies proposed on their research methods courses. In this, the traditional methodologies became a useful resource from which ideas and techniques could be appropriated and fashioned into something individual.

As we have seen, some members of the group stressed that they needed this knowledge as a basis from which to create unique, divergent ways forward. One cannot break with tradition unless one knows the tradition. Though some of the group felt constrained and frustrated by the seemingly 'set' methodologies they were meeting, these were also enabling in that they helped map out the methodological territory within which, ultimately, innovative approaches could be situated. Knowledge alone, of course, was not sufficient. These researchers also needed the capacity and freedom given to them in the institution, to take creative control of their methodology in order to 'do it my way'.

The project thus helped to clarify that our attention needed to be focused on issues of ethos and pedagogy. It has convinced us of the importance of introducing practitioner researchers to methodological diversity as an essential part of their learning, as well as actively encouraging the development of new methodological approaches in the light of individuals' questions, learning and representational styles. The project has also helped to underline the importance of making visible what the group called 'the person behind the research', so that other practitioner researchers can see how individuals' commitments, purposes, personal theories, experience, strengths and uncertainties all play a part in the methodological choices that they make.

In addition – and perhaps most critically – the project has helped us to see that it is *how* access to knowledge about established research traditions is provided, and the status and purposes accorded to them in the learning process, that is likely to determine whether such knowledge becomes enabling or constraining. If established methodologies, including action research, are seen as a set of resources from which practitioner researchers can select, adapt, modify, they are most likely to serve a creative and liberating function. If they are also offered as examples of approaches that have been developed and used for other purposes, other times and other contexts, then established methodologies can be studied for their situated value, so that lessons can be learned for one's own research.

If, however, methodological approaches are offered as the 'right' way in which one pursues research, then they may have a different, and less helpful, effect on the learning researcher. If research courses allow the particular methodological territories explored to be seen as the only valid territories, then this may not be helpful to the researcher whose purposes or learning styles do not seem to fit comfortably with what is offered. Such an approach to teaching about research may deny the appropriateness and power of researchers' own judgements in finding a methodological way through their enquiries. It may also fail to liberate the innovative researcher's creative talents.

If our aim is to create conditions that facilitate methodological inventiveness, we need to ensure as far as possible that our pedagogical approaches match the message that we seek to communicate. More important than adhering to any specific methodological approach, be it that of traditional social science or traditional action research, may be the willingness and courage of practitioners – and those who support them – to create enquiry approaches that enable new, valid understandings to develop; understandings that empower practitioners to improve their work for the beneficiaries in their care. Practitioner research methodologies are with us to serve professional practices. So what genuinely matters are the purposes of practice which the research seeks to serve, and the integrity with which the practitioner researcher makes methodological choices about ways of achieving those purposes. No methodology is, or should be, cast in stone, if we accept that professional intention should be informing research processes, not pre-set ideas about methods or technique.

Beyond orthodoxy

We are aware that our own interest in creating conditions that liberate practitioners to be creative and inventive has itself the potential to become constraining. We are not assuming that, in conditions that facilitate genuine methodological choice, most practitioners would necessarily choose to take an innovative route. As members of the group themselves stressed, innovation is not a virtue to be valued for its own sake. Methodological orthodoxies, be they old or new, may run the risk of turning research into a technical enterprise, in which practitioner researchers may come to adopt what they believe the institution values, rather than what their own situational creative judgement deems appropriate. Methodological orthodoxies may also run the risk of new researchers becoming dependent on the views of the research institution within which they are studying, rather than developing confidence in their own creative powers. Practitioner researchers may thus end up seeking to serve the institutional research agenda, rather than serve the needs of their research. These are dangers of which we must be aware in the pedagogical and institutional situation, lest by default we come to control the minds and research practices of practitioners in unhelpful ways.

The reality of the risk was brought home to us recently during an activity designed to assist teacher-researchers, newly embarked on their Masters' studies, in clarifying the criteria by which their written work would be assessed. Hoping to communicate to the new group that there was considerable flexibility within the criteria to use different styles of research and writing, course tutors had included Tish Crotty's study of perceptions of purpose for children's writing (Chapter 5) among samples of work examined. Sub-groups formed to discuss each piece of work. After a lively exchange of views about the strengths and limitations of Tish's study, one teacher suddenly looked at the tutor and asked 'So are you saying that it's good to be quirky?'

His question provided a powerful reminder that our efforts to extend opportunities and support for practitioner researchers to develop their work in the ways that they find most empowering may carry an unintentional subtext that work *must* be innovative in order to be valued highly by the academy, or that it will be valued more highly if it is innovative than if it uses conventional methods of enquiry and reporting. As skilled readers of institutional messages, practitioner researchers inevitably scan both our words and our deeds in order to discover what they need to do in order to maximise their chances of success in their studies. In this process, we need to be aware that institutional power relations can bestow upon our words and deeds meanings and messages that undermine our conscious purposes and intentions.

Innovation within the academy

The teaching institution clearly has a crucial role to play in setting a climate which allows for genuine methodological choice. This means not just valuing, and acknowledging as legitimate, diverse methodological approaches, but also actively fostering the creativity and courage needed for practitioners to be inventive. Without teaching and institutional support, innovative practitioner researchers can, as we have seen, take untold risks, especially in an award-bearing context in which the academy has power over the discourses which validate and legitimate research.

All of this leads to two key institutional issues for us in the context of the project. First, as we outlined in Chapter 9, we realise that we must acknowledge the problematic complexity of the notions of the 'academic' so that we do not fall into the trap of generalising, in a simplistic way, implications for supporting innovative practitioner research. When we talk about the institution constraining or supporting innovation, we recognise that we are talking about a complex interplay between the tutor who is teaching and supporting the work; the values, ethos, views of research and assessment criteria embodied within the diverse group of tutors making up the institution; and the institutional processes by which the research is discussed, judged and validated. The academic institution cannot be seen as a single entity, because of the diversity of people within it.

Second, the differences in background and perspectives of tutors may, therefore, despite standard criteria, lead to disagreements about the validity, quality and worthwhileness of particular studies, especially when these diverge from the mainstream style of work which passes through the institution.

We see that there are further practical implications in this for us as tutors supporting individual practitioner researchers at the same time as trying to advance our own understanding of practitioner research methodology and how it can be improved and legitimated within the academy. We have both experienced, over our years of working in this context, differences of views with colleagues about the quality, validity and worthwhileness of particular practitioner research studies. Many colleagues in our own and other academic institutions have had similar experiences in which there have been clashes of perspective and judgement. Such differences are not unusual within a judgmental award-bearing process.

We do, however, have choices about how we deal with these differences. They can either turn into debates and wrangles that mark out something of a methodological battleground, in which the purpose is to establish whose judgements of quality or view of the research is the 'right' or the 'legitimate' one; or they can become an intelligent opportunity to explore the nature of these differences with a view to understanding better our own individual perspectives, as well as testing out the validity of the criteria framework and views of practitioner research within which we are operating.

Our preference is certainly for the latter. If we can take differences of views in the academy as an opportunity for learning about ourselves and our own institutional practices, then we believe we can use them constructively within processes that mark out our workplace as a learning organisation, rather than one in which definitions are fixed, incontestable, taken for granted or the site of negative strife.

We have both, in general, been blessed by the opportunity to work in such learning organisational contexts where there has been opportunity for open discussion about evolving practices. Despite this, however, we also realise that we each have a responsibility to contribute to this continuous learning process by articulating our own understandings of practitioner research when, and if, such differences of views emerge with colleagues, or when institutional opportunities arise for practices to be reviewed and changed. Only thus can we contribute to articulating theories of practitioner research, and thereby help to move the debate forward. We know that this means being prepared to articulate our own thinking, to question the assumptions and practices of colleagues, as well as to open our own to challenge and critique by them. It means trying to contribute to a healthy climate of exchange in which these processes help us to understand our differences and move us forward as an organisation committed to supporting research that makes a difference to people's lives in professional contexts. It means, in essence, being open to new, innovative thinking ourselves about our own institutional practices in a bid to move them forward, so that we can continue to provide optimum conditions for practitioner research to do its work.

So research teaching which supports innovative methodology is best served by institutional values which are consonant with divergence and healthy, generative debate. Such values ought to help foster an institutional climate that encourages the growth of new possibilities in practitioner research, as well as in the institutional practices supporting it.

Innovation in the field of practitioner research

The project also implies, we suggest, an urgent need for further work to be done to gain acceptance for, and establish the legitimacy of, alternative methodologies for practitioner research on a wider scale. Wherever divergent forms of practitioner research continue to be judged by the standards and models of traditional social science research or action research, they will remain forever on the margins of perceived legitimate research methodology. In an age where, in the UK for example, there is growing interest in, and support for, practitioners to engage with research, such a position would be untenable, as well as dysfunctional to the growth of understanding about practitioner research and its potential for practice improvement.

As we were writing the final parts of this book, we were greatly encouraged by a new book representing the work of Stephen Fishman and Lucilla McCarthy (2000). In this book, the authors revisit their own methodological histories as practitioner researchers, reminding us that there have, in the past, been fairly fierce debates about which is the 'right' way for practitioners to study and understand their practice. As they review this methodological battleground, as we have chosen to call it, they conclude that such contrary positioning is not productive. Rather, we need to consider alternative approaches not necessarily as competing, but as different resources from which practitioner researchers can draw to realise their purposes of practice and professionalism.

This position adopted by Fishman and McCarthy working in the USA context, we saw, matched the outcomes of our thinking and research from the Darers' project. Fishman and McCarthy were posing the possibilities of a synthesis that seemed to parallel our own position about methodological choice. In this, we felt that their work, in some small way, contributed to the validity of ours and that, in turn, ours might perform the same purpose for theirs.

The responsibility to articulate our evolving theory and perspectives on practitioner research is an exacting one within the busy, pressured and overloaded contexts within which we work. Yet it is a necessary one to adopt, especially within a broader national and international context in which practitioner research is being taken more seriously than ever before by powerful government agencies, and in which better funding for practitioner researcher is emerging on an unprecedented scale. At the time of writing, for example, the Teacher Training Agency in England has been funding individual and collaborative teacher research projects for some three years, and now the Department for Education and Employment is investing £3 million in similar ventures.

In such a growing and optimistic climate, we feel that, as academics, we can use our professional responsibility to argue for the development of forms of practitioner research, in both an academic and other supported contexts, that actually enable practitioners to do what they set out to do, drawing on their personal strengths and professional commitments to their practice and wider audiences, in the best way they know how. Our current understanding suggests, as we have said, that a climate fostering, and providing the resources for, methodological choice and synthesis may be the most productive one for this to be realised. Our own role in that as teachers at higher education level, and the role of our own institutional context, now seem self-evident. We hope our experience and learning through the Darers' project might help to make a small contribution to the debate and to the growth of creative provision for the growing numbers of practitioner researchers.

Chapter 11

Keeping moving

In one sense, this is an end in that we have come to the concluding point of a fascinating and educative project. It has deepened our understanding of issues in practitioner research which we previously glimpsed, but which we understood in far less detail and complexity than we do now. In another sense, however, this point is another beginning. One rarely puts new understanding behind oneself. Rather, as Jacqui Potter suggests in her study (Chapter 3), new understanding begins to bed down into one's mind and practices to the point where one does not recognise it as new any longer. While this has not yet fully happened for us – it is early days – the learning we have undergone through the project has influenced us in subtle, as well as more obvious, ways, causing us to think and act differently.

At an overt and conscious level, the shifts in our tutor perspective and understanding which we outlined in Chapter 10 have affected the way we have approached our research methods teaching at postgraduate level. We have been much more aware than before of the value of emphasising methodological diversity, innovation and choice in the way we design and carry out our teaching with practitioner researchers. In addition, our awareness of the work and needs of innovative practitioner researchers has also, naturally, been heightened. We have noticed these changes; shared and discussed them, during the final stages of the project as well as in the aftermath. In that sense, the project is not finished but rolls forward with us in our professional lives.

We have not, consciously, decided to conduct a formal follow-on project tracking the effects of our changes on those practitioner researchers with whom we work. We have, however, spontaneously and informally engaged in a mental data gathering approach to our practice as tutors, born from these new awarenesses and the new, more watchful attitude which the project has generated.

In this short final chapter, we have selected two examples of practitioner researchers' innovative thinking taken from our steadily accumulating informal evidence. Together, these examples show that there is some validity in the speculations we offered at the beginning of Chapter 10 about ways in which others might be influenced by the project. We suggested that the examples of work and insights into the group's collective experience might, for example, provide: a stimulus to creative thinking; encouragement to pursue an innovative path; support in weighing up the risks and insight into the processes of learning to help others create the best possible conditions for their own. We see that these three effects have been realised in the examples from new innovative practitioners researchers which we share.

The first example looks at the work of Ken Thomas, a secondary learning support teacher, who was one of the participants in a thirty-hour Masters' course which Marion taught when she moved from Cambridge University to a new post at St Martin's College, Lancaster. The second example focuses on the work of Kevin O'Connell, a secondary teacher following the Cambridge Modular Masters' course on which Susan taught.

Example 1: re-thinking methodological possibilities

Marion writes:

This course was a short module of thirty hours within a full modular MA programme; not very long at all to help the practitioner researchers encounter and understand the very wide methodological field open to them, let alone take measured time to reflect upon the approaches that might best serve their needs.

Given the brevity of our time together on this course, the first session was spent looking at the notion of research as a plural, rather than a singular, concept, to emphasise the idea of diversity and difference in methodology. Although I had started other research courses in this way, I did so this time with greater confidence in the importance to the students of such an approach. This inevitably affected the emphasis I gave to it. For the second week, each member looked at a different published research project so that we could explore methodological diversity and the different ways in which researchers had approached their particular questions, purposes and audiences. This approach proved very generative as it brought before group members methodological approaches with which they were not familiar, such as narrative enquiry (Bateson 1989), autobiography (Simon 1998), anthropology (Sacks 1995) and subjective self-study approaches (Lomax 1994, Jalongo and Isenberg 1995), alongside the more traditional large scale, quantitative styles (Mortimore *et al.* 1988) and case study (Dadds 1995, Rowland 1984) which some were seeing as the only 'real' forms of research.

Some were excited to meet new approaches but expressed nervousness about their validity and respectability as forms of research. The inclusion of studies based on literary pen-portraits (Benedict 1991), diary and personal, reflective narrative (such as Chamberlain 1983, Forster 1995) fuelled a challenging debate about what is, and is not, 'real research', and what we can legitimately expect in the name of research. This debate, predictably, was left unresolved but recurred throughout the rest of the course.

Towards the end of the course, we began to consider issues related to writing up and dissemination. As part of this, we looked at Joe Geraci's research, as well as his account of the experience of coming to research innovatively, from which we drew the narrative summary presented here in Chapter 4. Many students were excited about Joe's innovative, personalised, reflective style as well as being able to identify with aspects of his rationale. Some, however, were still concerned about its validity as 'real research', as they were tending to judge it within the framework of larger-scale, quantitative studies. They were still unsure about the legitimacy of other approaches.

Some evidence has come through in the students' research essays (in which they develop their thinking in preparation for their major research project) that the new emphasis on methodological diversity, adaptability and creativity has had some influence. Ken Thomas, for example, wrote about the way in which he made a radical reappraisal of the research approach he planned to adopt for his school-based study of pupil performance, in the light of the new methodological possibilities he met on the course. Rather than pursue 'the ordered, characterised and systematic stasis doctrine' as he called it, of the mainstream quantitative school effectiveness research (which he had initially decided he should do), he came to think that 'a flexible approach is required that bends and moves with the pressures of enquiry rather than one that is stiff, inflexible and ultimately breaks'. He also came to see more clearly that his own preferred research, thinking and writing styles lay in qualitative, rather than quantitative research approaches. This had, he claimed, impacted more favourably on the practical outcomes from his previous research studies: 'in fact', he wrote, 'I have been able to find a practical application for my results and gained more satisfaction in writing in this manner'.

Added to this was the interest in narrative and anthropological approaches which had been stirred by his reading for the course of Oliver Sacks' (1995) work and that of Joe Geraci. Such approaches, he claimed, would allow him to express 'an insight and feeling for a situation that would be difficult to quantify'. In Ken's own words, encountering Sacks' and Geraci's work 'gave me the encouragement to pursue a reflective narrative approach, which is piloted in this assignment'. He took the opportunity in this planning essay, therefore, to try Joe Geraci's two-font technique to represent two different reflective modes within which he had been thinking, the 'academic' and the more personal and human. The essay was also an opportunity to develop his narrative written style.

Further than this, all of these forces – his preferred style, his interest in new approaches, his new understanding that he could explore his research question in more than one research style – came together into a creative plan to approach his forthcoming major research project in an innovative way. For this, he proposed to develop what he called a 'court room approach . . . possibly using the metaphor of a jury'. This would, he felt, allow him to represent the various voices and perspectives of those participating in his research, as well as other researchers' work, initially 'in an impartial way', to avoid premature judgement for the reader. (We had, on the course, looked at metaphor analysis as a way both of analysing data and structuring the research report, though it was not clear that this work had influenced Ken's decision). He planned to enhance the validity of his data and analysis by adopting triangulation techniques and by drawing upon the critical perspectives of a critical friend. From his data analysis, the emerging theory would be presented as argument for the 'defence'. Negative instances from data analysis would be presented as arguments for the prosecution. A reflective commentary on the arguments arising would be offered in 'reporter style'. The conclusion would be represented in a 'summing up by the "judge" directing points of action'.

Like some of the project group, Ken felt that he would be working against the mainstream, as he perceived it, and that this might carry risks. 'I am aware,' he wrote, 'that this represents a challenge and that it is probably in conflict with traditional methods'. But he felt, as had most of our research group, that he had to do it in his own way, despite knowing that the traditional 'recommended basic format' suggested in the course handbook was available to him, 'but it is one, that for me to accept, would be truly out of character'. (The traditional format for research reports, of Introduction, Literature Review, Methodology, Analysis, Conclusions – what Bassey (1995: 66) calls 'structured reporting' – is only a recommendation and not a compulsory requirement.)

Despite Ken's concerns about established approaches, however, we have evidence here that he planned to draw from a diverse range of resources from both traditional research (such as grounded theory, anthropology, triangulation) as well as Joe Geraci's more innovative work; that his plan was grounded in a number of methodological traditions, old and new. This suggests that the processes of his research might look fairly traditional, if eclectic, but that his final research text might be the site of the most innovative departure from convention.

At the time this chapter was being written, Ken was carrying out the field work for this major research project, so time only will tell whether or not his innovative plan will be realised. It is, as Ken intimated, a fairly high risk strategy. It will require good literacy and artistic skills, but it seems clear that the risk will be well worth taking if it allows Ken to draw upon the thinking and representational styles with which he is most comfortable and capable. It will also, if his previous qualitative studies are to be an indicator, be more likely to enable him to link the research to practical professional change.

Example 2: variations on the use of fiction as a research method

Susan writes:

Towards the end of his first year on the Cambridge Masters' course, Kevin O'Connell expressed dissatisfaction with the first piece of research that he had carried out for his Masters' degree. Kevin had looked at the attitudes and perceptions of colleagues who chose to use two different staff rooms in his school. His aim was to learn more about what he perceived as two different cultures associated with the two different staff rooms. He had used interview and other data collection techniques as means of gaining access to individuals' understandings and perspectives; but he was disappointed with the outcomes, despite receiving a pass grade. Looking back, he said that, although the topic that he had chosen had been – and still was – of great interest to him, he felt he had not been able to 'get close to' the issues that really mattered to him through the 'fairly standard' literature review that he had carried out and the methods of data collection that he had used for the investigation.

With the project fresh in my mind, I began to talk to him about alternative methodologies. I described some of the ways that members of the project group had used different forms of writing, including fictional writing, as part of their approaches. Kevin had not been aware that fictional writing could have a place in research, and the idea was immediately appealing because creative writing was such a strong part of his identity as an English teacher. He decided to find out more about the use of fictional writing as a means of research and professional development, and made this the focus for his second study.

> [Fictional writing] is such a big part of me – you just can't cut yourself off from it. . . . I feel in tune with the idea that, through creative writing, people genuinely express something about themselves and about the world, that doesn't get touched in other ways.

As part of this work, he also decided to give the ideas a try in practice so that he could assess their value, at least in part, on the basis of experience. He invited a group of colleagues to discuss a story he had written, using Richard Winter's 'fictional-critical' approach (Winter 1989, 1999), and then reflected upon what he had learned from their responses.

He went on to invent his own variations upon the fictional-critical method for the research carried out for his dissertation. He decided to explore the potential of fictional writing as a means of gaining access to the students' voice, focusing on their perceptions of problem behaviour. He set up two different approaches with two selected groups of five Year 9 students. With one group, he read a story that he had written himself about a classroom incident (viewed from the teacher's perspective) and asked them to discuss it. He was present for the discussion, but did not intervene once the task had been introduced. With the other group, he read the same story, but this time asked them to write their own version of the story as if they were a student in that class witnessing the incident. He then analysed the stories for the key themes that emerged, and presented these back to the group for discussion.

This innovative approach enabled him to capitalise on his experience and expertise as an English teacher, and seemed to hold out the promise of enabling him to get 'more deeply and more closely' to the reality of pupils' perceptions of problem behaviour through this means. This approach was more likely, he felt, to reach 'the person at centre of events', and also to 'perceive the blurred edges' and to 'recognise the complexity of it all'.

Kevin is still working with his data and deciding upon how to write up his thesis. While continuing to treat the methodology as experimental and open to question, he has found an approach that – for current purposes at least – has captured his interest. It has enabled him to work with the resourcefulness, intellectual energy, ownership and satisfaction that had been missing in the case of his first study.

A question worth pursuing

In both examples, we can see the way in which personal, professional and academic influences combined to produce an innovative approach that both Ken and Kevin believed would empower their thinking, enhance the quality and presentation of their learning, and consequently the practical outcomes of their research. Their experience provides some encouraging initial confirmation of the ideas emerging from our project. It underlines the importance of continuing to pursue the central question raised by the Darers' work: how can academic support for practitioner researchers be provided in ways which acknowledge and nurture the vital personal and professional dimensions of research upon which genuine methodological choice depends?

The more we understand about the human processes of practitioner research, the better we are able to develop our own supportive practices accordingly. It is our role, we now believe, to liberate practitioner researchers to conduct worthwhile research in ways that harmonise with their questions, professional purposes and talents. The need for further research in this area is crucial.

Appendix

Assessment criteria

As explained in Chapter 9, different approaches to assessment were in operation on the different courses from which the various studies presented in this book arose. The criteria for research and scholarship at Masters' level presented here are those currently in operation for the Cambridge Modular Masters' degree, although they have been slightly modified since Ros Frost carried out her study. The studies carried out by Linda Ferguson, Tish Crotty and Joe Geraci were assessed before a distinction was introduced between B and B+ grades.

Grade A: Work of distinguished quality

The work presented will demonstrate considerable skill in the organisation of the study, an extensive knowledge of the field, and evidence of an ability to select appropriately from relevant sources. Literature in the field will have been reviewed critically. The concepts and issues involved, both substantively and methodologically, will have been comprehensively understood and their implications identified. There will be evidence of original and imaginative insights into the theme involved and a high level of scholarship in the treatment and interpretation of evidence. The arguments presented will be logical and internally consistent with a thoughtful and thought-provoking presentation of evidence and argument. Where relevant, implications for future practice will have been explored in depth.

Grade B+: Work achieving a good pass standard

The work will demonstrate sound knowledge of the field of study and an ability to organise an appropriate investigation with attention to methodological issues. Pertinent issues will have been identified and a critical understanding of the relevant literature will have been demonstrated. The general impression will be one of a thorough attempt to examine the evidence and to draw appropriate conclusions. Where relevant, there will be reflection on implications for future practice. The arguments presented will be related to the theme under discussion and based on evidence. The structure and presentation of the exposition and argument will be careful and will demonstrate analysis and interpretation. There will be some indication of individual insight and the development of thinking. Premature judgements and unsupported generalisations will have been avoided. The work will conform to expected conventions of layout and presentation.

Grade B: Work achieving a pass standard

Work in this category will demonstrate knowledge of the field under study but may not recognise the complexities involved. The investigation will be appropriately organised in relation to the theme being studied, and methodological issues will have been addressed. However, more detailed consideration of structural and methodological issues might have been included. Relevant literature will have been drawn upon but there may be some omissions or limited critical discussion or commentary. The study will tend to be more descriptive than analytical and there may be weaknesses in interpretation and argument. Some thought will have been given to the relevance of the study to future practice, but this may be limited. Generally, presentation will be clear. In summary, the study will be adequate and just reaches the standard of an M.Ed.

Grade F: Work that fails

Work which tends to reflect an inadequacy of coverage, or where the major sources are not represented, or where any investigation is characterised by confusion will not meet the required standard for a Masters' degree. The grasp of issues is likely to be uncertain or distorted and include evidence of misunderstanding of the arguments involved. It may also be characterised by unsupported generalisation. There will be no clearly articulated line of argument in the discussion and evidence will remain largely unexamined, with a tendency to quote verbatim with little or no discussion of the implications of the material included. Work with a poor standard of presentation, with errors, gaps and inconsistencies, or where plagiarism is present, will be placed in this category.

Work is assessed independently by two internal examiners who then meet and decide upon a provisional grade. The final grade is confirmed at the Examination Board held following the end of the two-year course.

Bibliography

Abercrombie, M. L. J. (1989) *The Anatomy of Judgement: An Investigation into the Reasoning Processes of Perception and Reasoning*, London: Free Association Books.

Adlam, R. (1998) 'Developing ethics education for police leaders and managers: action research and critical reflection for curriculum and personal development', *Educational Action Research* 6(1): 112–31.

Alexander, R., Rose, J. and Woodhead, C. (1992) *Curriculum Organisation and Classroom Practice in Primary Schools*, London: DES.

Arnot, M. and Barton, L. (eds) (1992) *Voicing Concerns: Sociological Perspectives on Contemporary Education Reforms*, Wallingford: Triangle.

Association of Heads and Teachers of Adults and Children with Autism (AHTACA) (1985) *The Special Curricular Needs of Autistic Children,* Leicester: Quorn Selective Repro.

Baron-Cohen, S. (1995) 'First lesson in mind reading', *Times Higher Education Supplement* (June 16): 18–19.

—— (1989) 'The autistic child's theory of mind: a case of specific developmental delay', *Journal of Child Psychology and Psychiatry* 30(2): 285–97.

Barrows, H. S. and Tamblyn, R. (1980) *Problem Based Learning: An Approach to Medical Education*, New York: Springer.

Barton, D. (1991) 'The social nature of writing', in Barton, D.and Ivanic, R. (eds), *Writing in the Community*, California: Sage.

Barton, L. and Oliver, M. (1992) 'Special needs: personal trouble or public issue?' in Arnot, M. and Barton, L. (eds), *Voicing Concerns: Sociological Perspectives on Contemporary Educational Reforms*, Wallingford: Triangle.

Bassey, M. (1992) 'Creating education through research', *British Education Research Journal* 18(1): 3–16.

Bassey, M. (1995) *Creating Education Through Research*, Newark: Kirklington Moor Press.

Bateson, M. C. (1990) *Composing a Life,* New York: Plume.

Benedict, H. (1991) *Portraits in Print,* New York: Columbia University Press.

Benner, P. (1984) *From Novice to Expert: Excellence and Power in Clinical Nursing Practice*, California: Addison-Wesley.

Bereiter, C. (1980) 'Development in writing', in Gregg, L. W. and Steinberg E. R. (eds), *Cognitive Processes in Writing*, Hillsdale, NJ: Lawrence Erlbaum.

Berthoff, A. (1987) 'The teacher as researcher', in Goswami, D. and Stillman, P.

(eds), *Reclaiming the Classroom: Teacher Research as an Agency for Change*, Upper Montclair, NJ: Boynton/Cook.

Boshuizen, H. P. A. and Schmidt, H. G. (1992) 'On the role of biomedical knowledge in clinical reasoning by experts, intermediates and novices, *Cognitive Science* 16: 153–84.

Bourne, J. (1994) 'A question of ability' in Bourne, J. (ed.), *Thinking Through Primary Practice*, London: Routledge.

Bourne, J. (ed.) (1994) *Thinking Through Primary Practice*, London: Routledge.

British Broadcasting Corporation (BBC) (1995) *A Nice Safe Place*, London: Disability Programmes Unit for the BBC.

Britton, J., Burgess, T., Martin, N., McLeod, A. and Rosen, H. (1975) *The Development of Writing Abilities (11–18)*, Basingstoke: Macmillan.

Calkins, L. M. (1983) *Lessons from a Child: On the Teaching and Learning of Writing*, Portsmouth, NH: Heinemann.

Chamberlain, M. (1983) *Fenwomen: A Portrait of Women in an English Village*, London: Routledge and Kegan Paul.

Childs, V., Franklin, F. and Kemp, P. (1997) *Action Research in Social Services and Health Care Settings,* vol. 1, Cambridge: Anglia Polytechnic University.

Christie, F. (1990) 'The changing face of literacy', in Christie, F. (ed.), *Literacy For A Changing World*, Victoria: Acer.

Cline, T. and Frederickson, N. (1991) *Bilingual Pupils and the National Curriculum: Overcoming Difficulties in Teaching and Learning,* London: University College London.

—— (1996) 'The development of a model of curriculum related assessment', in Cline, T. and Frederickson, N. (eds), *Curriculum Related Assessment, Cummins and Bilingual Behaviour*, Clevedon: Multilingual Matters.

Cochran-Smith, M. and Lytle, S. L. (1993) *Inside Outside: Teacher Research and Knowledge*, New York: Teachers College Press.

Convery, A. (1993) 'Developing fictional writing as a means of stimulating teacher reflection: a case study', *Educational Action Research* 1(1): 112–35.

Cope, B. and Kalantzis, M. (1993) *The Powers of Literacy: A Genre Approach to Teaching Writing*, London: Falmer.

Cummins, J. (1984) *Bilingualism and Special Education Issues in Assessment and Pedagogy*, Clevedon: Multilingual Matters.

Czerniewska, P. (1992) *Learning about Writing*, Oxford: Blackwell.

Dadds, M. (1994) 'Can INSET essays change the world for children?' in Constable, H. (ed.), *Change in Classroom Practice*, Lewes: Falmer.

—— (1995) *Passionate Enquiry and School Development: A Story About Teacher Action Research*, London: Falmer.

—— (1996) 'Supporting practitioner research: a challenge', *Educational Action Research* 6(1): 39–52.

Davies, G. (1989) 'Discovering a need to write: the role of the teacher as collaborator', in Styles, M. (ed.), *Collaboration and Writing*, Milton Keynes: Open University Press.

Day, C. (1990) 'Series editor's introduction' in Elliott, J., *Action Research for Educational Change,* Milton Keynes: Open University Press.

Delamont, S. (1992) *Fieldwork in Educational Settings: Methods, Pitfalls and Perspectives*, London: Falmer.

Department for Education (DfE) (1978) *Report of the Committee of Enquiry into the Education of Handicappd Children and Young People* London: HMSO.

—— (1995) *Key Stages 1 and 2 of the National Curriculum*, London: HMSO.

Donoghue, J. (1991) 'Entitlement for all: race, gender and ERA. A perspective from the NCC', *Multicultural Teaching* 10(1): 3–22.

Drummond, M. J. (1993) *Assessing Children's Learning,* London: David Fulton.

Dunham, J. (1992) *Stress in Teaching*, London: Routledge.

Dyson, A. (1990) 'Special Educational Needs and the concept of change', *Oxford Review of Education* 16(1): 55–66.

Ebbutt, D. (1983) *'Educational action research: some general concerns and specific quibbles',* Cambridge Institute of Education, mimeo.

Elbow, P. (1981) *Writing with Power*, New York: Oxford University Press.

Elliott, J. (1990) 'Educational research in crisis: performance indicators and the decline in excellence', *British Educational Research Journal* 16(1): 3–18.

Ellis, A. and Beattie, G. (1986) *The Psychology of Language and Communication*, London: Weidenfeld and Nicolson.

Ely, M., Vinz, R., Downing, M. and Anzul, M. (1997) *On Writing Qualitative Research*, London: Falmer.

Emig, J. (1983) *The Web of Meaning*, Montclair, NJ: Boynton/Cook.

Eraut, M. (1994) *Developing Professional Knowledge and Competence*, London: Falmer.

Evans, P. and Ware, J. (1987) *Special Care Provision – The Education of Children with Profound and Multiple Learning Difficulties*, Windsor: NFER – Nelson.

Ewen, R. B. (1984) *Introduction to Theories of Personality* 2nd edn, Orlando: Academic Press.

Fergusson, A. (1994) 'Planning for communication', in Rose, R., Fergusson, A., Coles, C., Byers, R. and Banes, D. (eds), *Implementing the Whole Curriculum for Pupils with Learning Difficulties*, London: David Fulton.

Fishman, S. and McCarthy, L. (2000) *Unplayed Tapes*, New York: Teachers' College Press.

Flanagan, J. C. (1954) 'The critical incident technique', *Psychological Bulletin* 51(4): 327–59.

Flower, L. and Hayes, J. (1981) 'A cognitive process theory of writing', *College Composition and Communication* 32(4): 365–87.

Forster, M. (1995) *Hidden Lives,* London: Viking.

Frith, U. (1989) *Autism: Explaining the Enigma*, Oxford: Blackwell.

Gilbert, P. (1989) *Writing, Schooling and Deconstruction. From Voice to Text in the Classroom,* London: Routledge.

Gipps, C. (1995) 'What do we mean by equity in relation to assessment?' *Assessment in Education: Principles, Policy and Practice* 2(3): 271–81.

Gipps, C. and Murphy, P. (1994) *A Fair Test? Assessment, Achievement and Equity*, Buckingham: Open University Press.

Goldbart, J. (1988) 'Communication for a purpose' in Coupe, J. and Goldbart, J. (eds), *Communication Before Speech*, Kent: Croom Helm.

—— (1994) 'Opening the communication curriculum to students with PMLDs', in Ware, J. (ed.) *Educating Children with Profound and Multiple Learning Difficulties,* London: David Fulton.

Graham, M. (1973) *The Notebooks of Martha Graham,* New York: Harcourt Brace Jovanovich.

Graves, D. (1983) *Writing: Teachers and Children at Work,* London: Heinemann.

Gregory, E. (1993) 'Sweet and sour: learning to read in a British and Chinese school, *English in Education* 27(3): 52–9.

Gregory, E. and Kelly, C. (1994) 'Bilingualism and assessment', in Bourne, J. (ed.) *Thinking through Primary Practice,* London: Routledge.

Hall, N. (1987) *The Emergence of Literacy,* London: Hodder and Stoughton.

Hammersley, M. (1990) *Reading Ethnographic Research: A Critical Guide,* London: Longman.

Happe, F. (1994) *Autism: An Introduction to Psychological Theory,* London: UCL Press.

—— (1995) 'The role of age and verbal ability in the theory of mind task performance of subjects with autism', *Child Development* 66(3): 843–55.

Harrison, J., Lombardina, L. and Stapell, J. (1987) 'The development of early communication: using developmental literature for selecting communication goals', *Journal of Special Education* 20(4): 463–73.

Hart, S. (1995a) 'Action-in-reflection', *Educational Action Research* 3(2): 211–32.

—— (1995b) 'Down a different path', from Discussion Papers 1, *Schools' Special Educational Needs Policies Pack,* London: National Children's Bureau.

Heath, S. B. (1983) *Ways with Words,* Cambridge: Cambridge University Press.

Higgs, J. (1990) 'Fostering the acquisition of clinical reasoning skills', *New Zealand Journal of Physiotherapy* 18: 13–17.

—— (1992a) 'Developing clinical reasoning competencies', *New Zealand Journal of Physiotherapy* 78(8): 575–81.

—— (1992b) 'Managing clinical education: the educator-manager and the self-directed learner', *New Zealand Journal of Physiotherapy* 78(11): 822–8.

—— (1993) 'Managing clinical education: the programme', *New Zealand Journal of Physiotherapy* 79(4): 239–46.

Hitchcock, G. and Hughes, D. (1989) *Research and the Teacher: A Qualitative Introduction to School-based Research,* London: Routledge.

Hollingsworth, S. (1994) *Teacher Research and Urban Literacy: Lessons and Conversations in a Feminist Key,* New York: Teachers' College Press.

—— (ed.) (1997) *International Action Research: A Casebook of Educational Reform,* London: Falmer.

Holyroyd, S. and Baron-Cohen, S. (1993) 'Brief report: how far can people with autism go in developing a theory of mind?' *Journal of Autism and Developmental Disorders* 23(2): 379–85.

Howlin, P. (1996) 'Asperger syndrome and the needs of more able people with autism', lecture, London: National Autistic Society.

Hughes, T. (1967) *Poetry in the Making,* London: Faber.

Hunt, P. (1991) *Criticism, Theory and Children's Literature,* Oxford: Blackwell.

Jalongo, M. R. and Isenberg, J. P. (1995) *Teachers' Stories,* San Francisco: Jossey-Bass.

Jordan, R. and Powell, S. (1996) *Understanding and Teaching Children with Autism,* Chichester: Wiley.

Jorgensen, D. (1989) *Participant Observation: A Methodology for Human Studies,* London: Sage.

Kopchick, G. A. and Lloyd, L. L. (1976) 'Total communication programming for the severely language impaired: a 24-hour approach' in Lloyd, L. L. (ed.) *Communication Assessment and Intervention Strategies*, Md.: University Park Press.

Lomax, P. (1994) *Narrative of an Educational Journey – or Crossing the Track*, Kingston: Kingston University School of Education.

Lomax, P. and Parker, Z. (1995) 'Accounting for ourselves: the problematics of representing action research', in *Cambridge Journal of Education* 25(3): 301–14.

Martin, A. (1988) 'Teachers and teaching: screening, early intervention and remediation – obscuring children's potential', *Harvard Educational Review* 58(4): 488–501.

May, J. P. (1995) *Children's Literature and Critical Theory*, Oxford: Oxford University Press.

Medwell, J. (1994) 'Contexts for writing: the social construction of written composition', in Wray, D. and Medwell, J. (eds), *Teaching Primary English: The State of the Art*, London: Routledge.

Mellor, N. J. (1999) 'From exploring practice to exploring enquiry: a practitioner researcher's experience', Ph.D. thesis, University of Northumbria, Newcastle.

Mesibov, G. (1996) 'TEACCH Structured Teaching Model: Basic Concepts', lecture, Sheffield: National Autistic Society.

Middleton, S. (1995) 'Doing feminist educational theory: a post-modernist perspective', *Gender and Education* 7(1): 87–100.

Miles, M. B. and Huberman, A. M. (1994) *Qualitative Data Analysis*, 2nd edn, London: Sage.

Mortimore, P., Sammons, P., Stoll, L., Lewis, D. and Ecob, R. (1988) *School Matters*, Wells: Open Books.

Mortlock, J. (1996a) 'Working with people with autism – addressing challenging behaviour', lecture, London: National Autistic Society.

—— (1996b) 'Working with people with autism – addressing the triad of impairments', lecture, Birmingham: National Autistic Society.

Moustakas, C. (1994) *Phenomenological Research Methods*, London: Sage.

Murphy, P. (1995) 'Sources of inequity, understanding students' responses to assessment', *Assessment in Education* 2(3): 249–70.

National Writing Project (1990) *Perceptions of Writing*, Walton on Thames: Nelson.

Newson, J. (1978) 'Dialogue and development', in Locke, A. (ed.), *Action, Gesture and Symbol: The Emergence of Language*, New York: Academic Press.

Nichols, R. (1997) 'Action research in healthcare: the collaborative action research network health care group', *Educational Action Research* 5(2): 185–92.

Nind, M. and Hewett, D. (1994) *Access to Communication*, London: David Fulton.

Peacock, G. *et al.* (1996) 'Autism – a range of educational provision for a spectrum disorder', lecture, Edinburgh: National Autistic Society and Scottish Society for Autistic Children.

Polanyi, M. (1958) *Personal Knowledge: Towards a Post-Critical Philosophy*, London: Routledge.

Pollard, A. and Tann, S. (1987) 'Investigating Classrooms', in *Reflective Teaching in the Primary School*, London: Cassell.

Purkey, W. W. (1970) *Self-Concept and School Achievement*, Englewood Cliffs, NJ: Prentice Hall.

Robson, C. (1993) *Real World Research: A Resource for Social Scientists and Practitioner Researchers*, Oxford: Blackwell.

Rouse, M. (1992) *Principles and Purposes of Assessment. Learning Difficulties*, Birmingham: School of Education, University of Birmingham.

Rowland, S. (1984) *The Enquiring Classroom*, Lewes: Falmer.

Sacks, O. (1995) *An Anthropologist on Mars*, London: Picador.

Saint-Exupéry, A. de (1945) *The Little Prince*, London: Heinemann.

Schein, E. H. (1972) *Professional Education: Some New Directions*, New York: McGraw Hill.

Schindele, R. (1985) 'Researching Methodology in Special Education: a framework approach to special problems and solutions', in Hegarty, S. and Evans, P. (eds), *Research and Evaluation Methods in Special Education*, Berkshire: NFER – Nelson.

Schön, D. A. (1983) *The Reflective Practitioner*, London: Maurice Temple Smith.

—— (1990) *Educating the Reflective Practitioner*, Oxford: Jossey Bass.

Simon, B. (1998) *A Life in Education*, London: Lawrence and Wishart.

Smith, F. (1982) *Writing and the Writer*, London: Heinemann.

Street, J. and Street, B. (1991) 'The schooling of literacy', in Barton, D. *et al.* (eds), *Writing in the Community*, California: Sage.

Stengelhofen, J. (1993) *Teaching Students in Clinical Settings*, London: Chapman and Hall.

Stenhouse, L. (1975) *An Introduction to Curriculum Research and Development*, London: Heinemann.

Strauss, A. (1987) *Qualitative Analysis for Social Scientists*, Cambridge: Cambridge University Press.

Teale, W. and Sulzby, E. (eds) (1986) *Emergent Literacy*, Norwood, NJ: Ablex.

Titchen, A. and Binnie, A. (1993) 'A unified action research strategy in nursing', *Educational Action Research* 1(1): 8–25.

Tizard, B. and Hughes, M. (1984) *Young Children Learning: Talking and Thinking at Home and at School*, London: Fontana.

Tomlinson, S. (1982) *A Sociology of Special Education*, London: Routledge.

Tripp, D. (1993) *Critical Incidents in Teaching*, London: Routledge.

Walshe, R. (1981) *Donald Graves in Australia*, Rosebery, NSW: Primary English Teaching Association of New South Wales.

Ware, J. (1994) 'Using interaction in the education of pupils with PMLDs', in Ware, J. (ed.), *Educating Children with Profound and Multiple Learning Difficulties*, London: David Fulton.

Wells, G. (1986) *The Meaning Makers: Children Learning Language and Using Language to Learn*, London: Hodder and Stoughton.

Wilkinson, A., Barnsley, G. and Hanna, P. (1980) *Assessing Language Development*, Oxford: Oxford University Press.

Williams, D. (1994) *Nobody Nowhere*, London: Bantam.

—— (1995) *Inside Out – Jam Jar*, a Channel Four television production.

—— (1996) *Autism: An Inside-Out Approach*, London: Kingsley.

Wing, L. (1996) *The Autistic Spectrum: A Guide for Parents and Professionals*, London: Constable.

Winter, C. (1996) 'Creating quality care for children in the family centre', *Educational Action Research* 4(1): 49–57.

Winter, R. (1988) 'Fictional – critical writing: an approach to case study research by practitioners and for in-service and pre-service work with teachers', in Nias, J. and Groundwater-Smith, S. (eds), *The Enquiring Teacher*, London: Falmer.

—— (1989) *Learning from Experience: Principles and Practice in Action Research*, Lewes: Falmer.

—— (1991) 'Interviewers, interviewees and the exercise of power (fictional-critical writing as a method for educational research)', *British Educational Research Journal* 17(3): 251–62.

Winter, R., Buck, A. and Sobiechowska, P. (1999) *Profesional Experience and the Investigative Imagination – The ART of Reflective Writing*, London: Routledge.

Wray, D. (1994) *Literacy and Awareness*, London: Hodder and Stoughton.

Yin, R. (1989) *Case Study Research, Design and Methods*, California: Sage.

Index